Louise Brooks

A Life in Pictures

Bill LeFurgy

High Kicker Books

LCCN:

ISBN: 979-8-9916325-1-5 (paperback)

ISBN: 979-8-9916325-2-2 (eBook)

ALSO FROM HIGH KICKER BOOKS

Is Your Cat an Alien? An Adult Activity Book with Illustrations and a Quiz to Learn if Your Cat is Plotting World Domination, 2024

Series: Adult Swearing Coloring Books

Chill, Smile & Swear: Curse Words to Color and Laugh, 2024

Swear Your Stress Away: Coloring Naughty Words for Fun and Relaxation, 2024

Cursing Therapy: Dirty Words to Color and Gain Inner Peace, 2024

Swearing Food Adult Coloring Book: Relaxation and Stress Relief for Women and Men Who Swear, 2024

Sassy Cats: An Adult Swearing Coloring Book For Cat Lovers, 2024

Swearing Cats Coloring Book for Adults: Relaxation and Stress Relief for Women and Men Who Like Cattitude, 2024

Swearing Cats Coloring Book for Adults, Book 2: Stress Busting Fun, 2024

Books by Bill LeFurgy

Fiction

Into the Suffering City: A Novel of Baltimore, 2020

Murder in the Haunted Chamber, 2021

Non-fiction

Criminal Slang: Annotated Edition of the 1908 Dictionary of the Vernacular of the Underworld, 2020

Sex, Art, and Salome: Historical Photographs of a Princess, Dancer, Stripper, and Feminist Inspiration, 2022

CHECK THEM OUT ON AMAZON.COM!

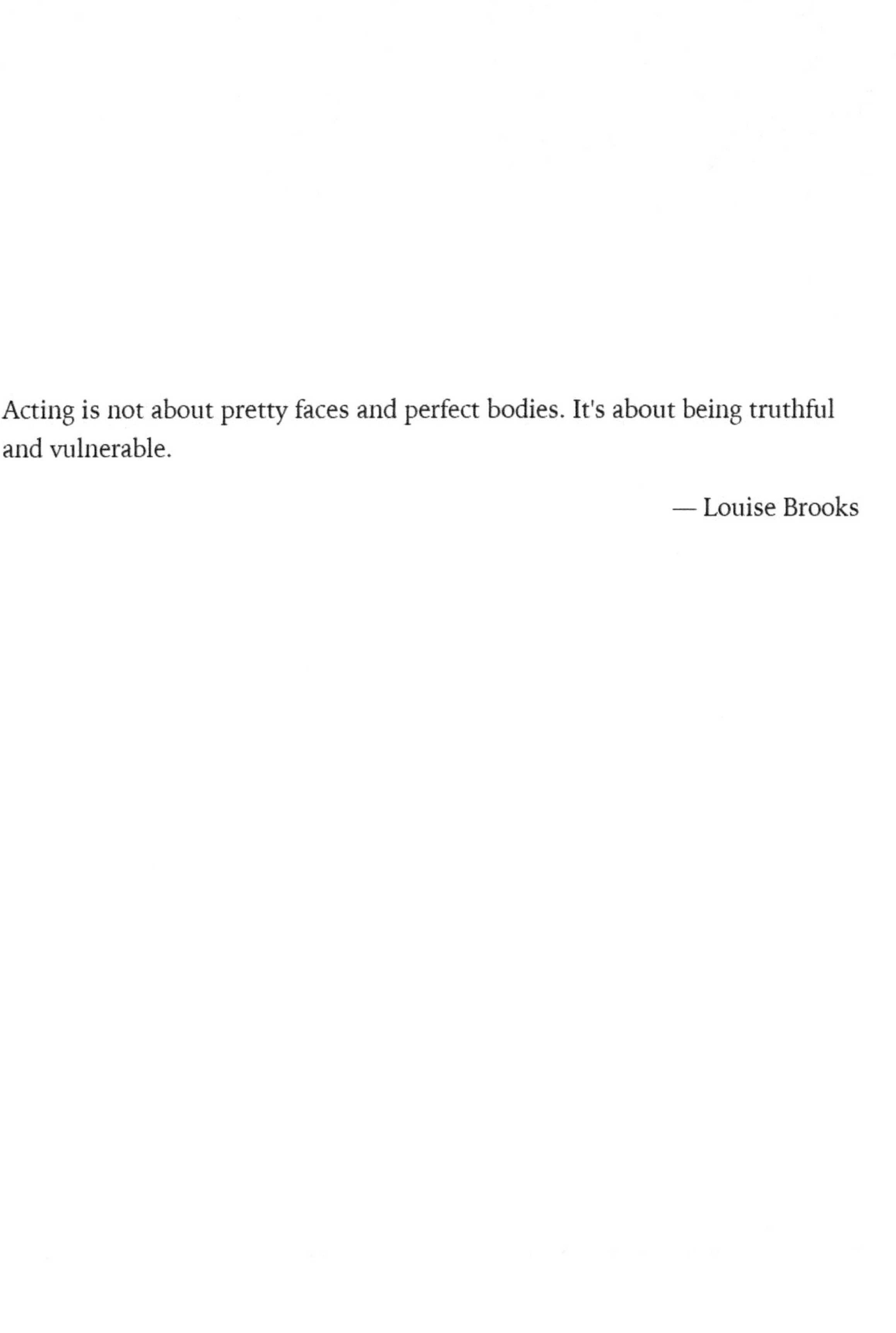

Acting is not about pretty faces and perfect bodies. It's about being truthful and vulnerable.

— Louise Brooks

INTRODUCTION

Images of the actress Louise Brooks (1906–1985) persist in popular memory to a remarkable degree. Show someone her picture—even someone who knows nothing about her—and they will instantly recognize the prototypical 1920s Jazz Age modern woman (a flapper, if you will), complete with bold expression and short bob haircut.

We remember Brooks for two fundamental reasons. First, her star power blazed during the height of the Roaring Twenties, from 1925 to 1929. She made over a dozen films during that period and appeared constantly in the popular press. Her image was a captivating blend of innocence and modernity, embodying the cute tomboy next door and the sophisticated coed at ease in a downtown speakeasy.

The second, and more significant, reason for Brooks' enduring hold on our imagination is her remarkable beauty. Her open face features large, wide-set eyes, a straight nose, firm lips, and a perfectly pointed chin. Early in her career, her black bangs hung straight above delicate, expressive eyebrows. In later years, her bangs were swept to the side, revealing a high, intelligent forehead that enhanced her beauty further.

While Brooks is undeniably beautiful, there is something else at play in her photographs (as well as in her best films). Her expression is unaffected, with little mugging, vamping, or calculated posturing. Instead, her demeanor is natural and introspective, as though she is immersed in her own world, inviting us to witness without demanding our attention.

Brooks achieves this in photo after photo, whether taken by hacks or the most talented photographers of the day. She somehow manages to communicate something both intimate and profound, drawing us into her world and compelling us to ponder her mystery and allure. She is undeniably radiant and iconic, but beyond that façade lies a deeply layered human experience. As Kenneth Tynan once noted, her photos seem to "smuggle personality past the camera," inviting us to connect on a level deeper than mere beauty and stardom.

The impact of Brooks' photographs intensifies as one delves into her life, which is a rich and complex story marked by success, struggle, and self-sabotage as well as a steadfast refusal to indulge in self-pity. Her story in brief:

- Born to a well-to-do lawyer and a mother who told him that "any squalling brats she produced could take care of themselves."
- Sexually abused by a neighbor, "Mr. Feathers," at age nine. Her mother reportedly said she "must have led him on."
- After a successful local career as a dancer, she moved to New York City at fifteen to join the Denishawn Dance Company, a pioneering force in American modern dance.
- Expelled from Denishawn at eighteen for lack of focus, she worked as a showgirl on Broadway, eventually becoming a "specialty dancer" in the Ziegfeld Follies.
- Signed a movie contract with Paramount Pictures at nineteen, quickly becoming a well-known movie actress.
- Married a film director in 1926; divorced within two years after she became involved with a wealthy older man.
- Starred in *The Canary Murder Case* as a silent film; Paramount decided to remake it as a "talkie," but Brooks refused to dub her character's voice, enraging the studio.
- Traveled to Germany to star in *Die Büchse der Pandora* (*Pandora's Box*), portraying her most famous character, Lulu, a scandalous mistress. Now regarded as one of the greatest silent film performances, critics at the time panned her work.
- Returned to Hollywood to find herself labeled as difficult to work with and struggled to find roles. She declared bankruptcy in 1932 and appeared in her last film with a then-unknown John Wayne in 1937.
- Married a wealthy polo player in 1933; divorced him five months later.
- Worked as a ballroom dancer in nightclubs during the early to mid-1930s.
- Lived as the mistress of a series of wealthy men in New York City during the 1940s and early 1950s, drinking heavily.
- Rediscovered by cinephiles in the mid-1950s, she wrote acclaimed articles about her career and lived as a recluse until her death at age 78 in 1985.

Brooks enjoyed cultivating an air of intellectual sophistication to set herself apart from her Hollywood peers. Though she had no formal education beyond high school, she took great pride in her love of literature, immersing herself in the works of Marcel Proust, Samuel Johnson, and Arthur Schopenhauer. "I'm probably one of the best-read idiots in the world," she remarked with characteristic self-lacerating wit.

Gifted with brains, she also possessed a remarkable natural talent as an actress. In an era when silent movie acting often relied on exaggerated expressions to compensate for the absence of sound, Brooks appeared entirely natural on screen. Her finest role, that of Lulu in *Pandora's Box*, showcased a fascinatingly incongruous mix of childlike innocence, adult hedonism, and selfish focus on her own desires—unbound by moral constraints or societal expectations. She moved with lively grace throughout the film, in stark contrast to the other actors, whose performances often seem, to modern eyes, overly affected. The role came easily to her, she later remarked, because "Lulu's story is as near as you'll get to mine."

I've included a small selection of Brooks photographs for this book, as well as posters, magazine covers, and lobby cards (hand-colored placards illustrating scenes from her films, displayed in theater lobbies to attract audiences and preview the movie's highlights).

The hundred or so images are arranged in rough chronological order. The exact dates of many of Brooks' publicity shots are unknown, but I've made approximations.

Unless otherwise noted in the captions, all images are sourced from Wikimedia Commons, an open-access digital media repository available at https://commons.wikimedia.org.

PHOTOGRAPHS

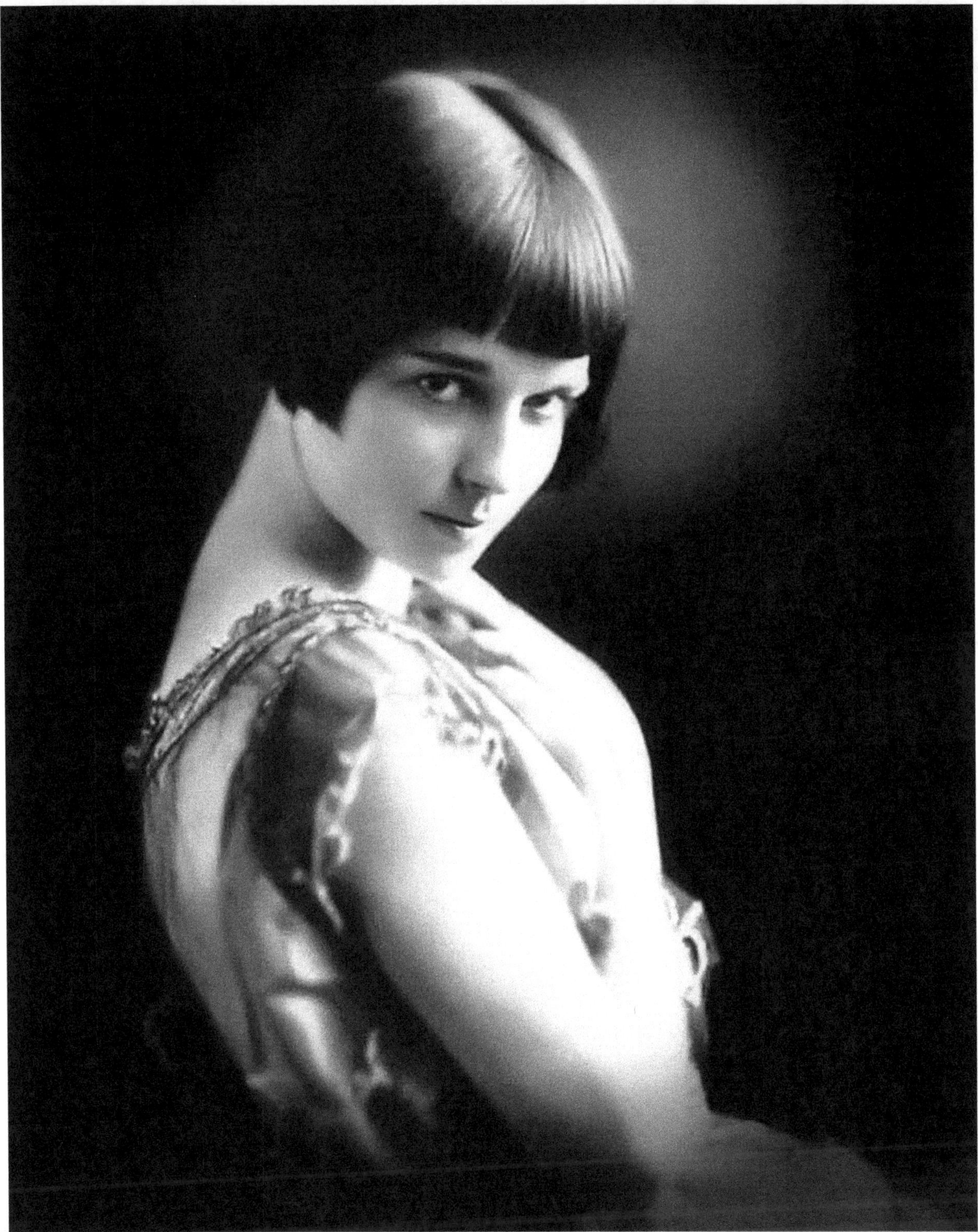

Image 1: Brooks before joining the Denishawn Dance Company in New York City, ca. 1922.

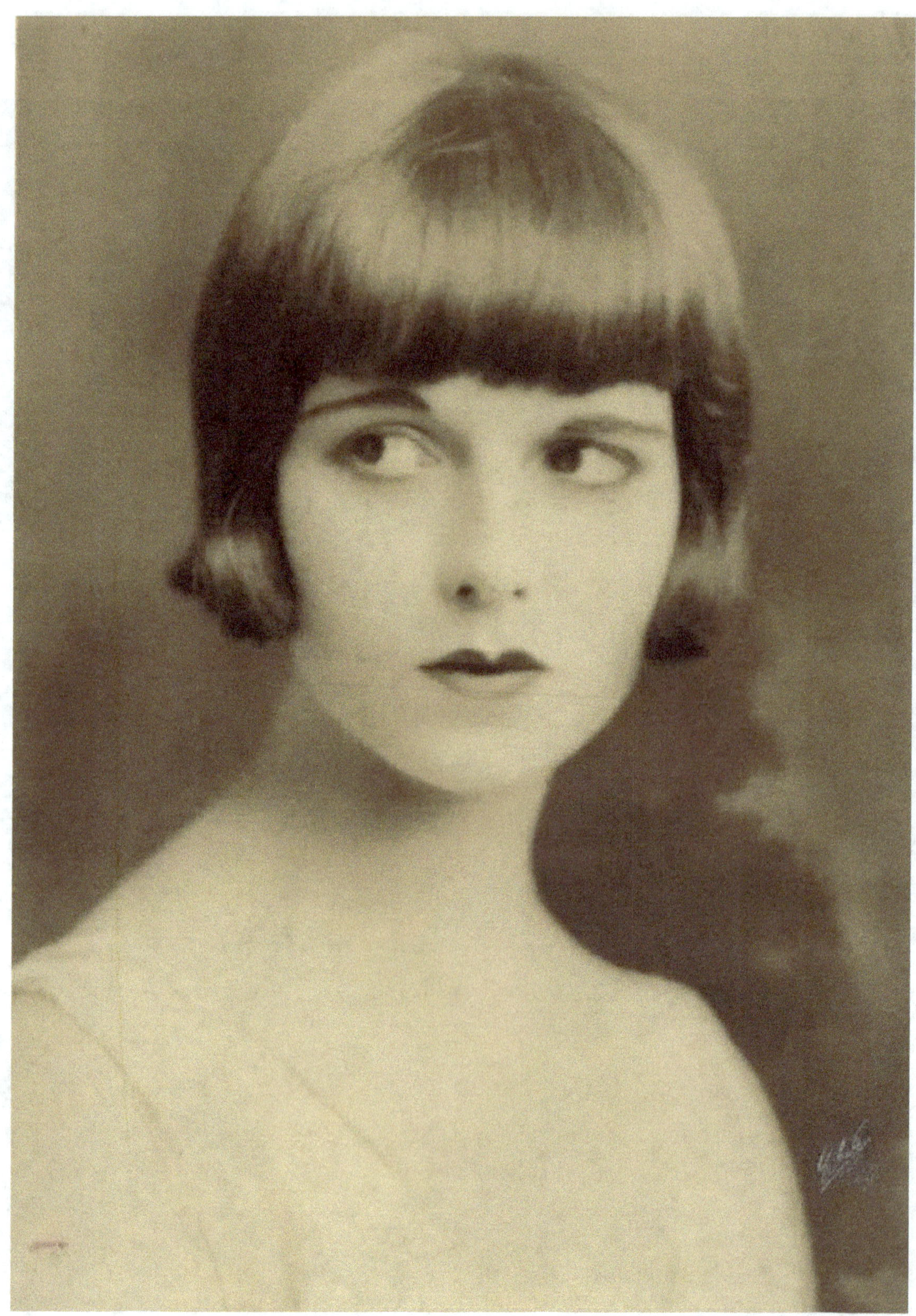

Image 2: As a Denishawn dancer, 1923.

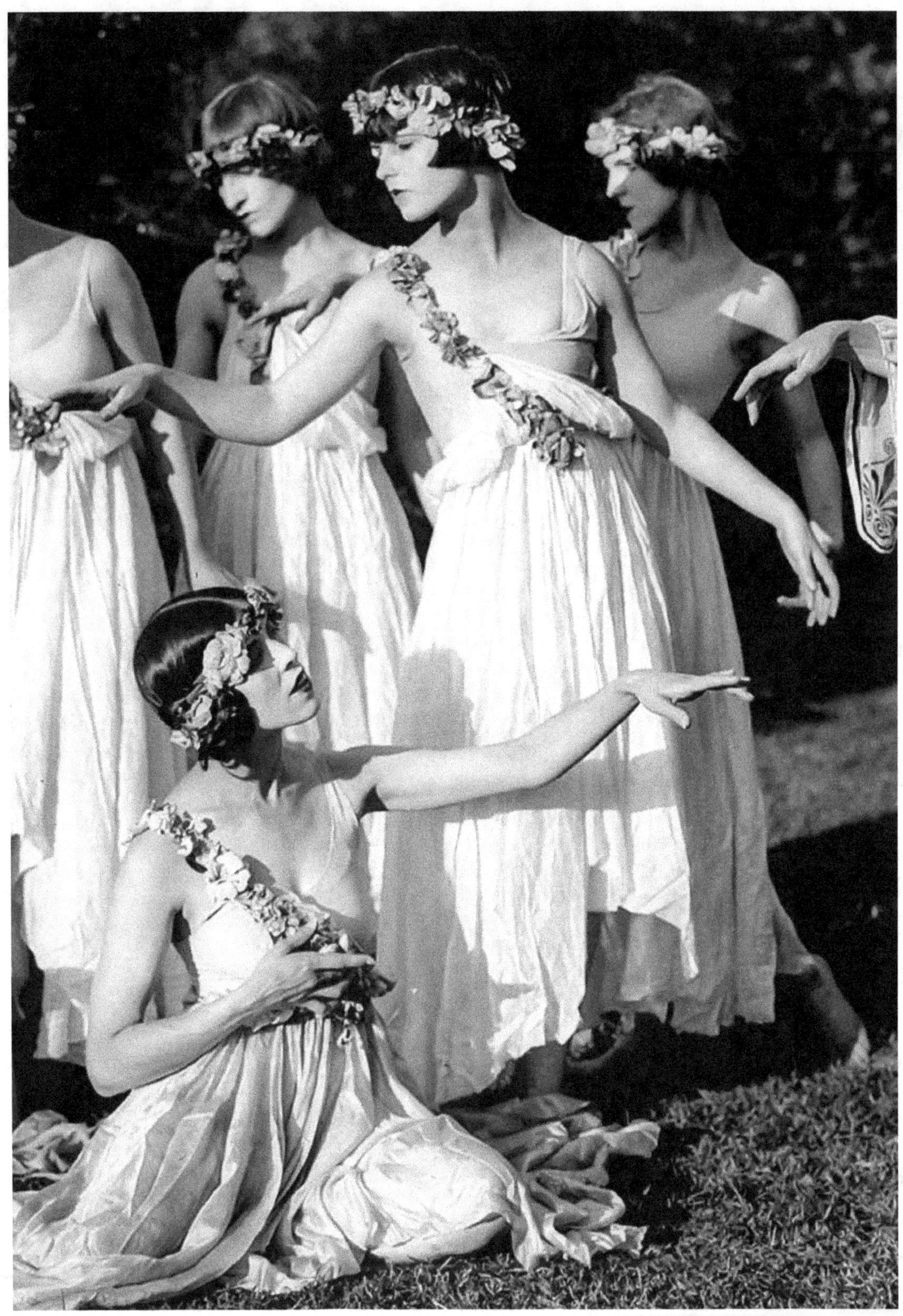

Image 3: Brooks in center and Martha Graham kneeling with the Denishawn Dance Company, 1923 or early 1924.

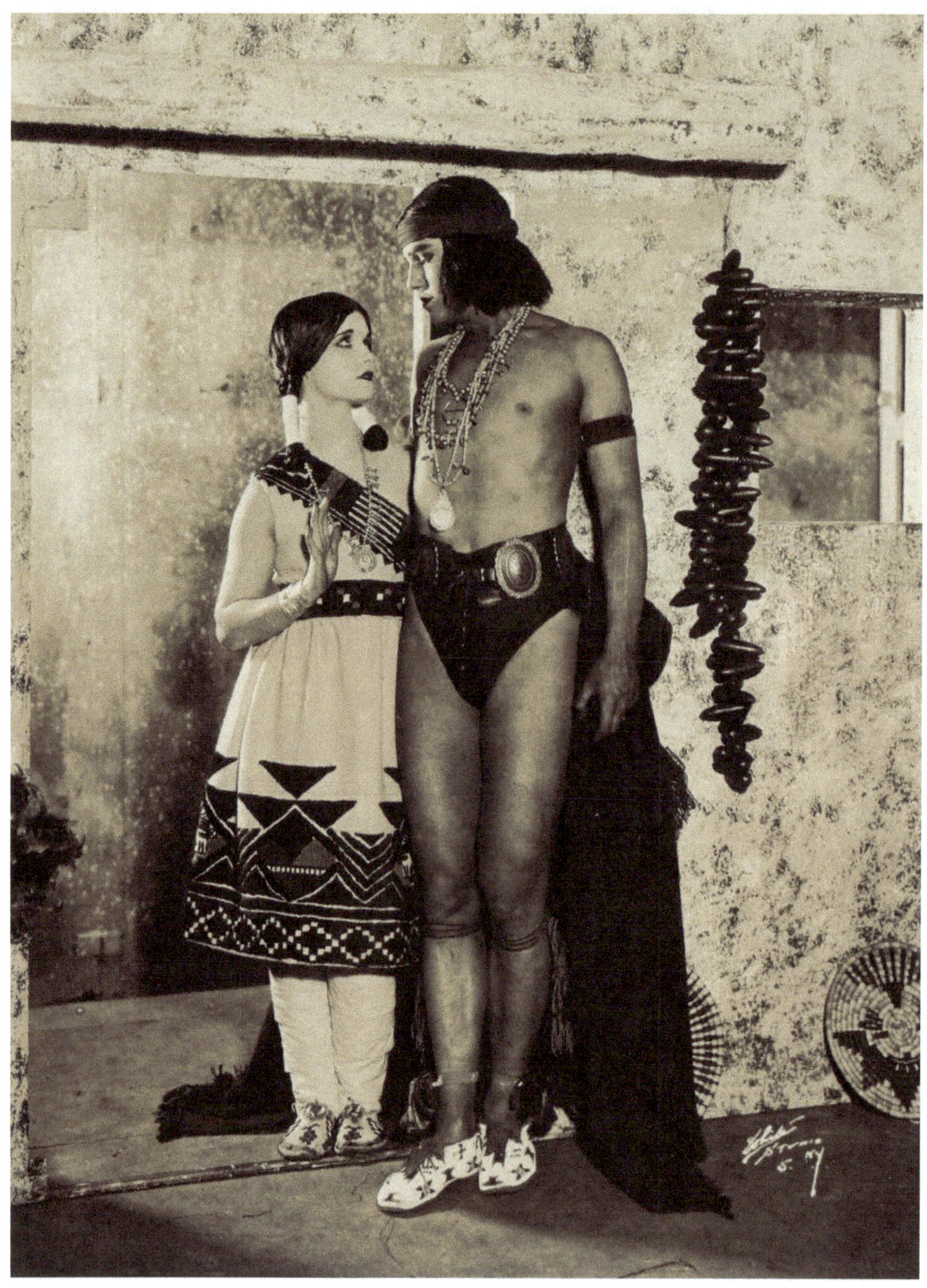

Image 4: With Ted Shawn in "Feather of the Dawn," 1923; Source: The New York Public Library Digital Collections.

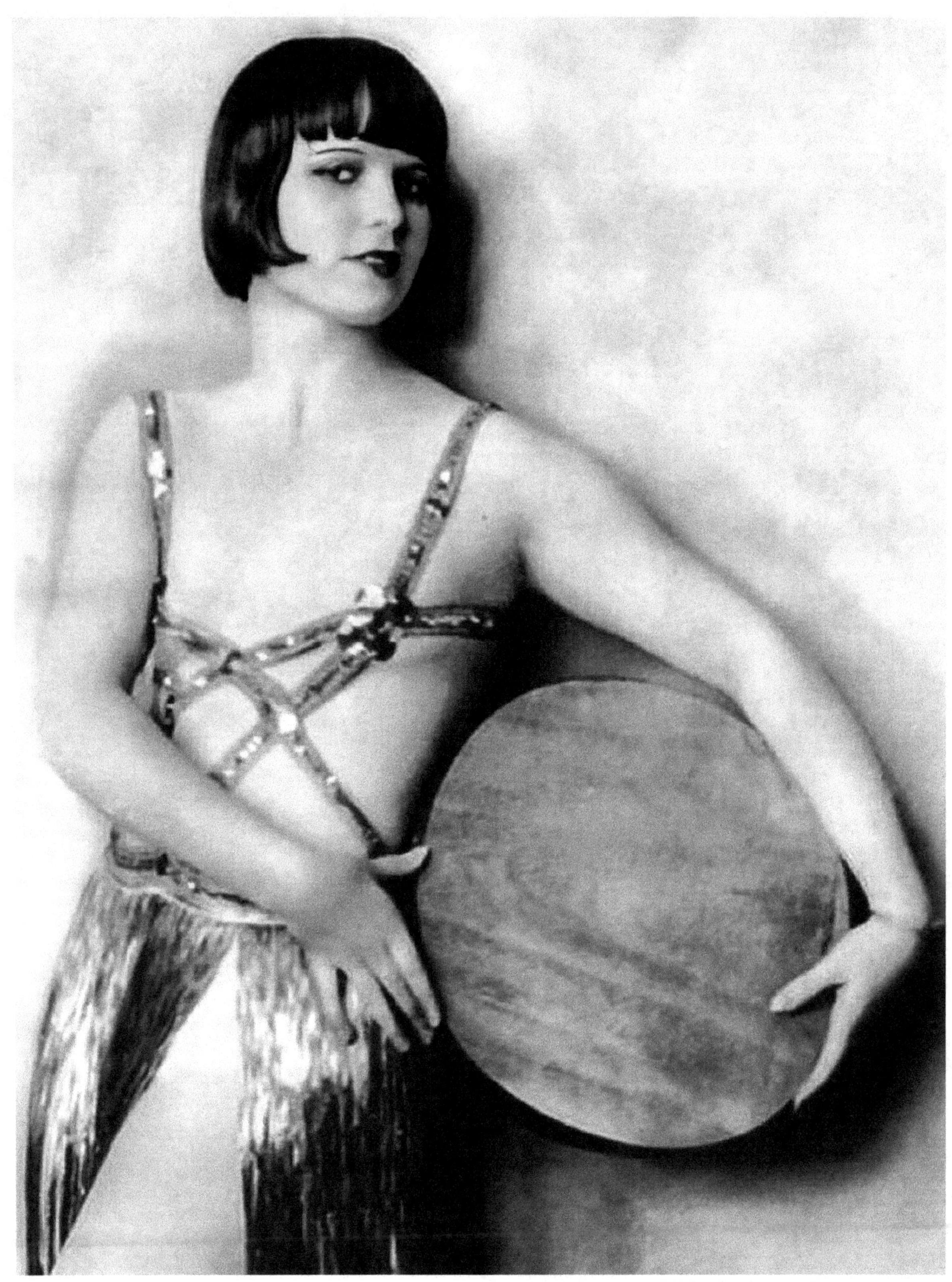

Image 5: Promotional photo by Alfred Cheney Johnston, well-known photographer of the Ziegfeld Follies and other Broadway showgirls, 1924-1925.

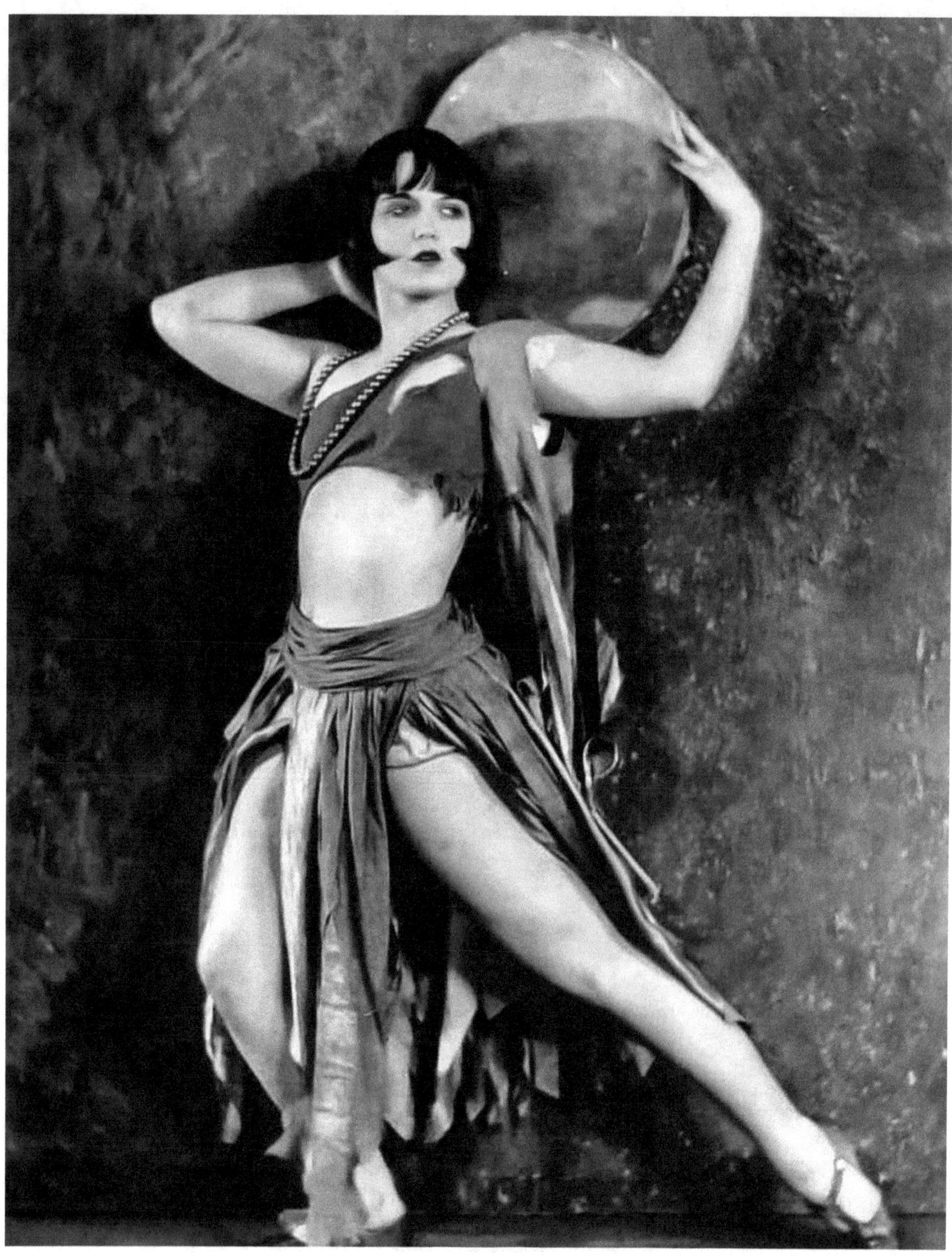

Image 6: Promotional photo, 1924-1925.

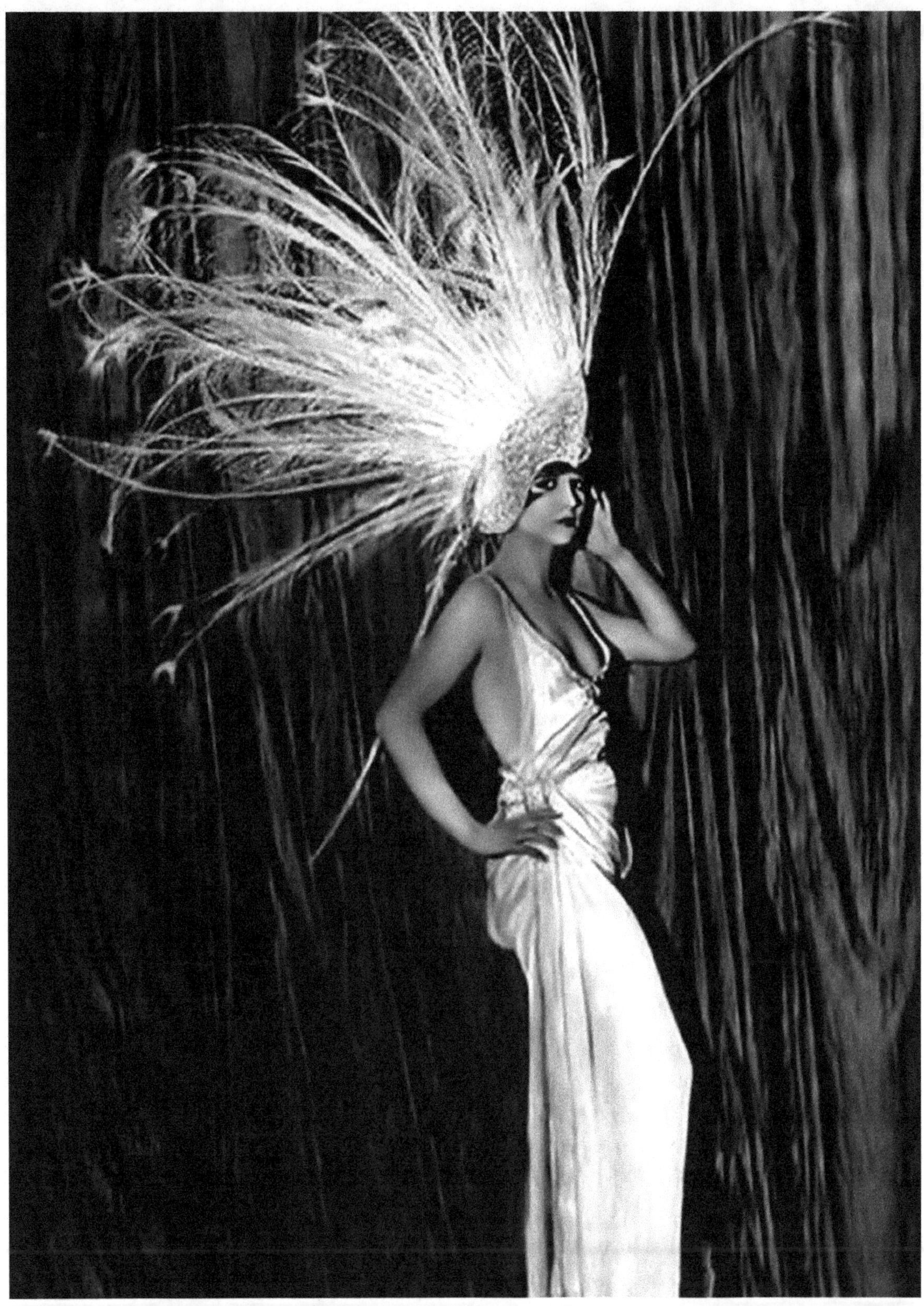

Image 7: In a costume for the Ziegfeld Follies, 1925.

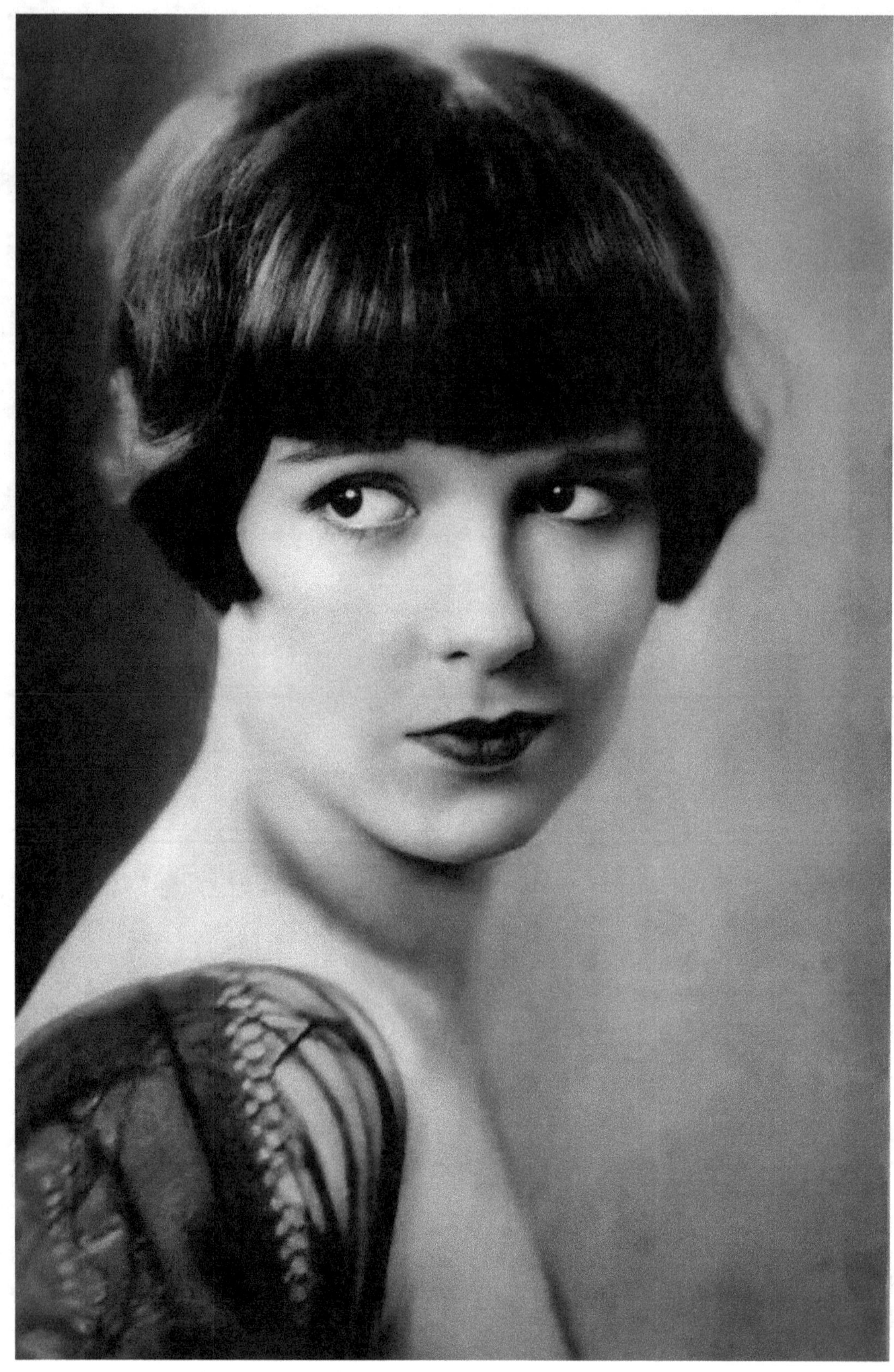

Image 8: Promotional photo by John De Mirjian, ca. 1924-1925.

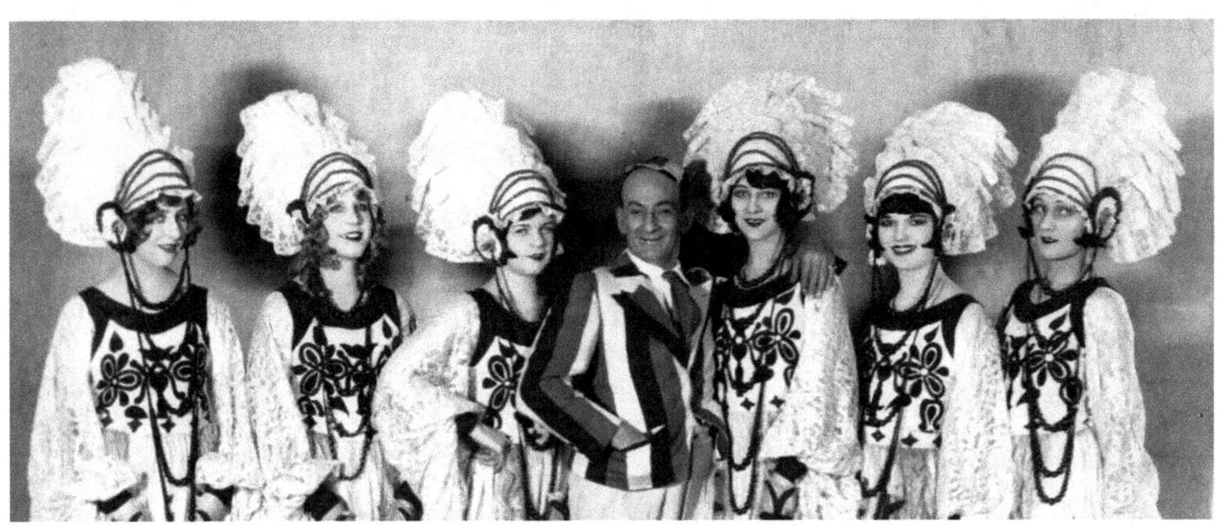

Image 9: From left: Gertrude McDonald, Dixie Boatwright, Catherine Littlefield, Leon Errol, Anastasia Reilly, Louise Brooks, and Helen Frances, Ziegfeld Follies, 1925.

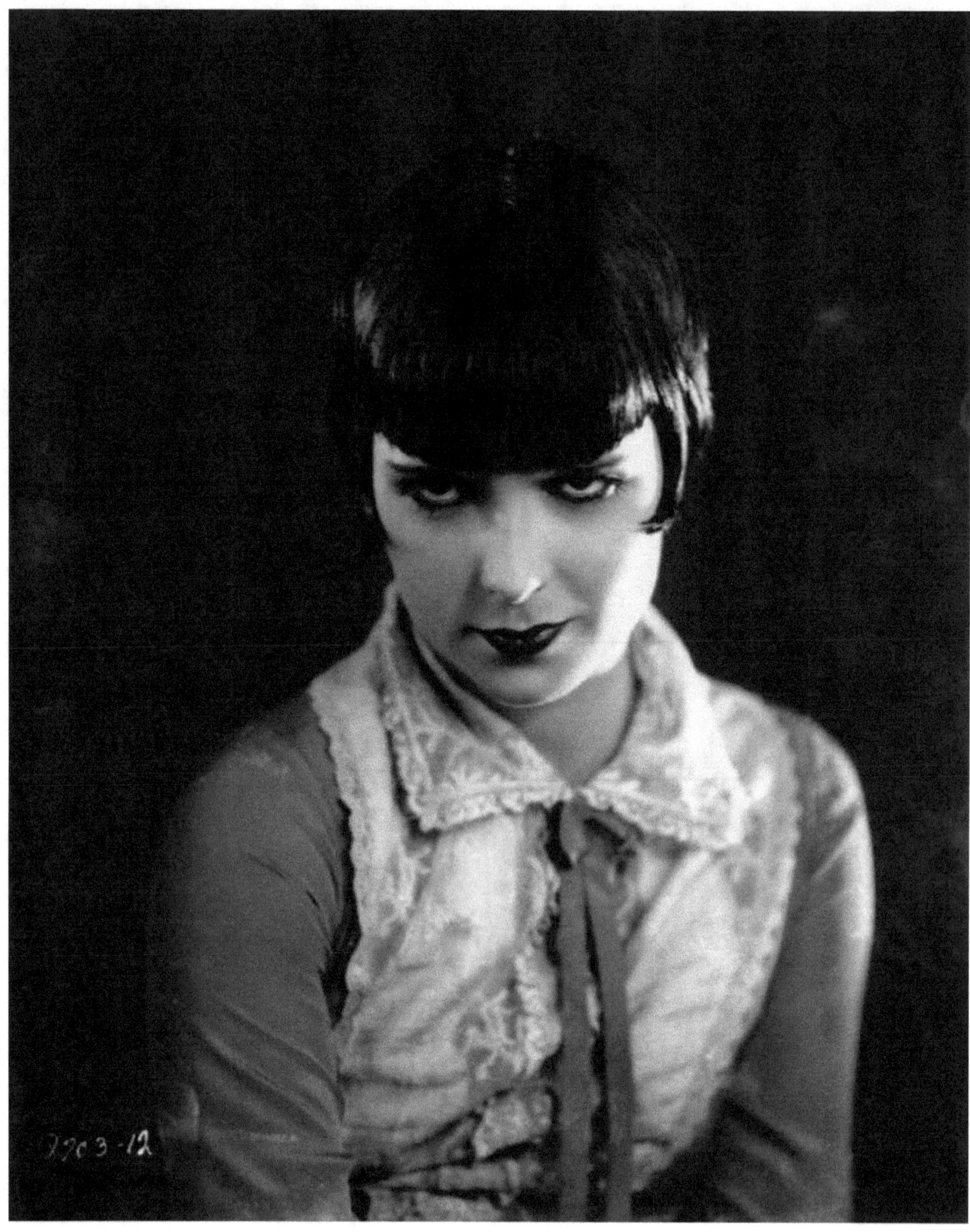

Image 10: Shortly after signing with Paramount Pictures in 1925.

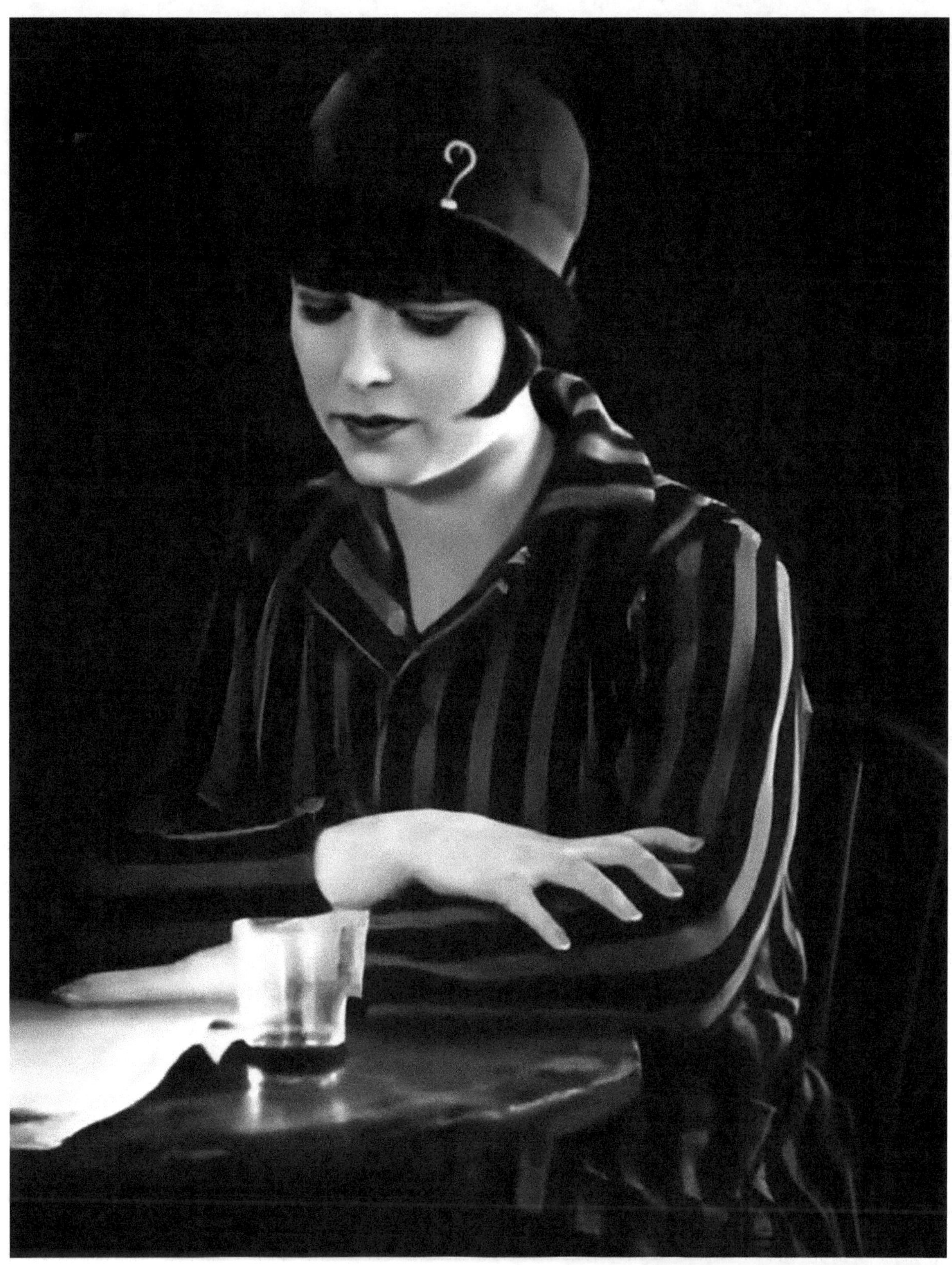

Image 11: *The Street of Forgotten Men*, 1925.

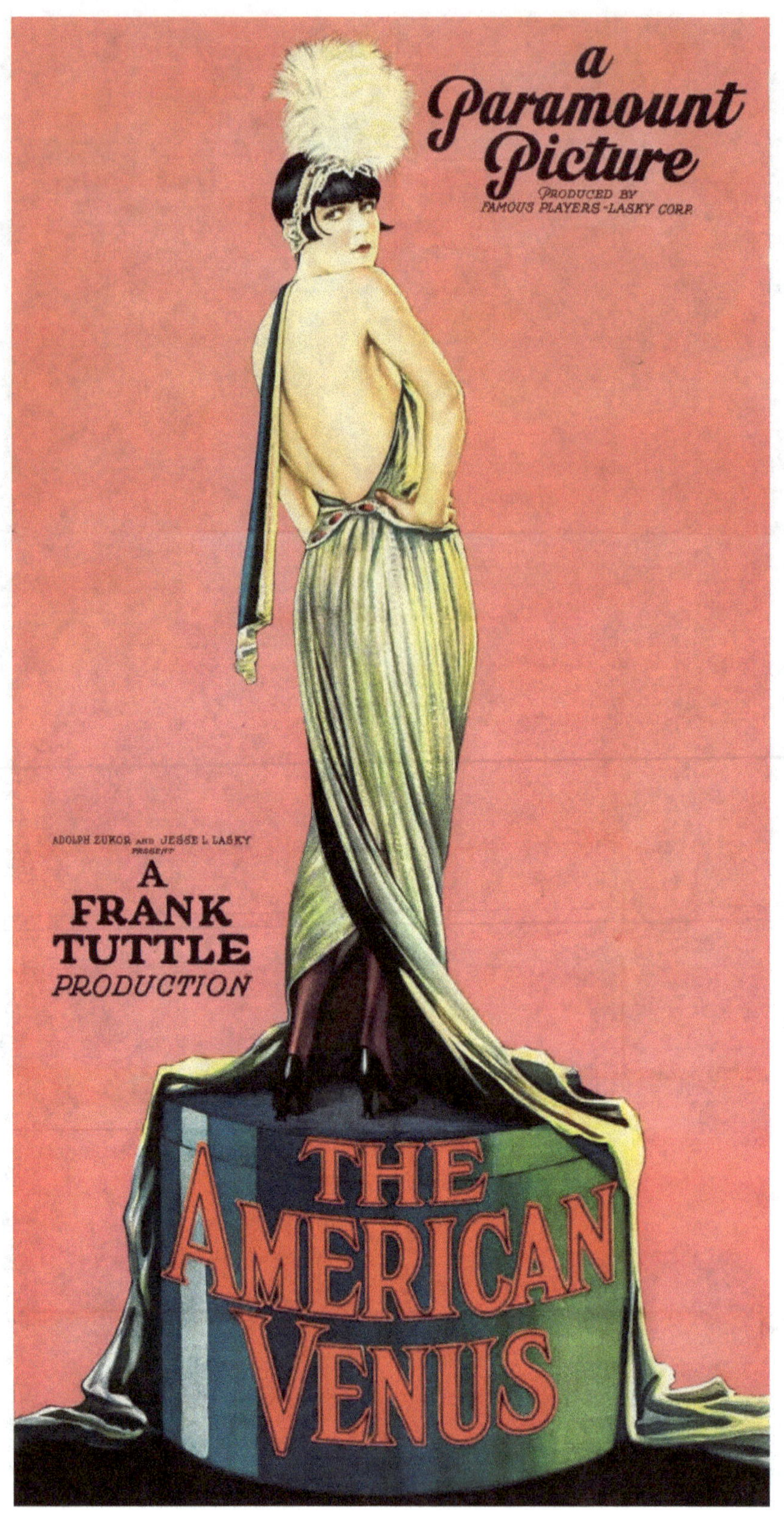

Image 12: Poster for *The American Venus,* 1926.

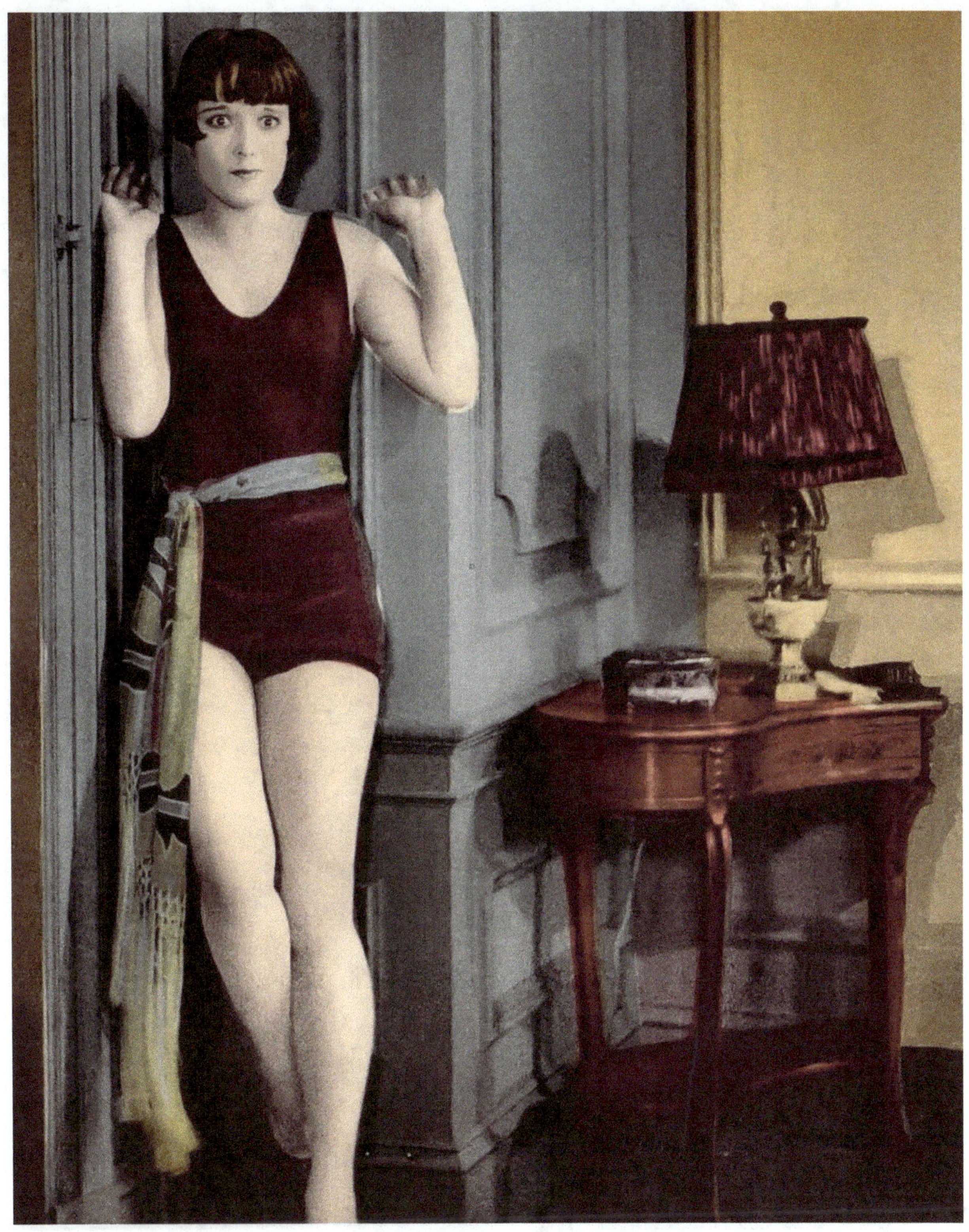

Image 13: Lobby card detail for *The American Venus,* 1926.

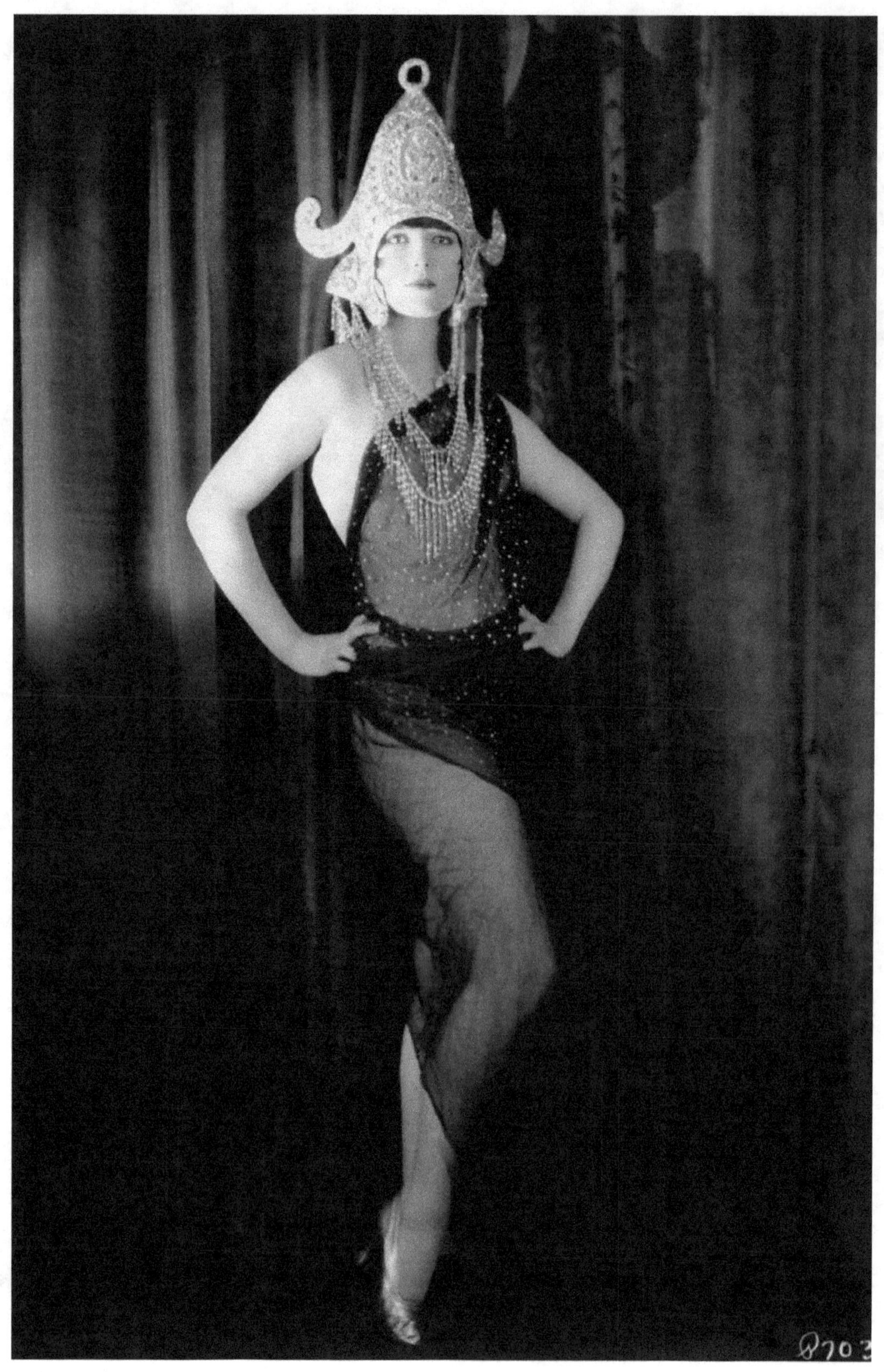

Image 14: *The American Venus*, 1926.

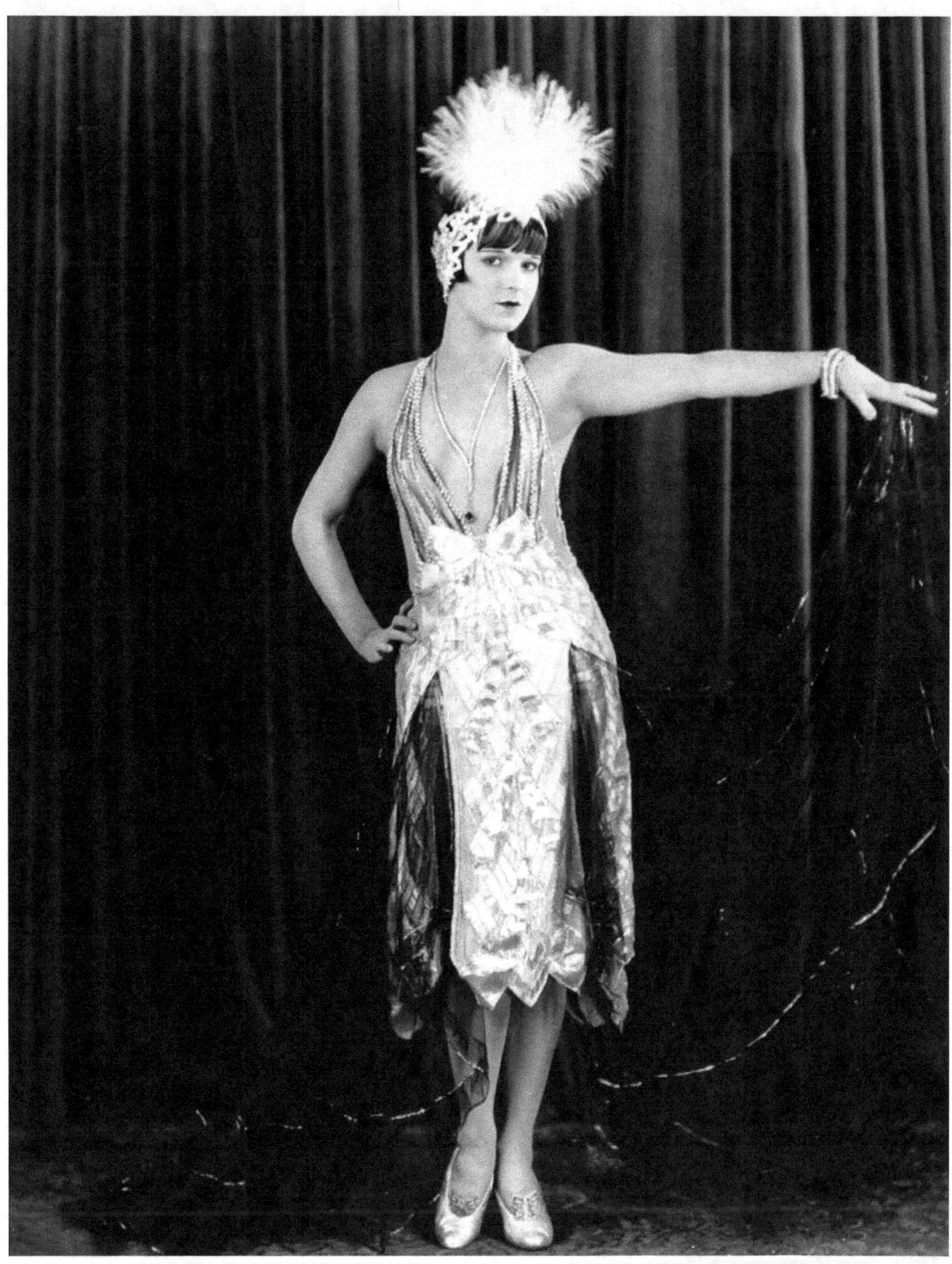

Image 15: *The American Venus*, 1926.

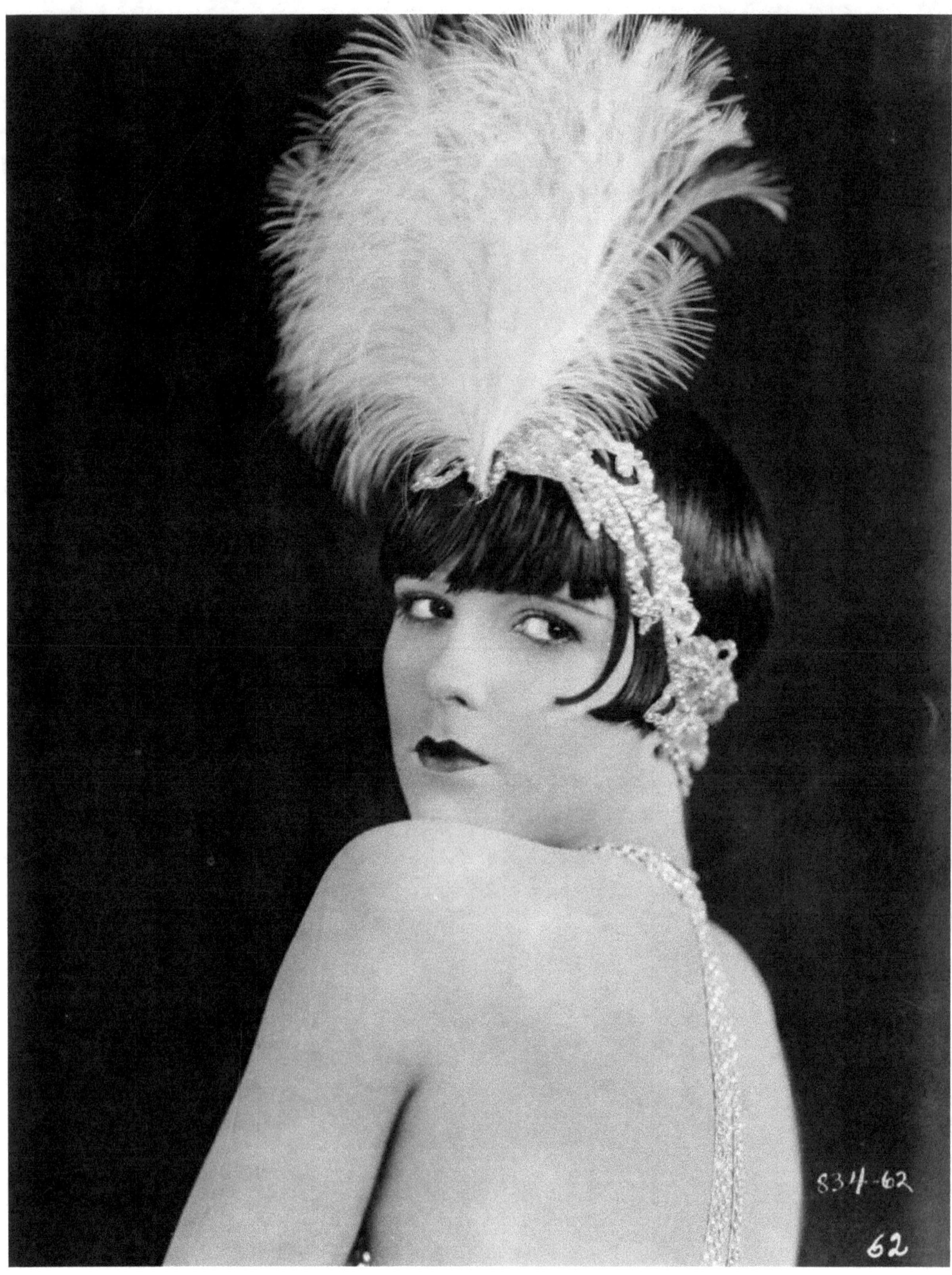

Image 16: *The American Venus*, 1926.

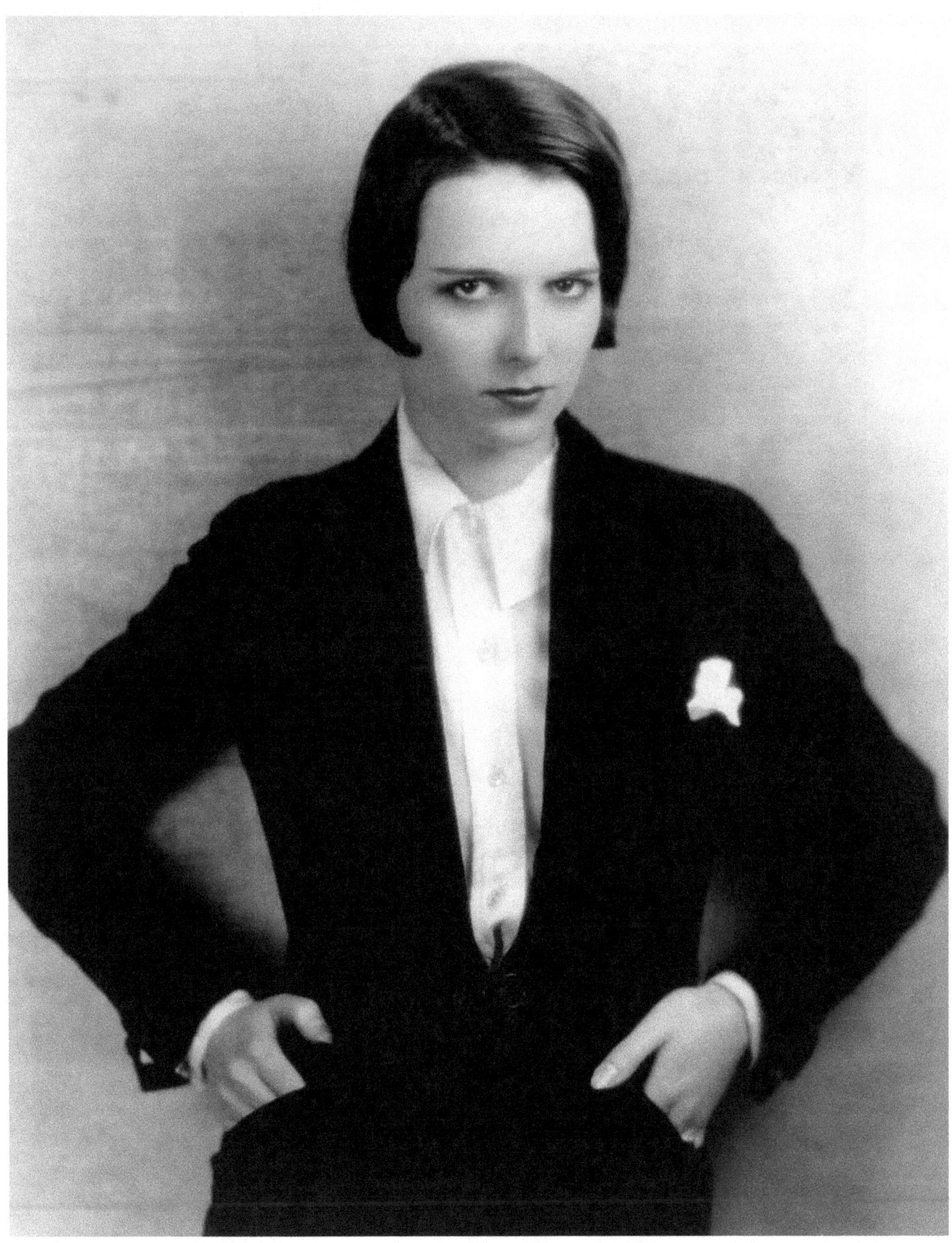

Image 17: Promotional photo, ca. 1926.

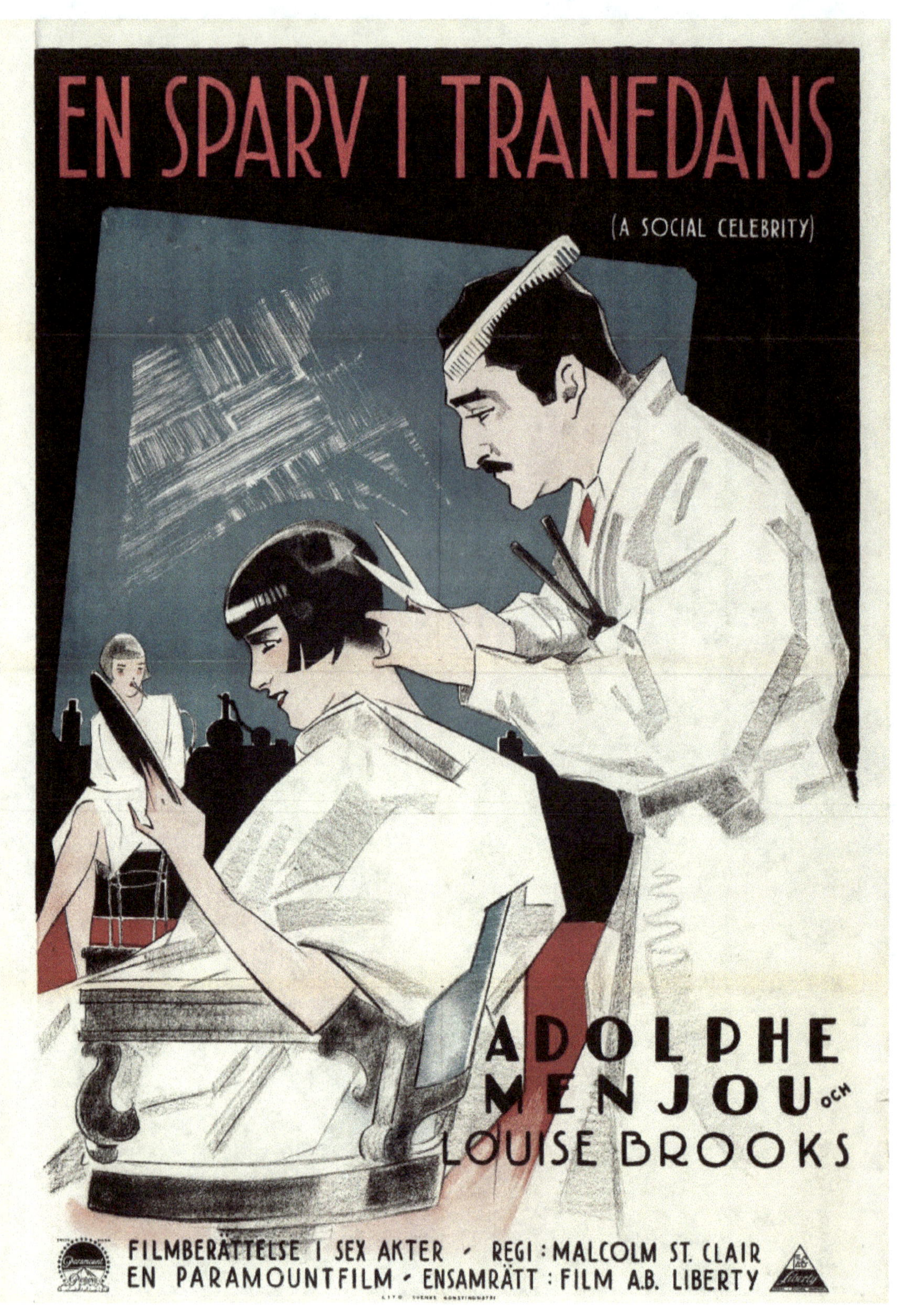

Image 18: Poster for *A Social Celebrity*, 1926.

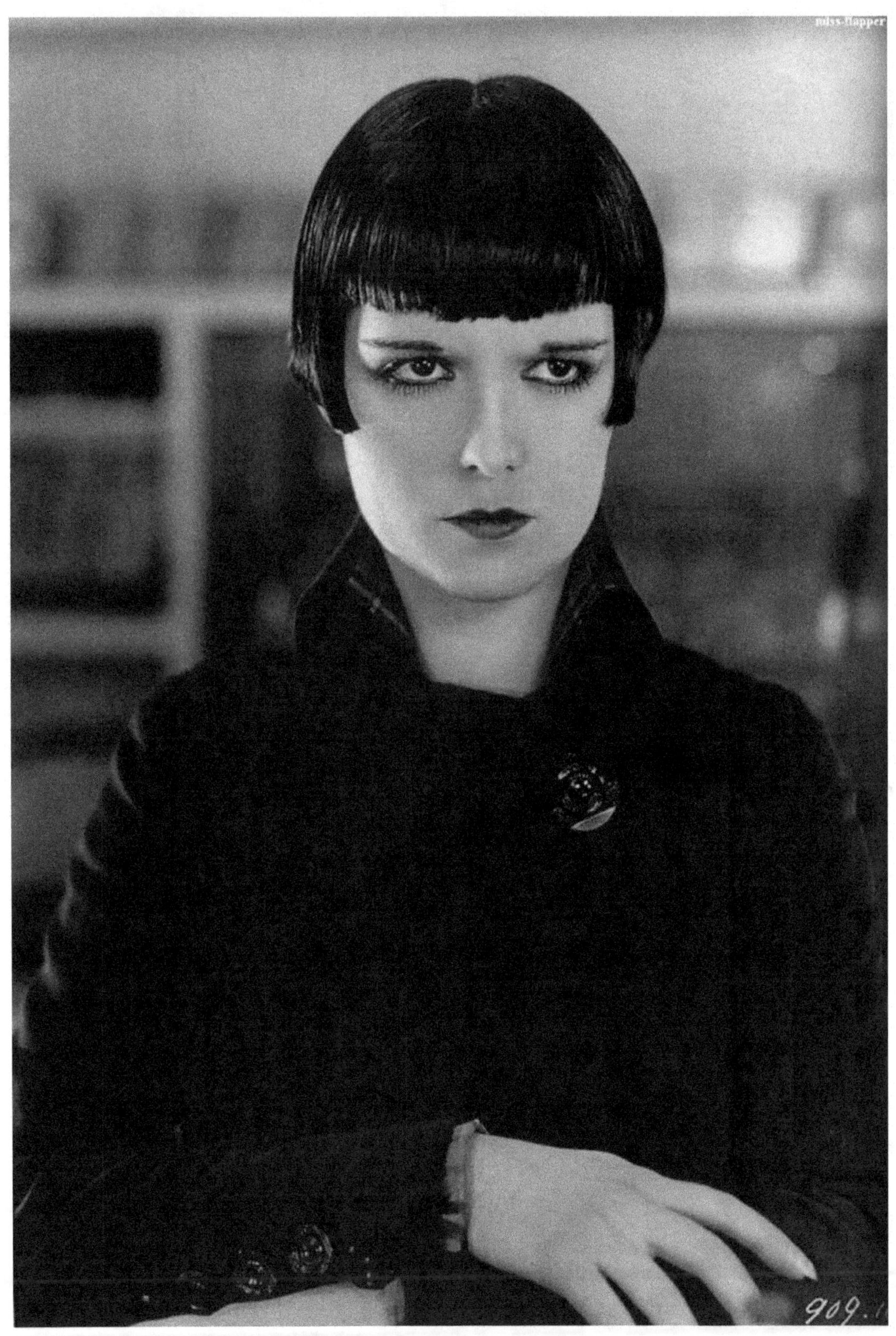

Image 19: *A Social Celebrity, 1926.*

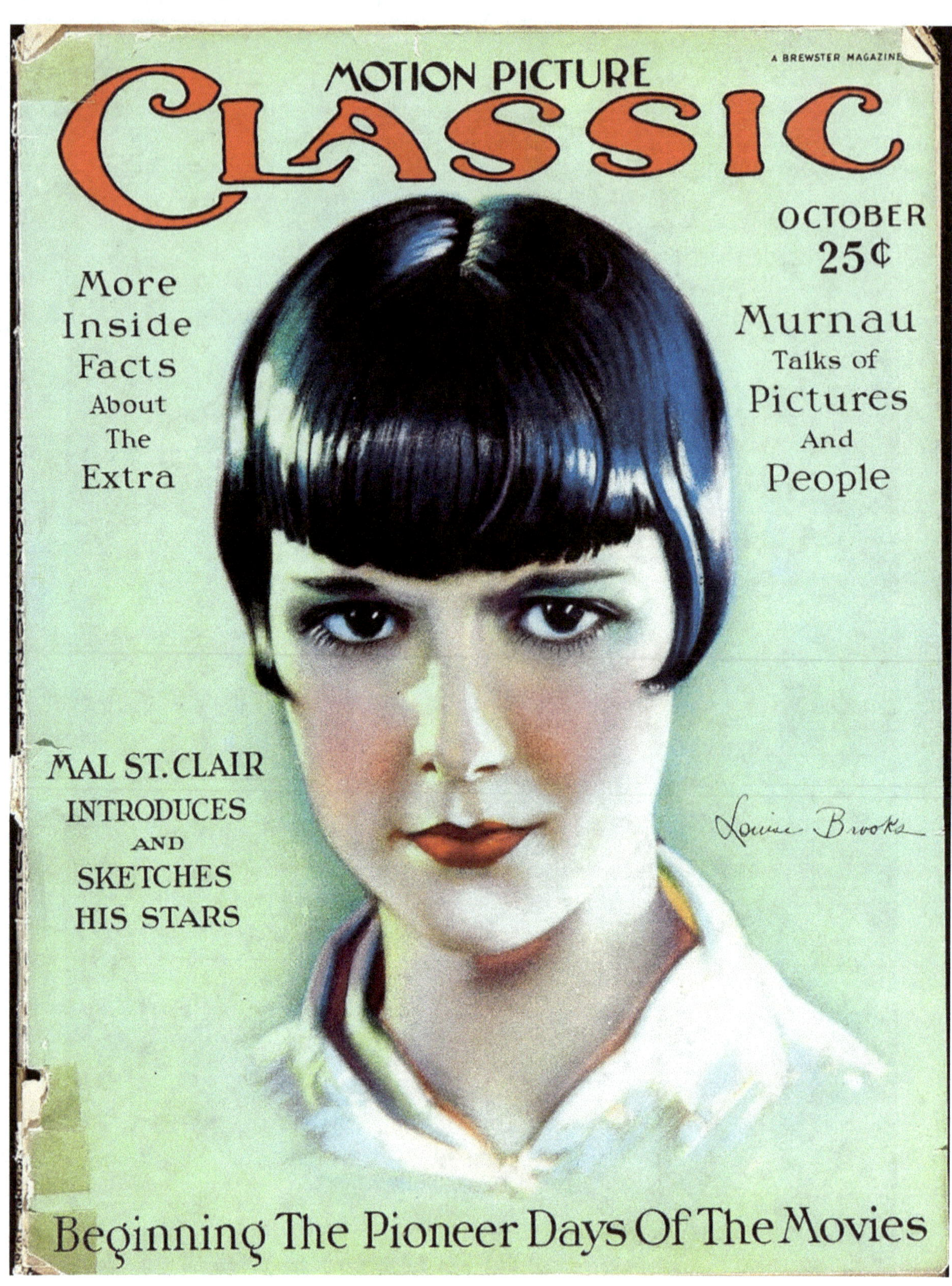

Image 20: Cover of a fan magazine, Oct, 1926.

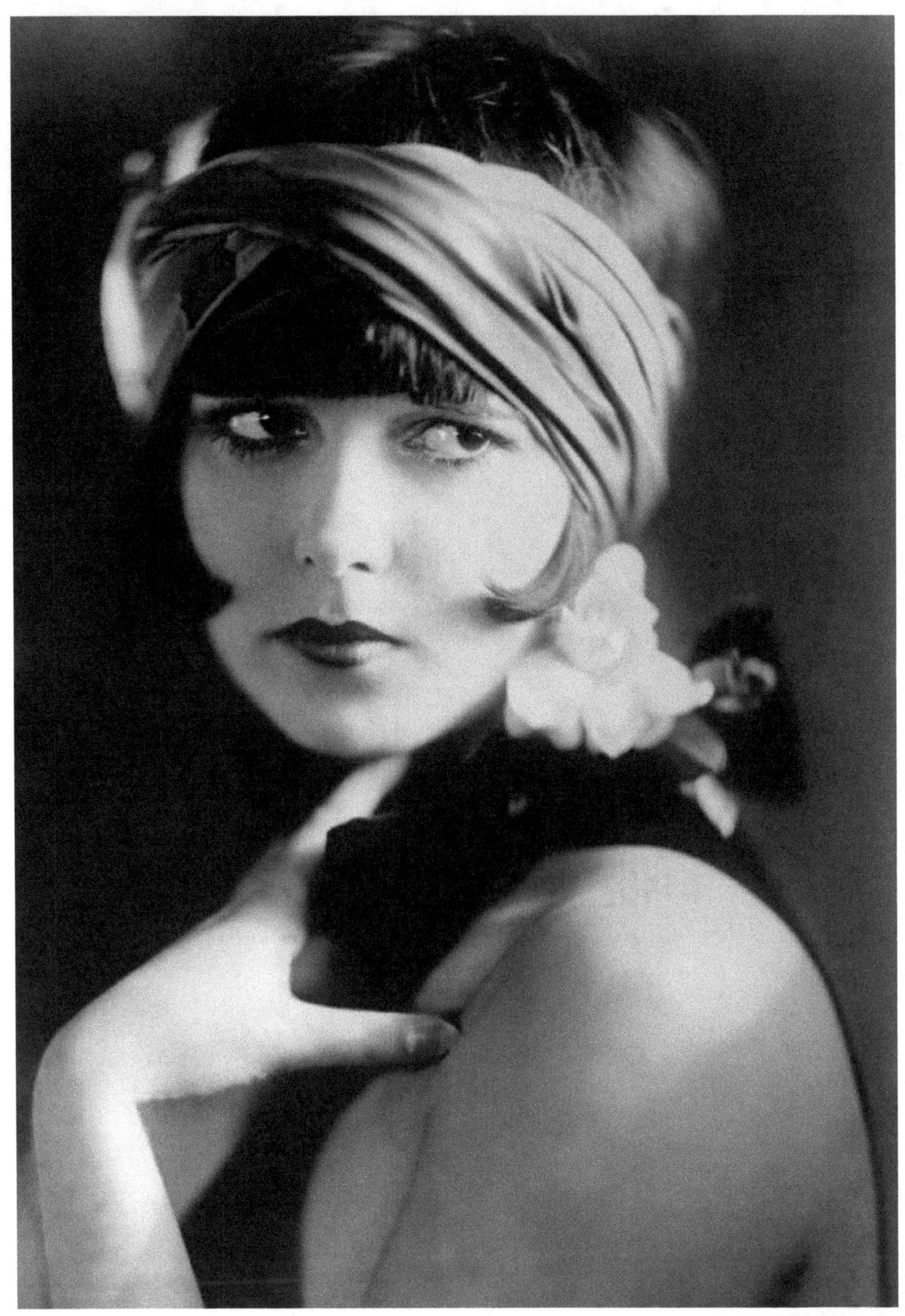

Image 21: Publicity photo, ca. 1926.

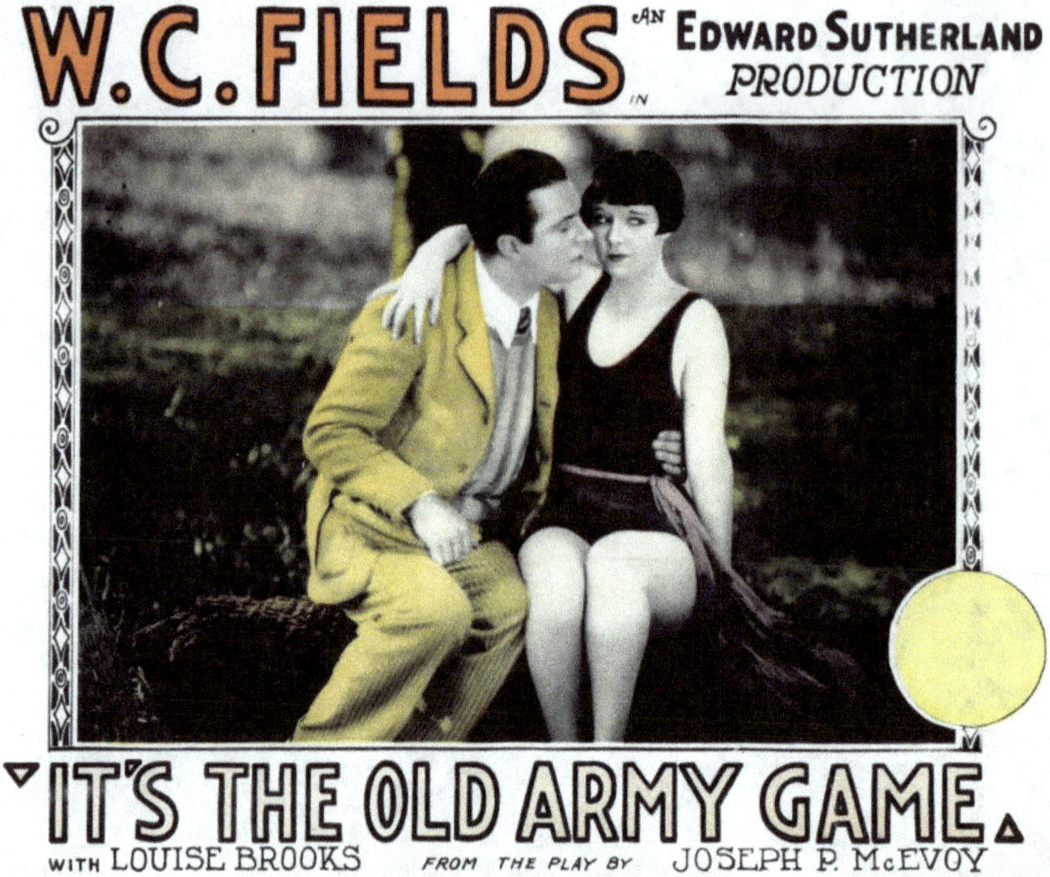

Image 22: Lobby card for *It's the Old Army Game,* 1926.

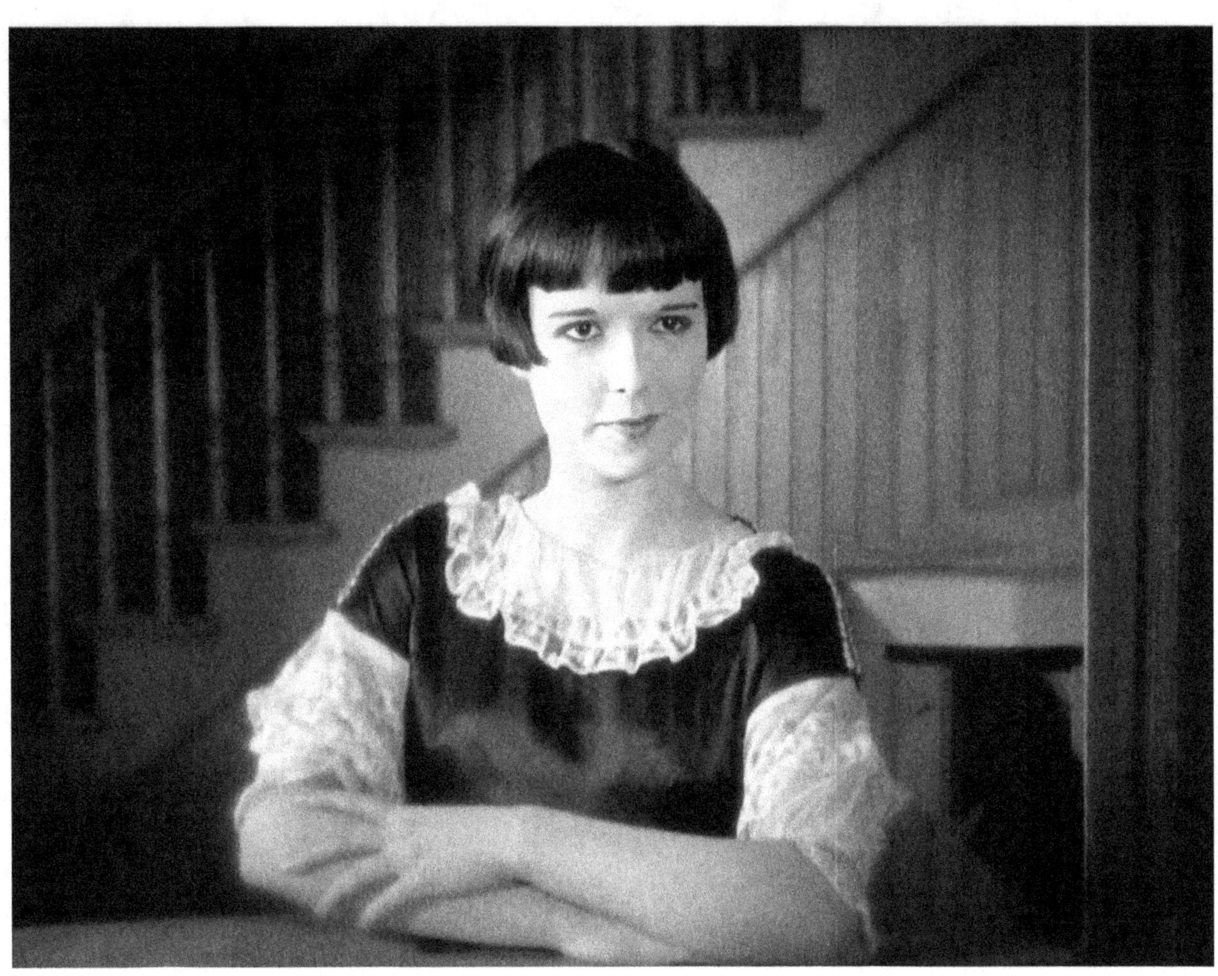

Image 23: *It's the Old Army Game*, 1926.

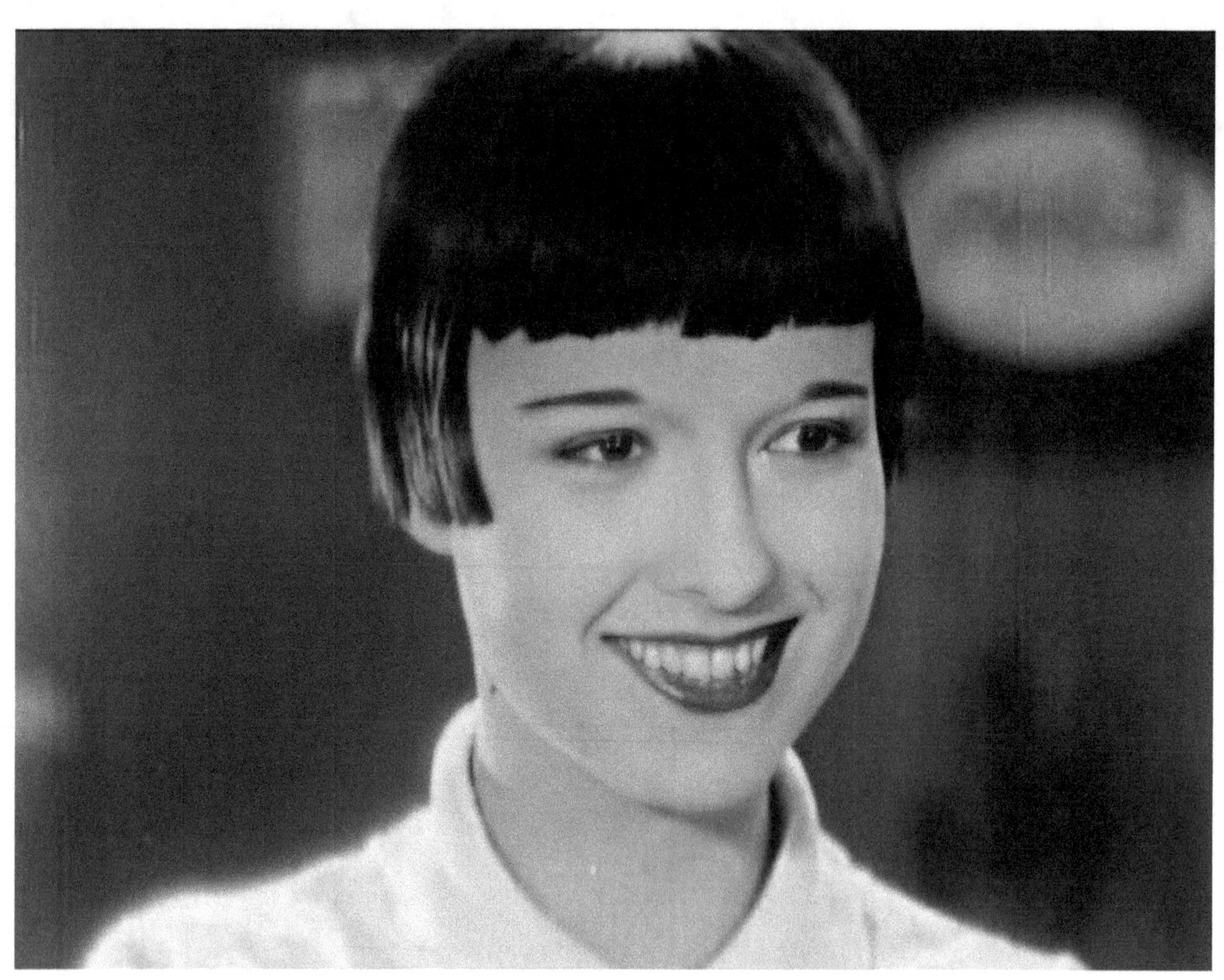

Image 24: *It's the Old Army Game*, 1926.

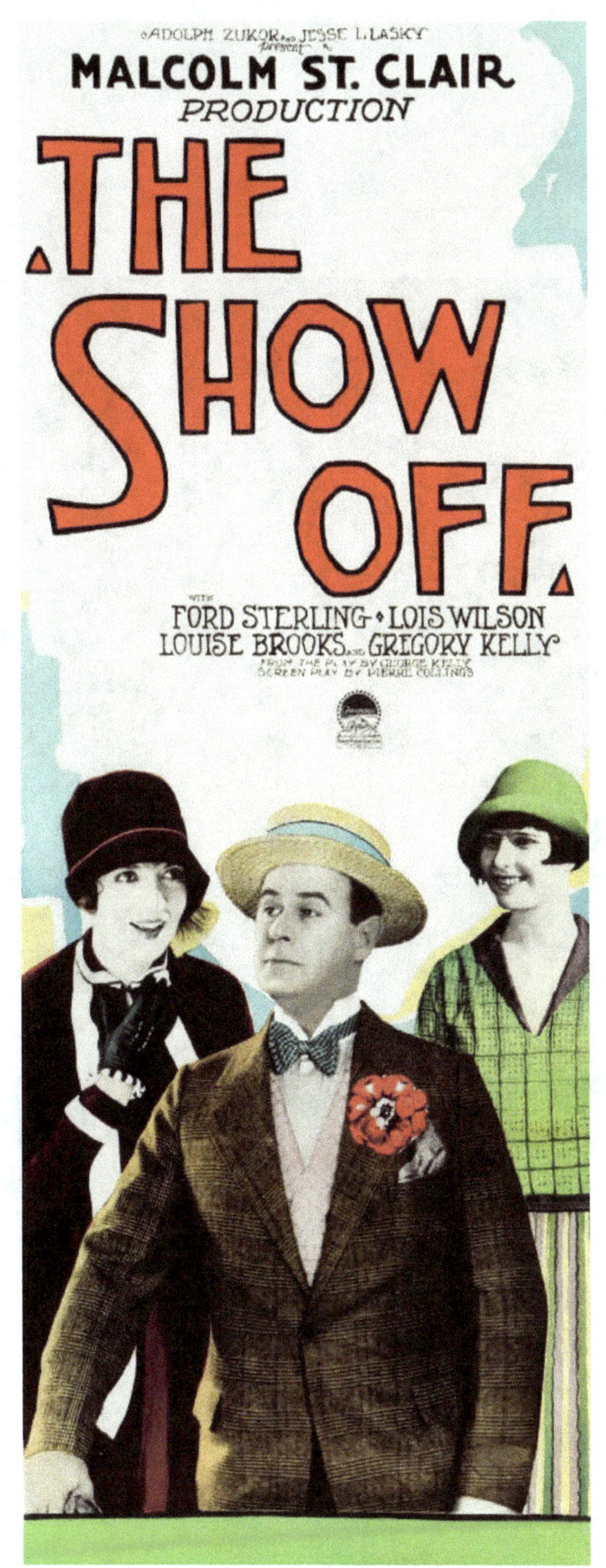

Image 25: Poster for *The Show Off*, 1926.

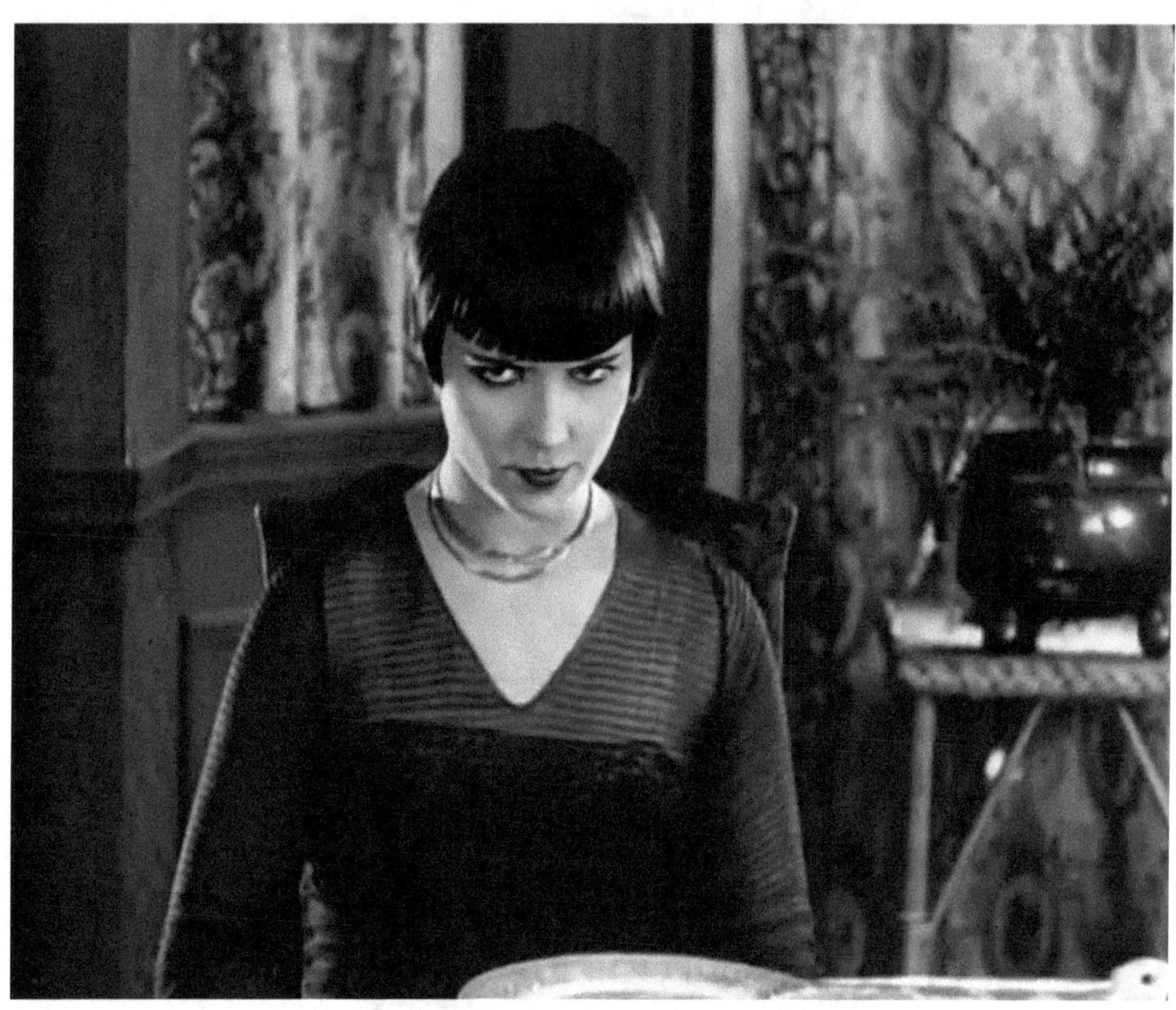

Image 26: *The Show Off*, 1926.

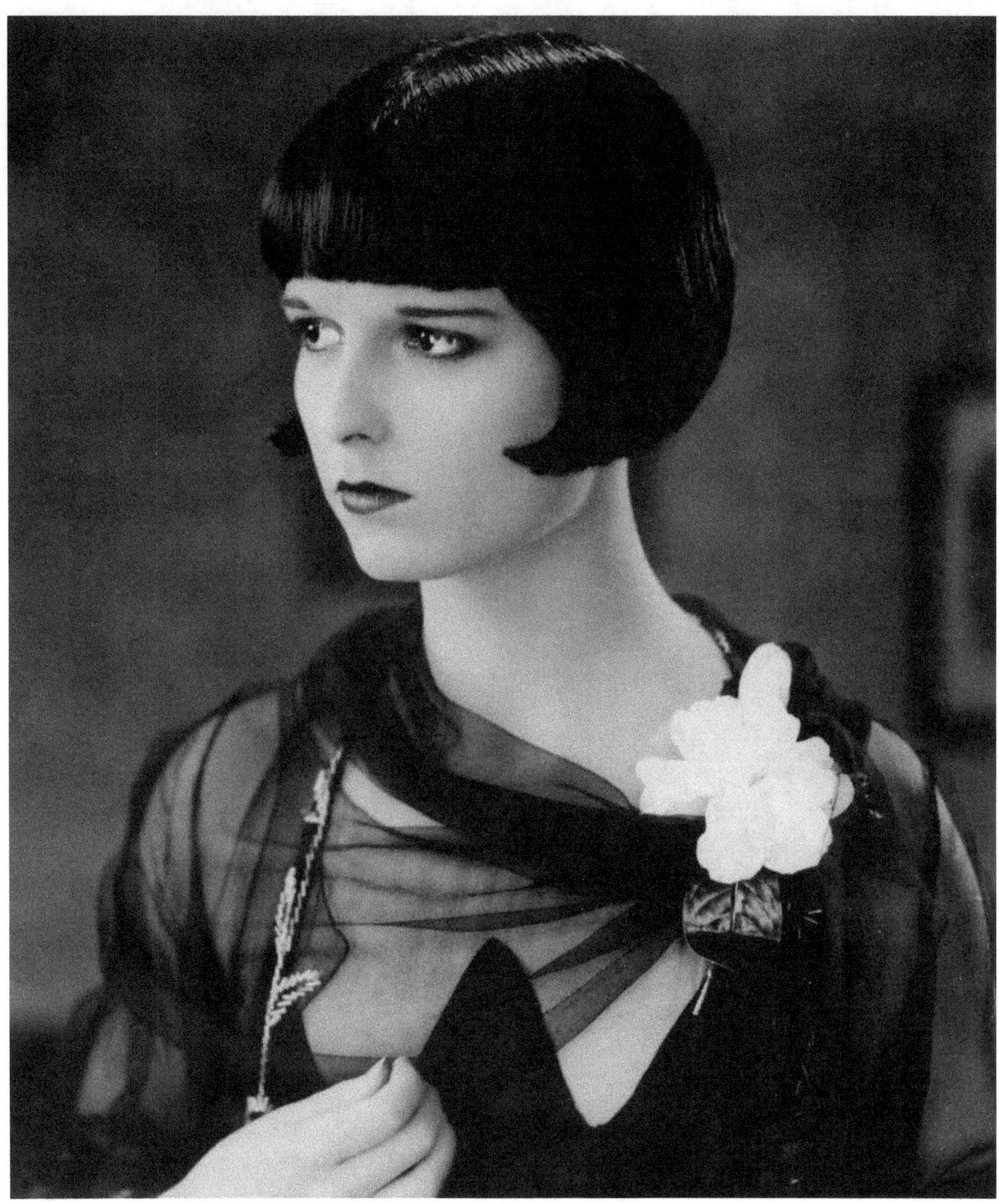

Image 27: Promotional photo, ca. 1926.

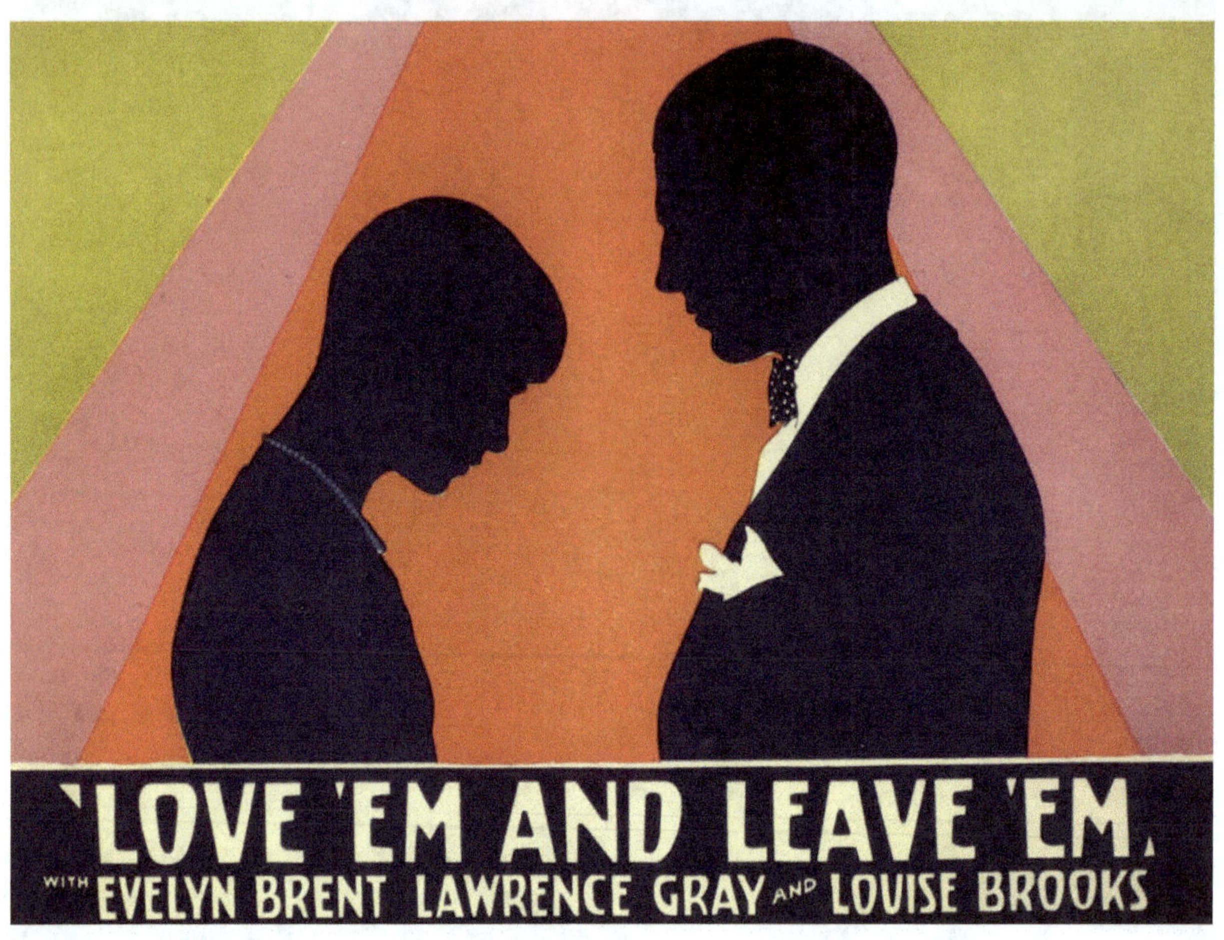

Image 28: Poster for *Love 'Em and Leave 'Em*, 1926.

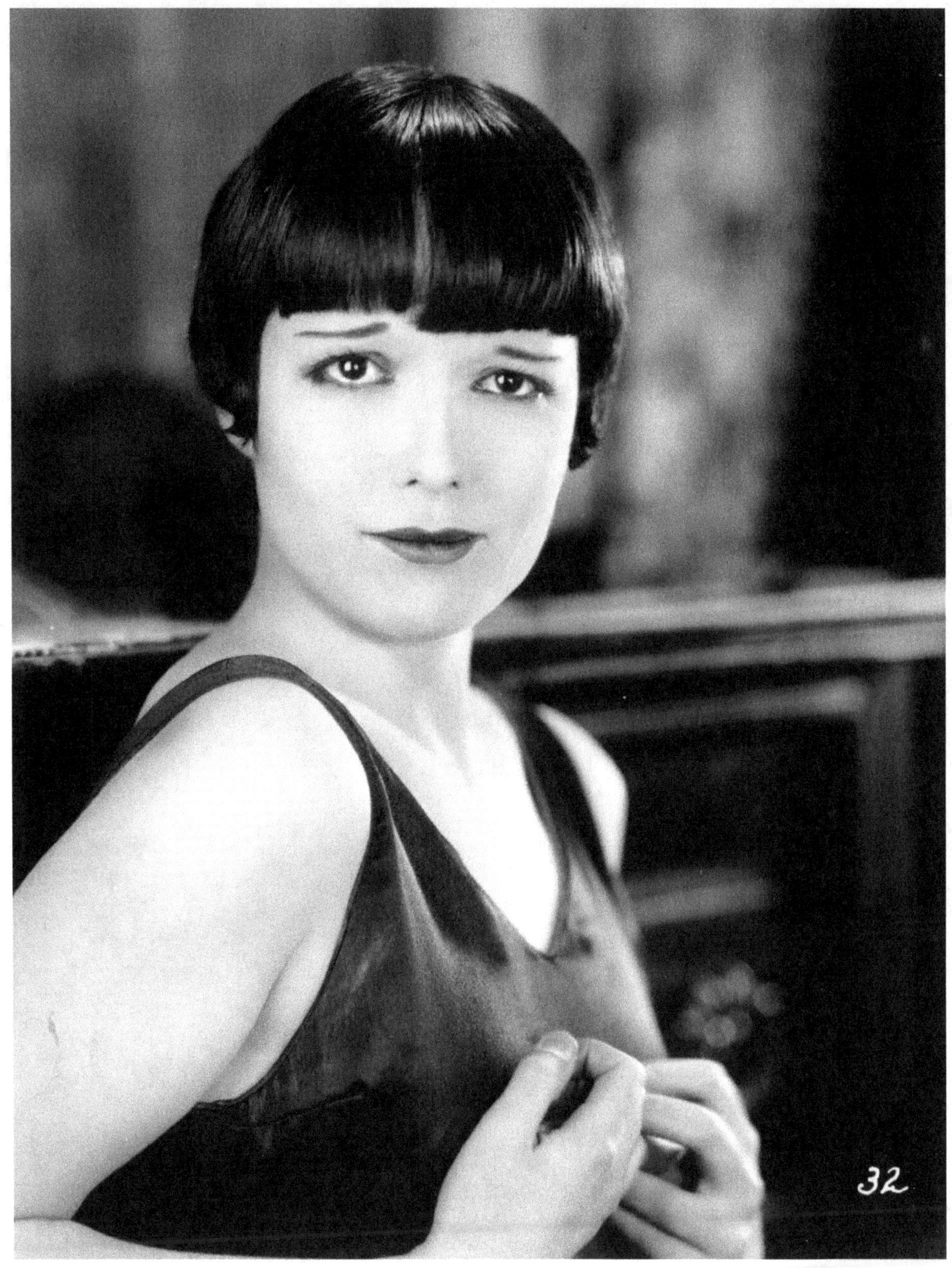

Image 29: *Love 'Em and Leave 'Em*, 1926.

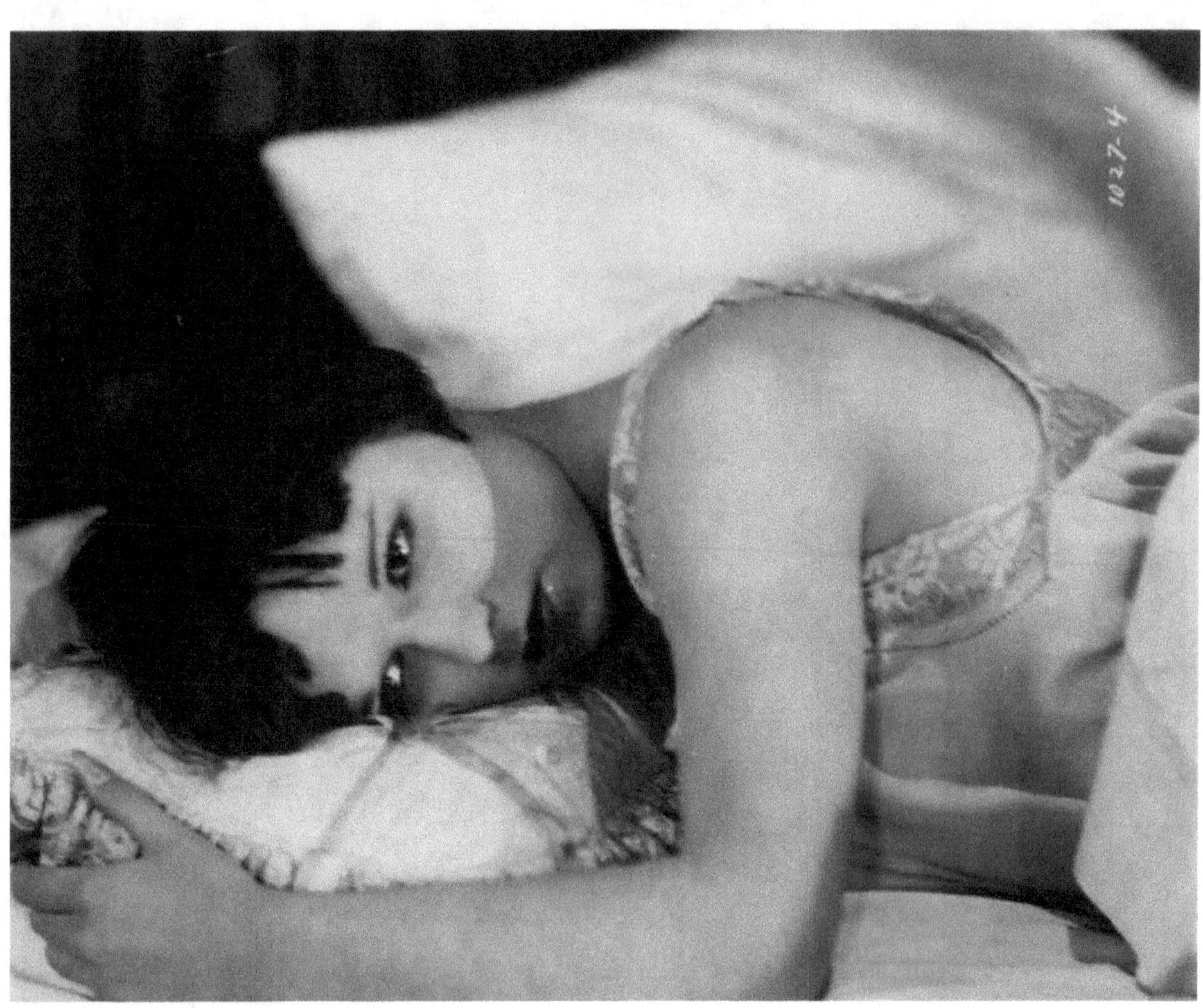

Image 30: *Love 'Em and Leave 'Em*, 1926.

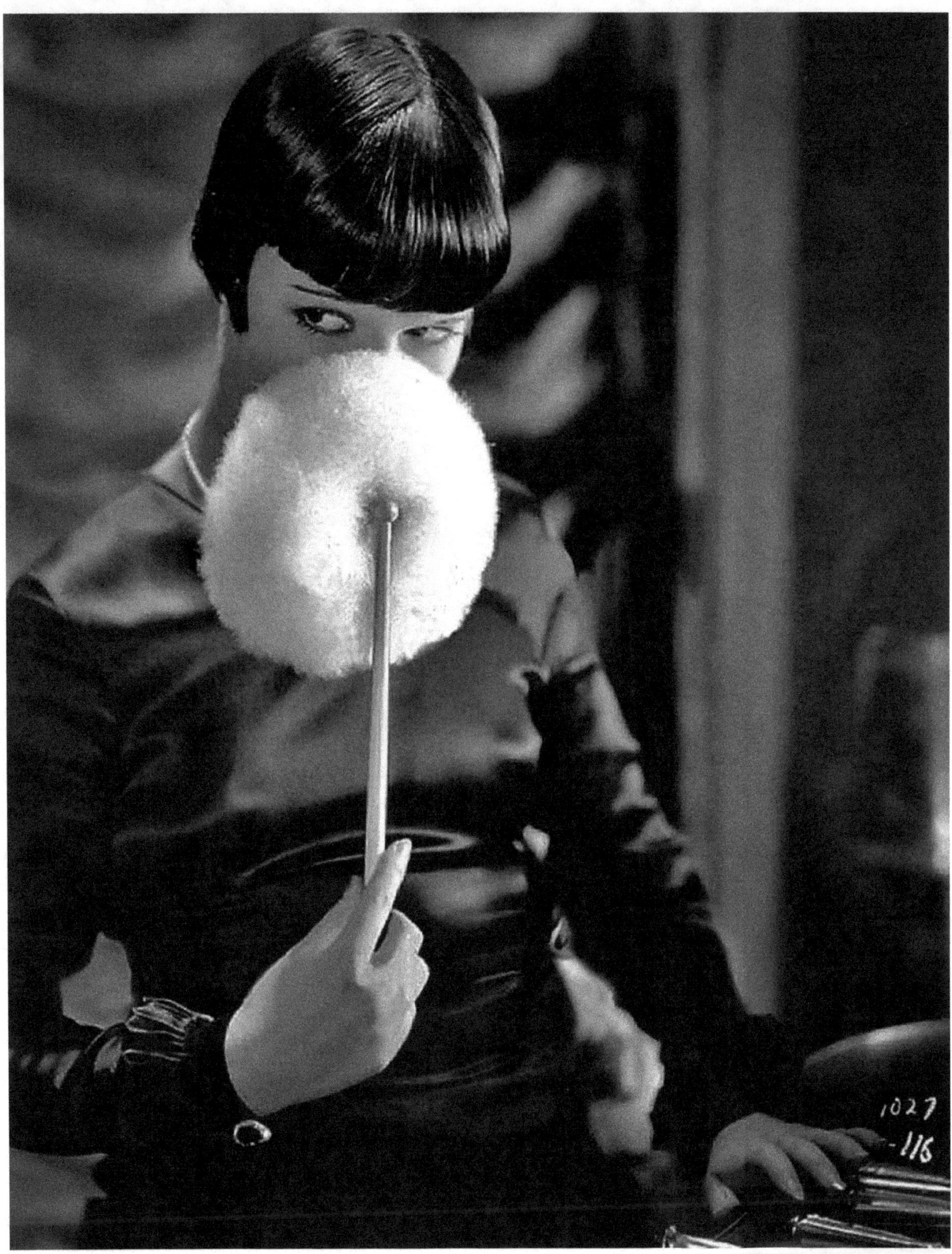

Image 31: *Love 'Em and Leave 'Em,* 1926.

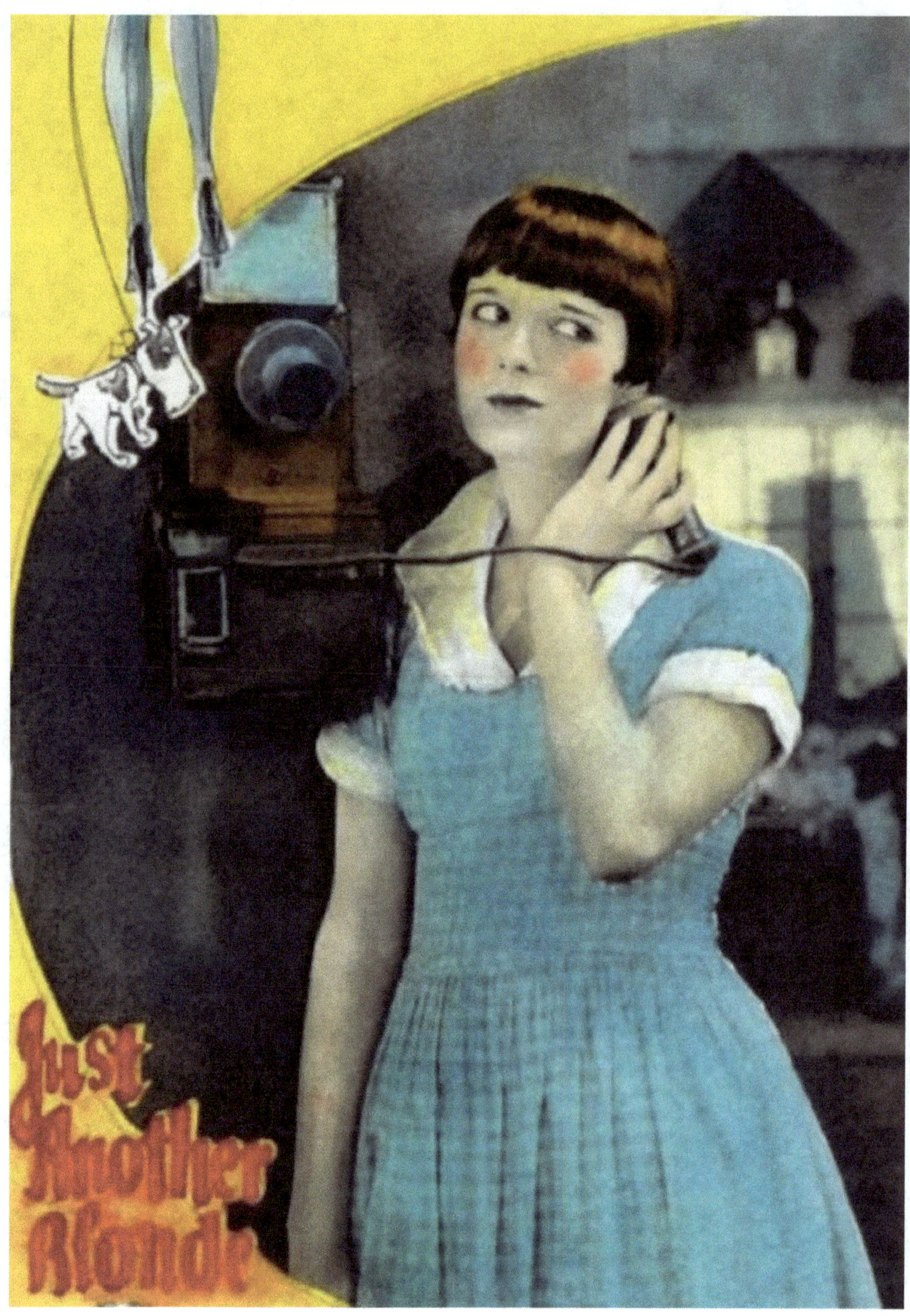

Image 32: Lobby card detail for *Just Another Blonde*, 1926.

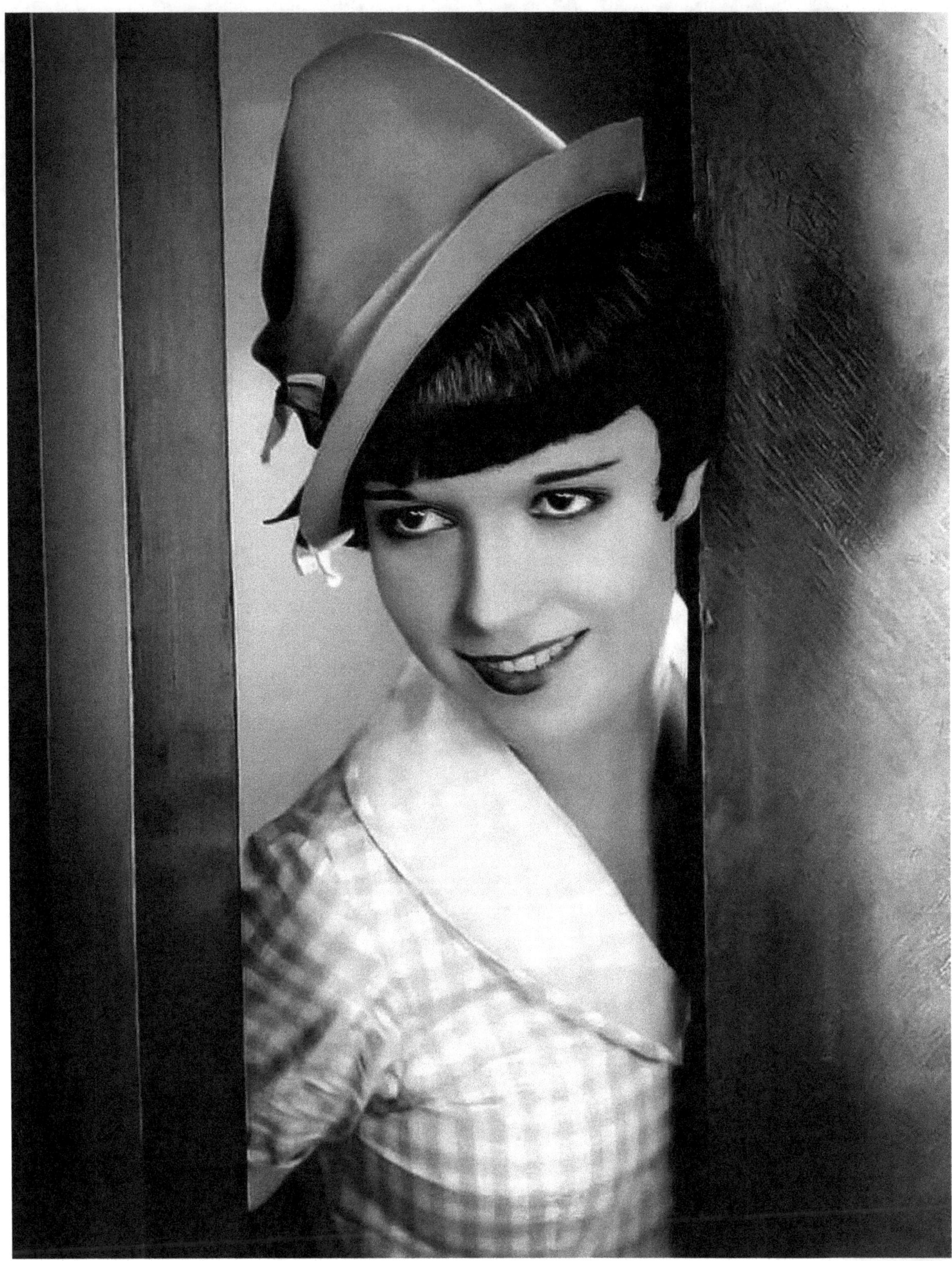

Image 33: *Just Another Blonde*, 1926.

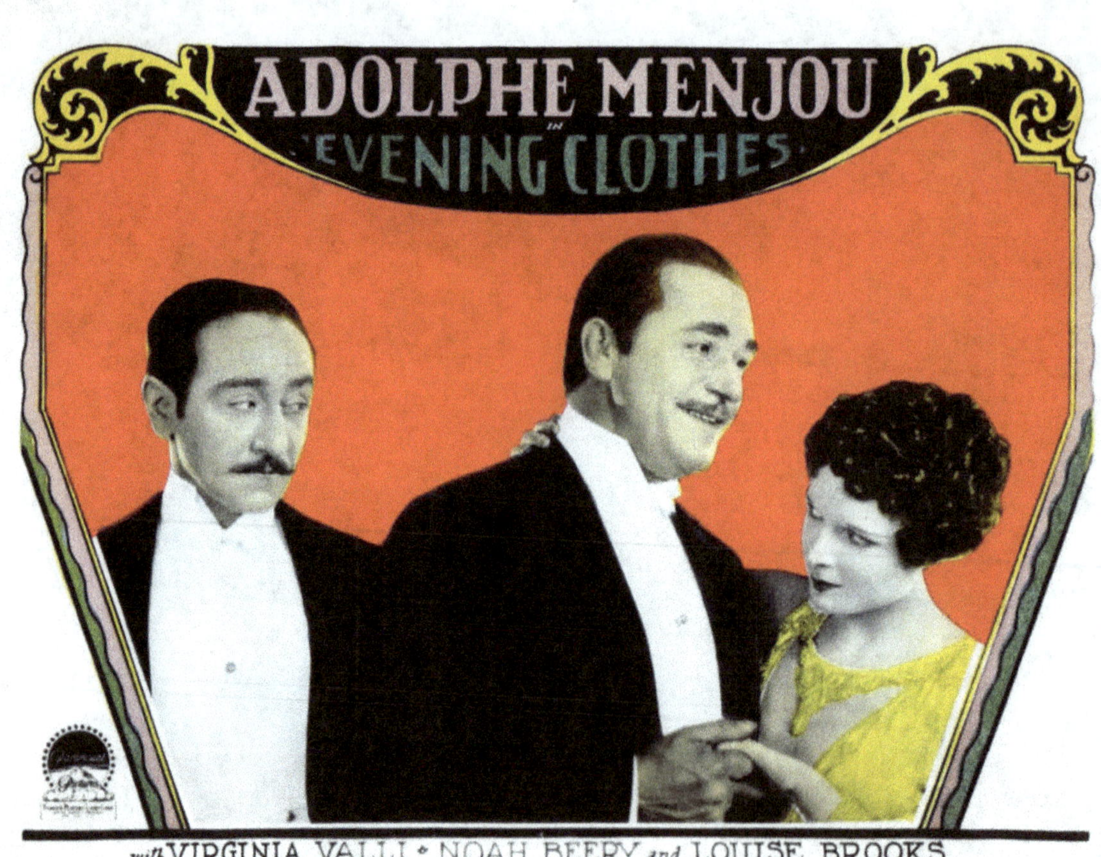

Image 34: Lobby card for *Evening Clothes*, 1927.

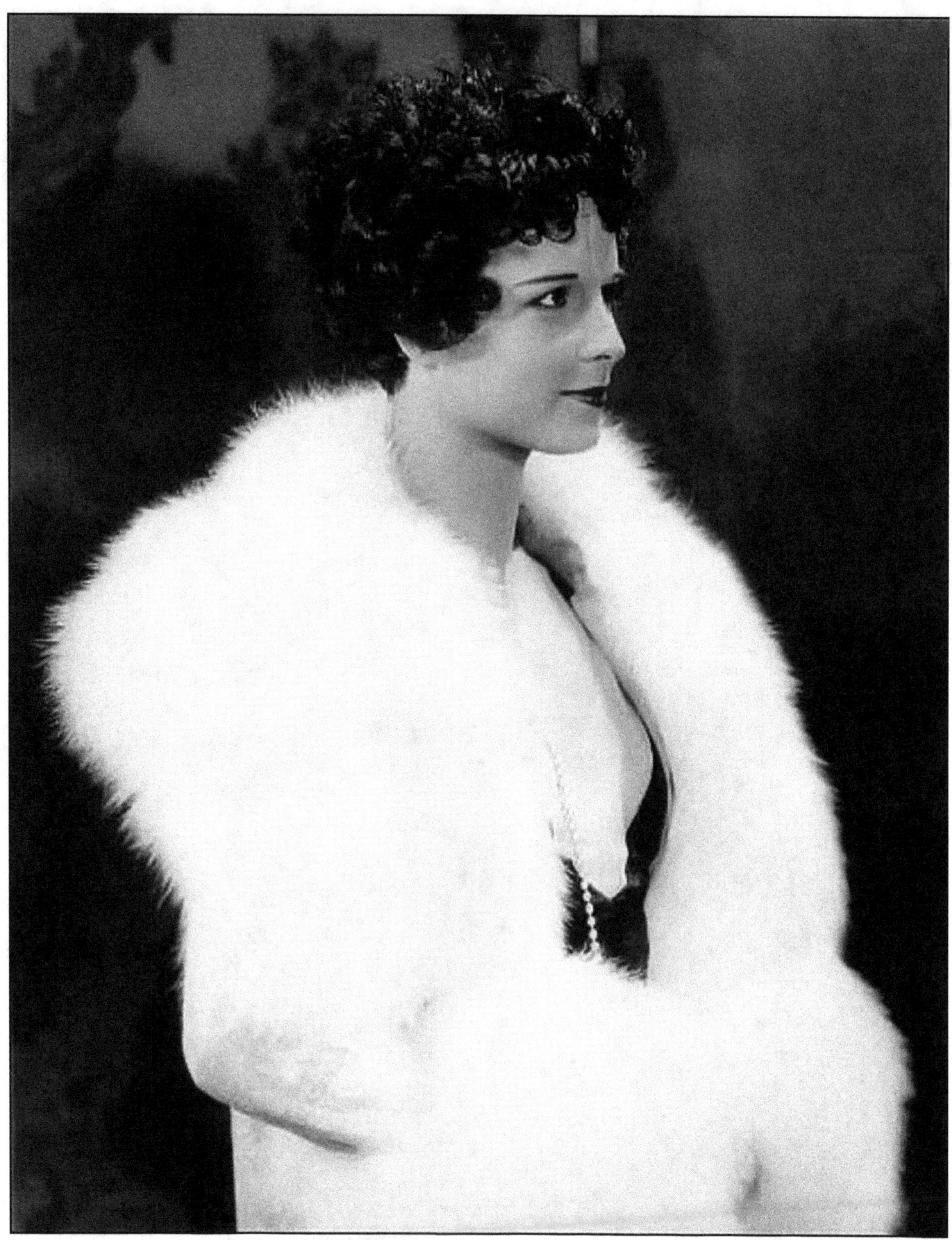

Image 35: *Evening Clothes,* 1927.

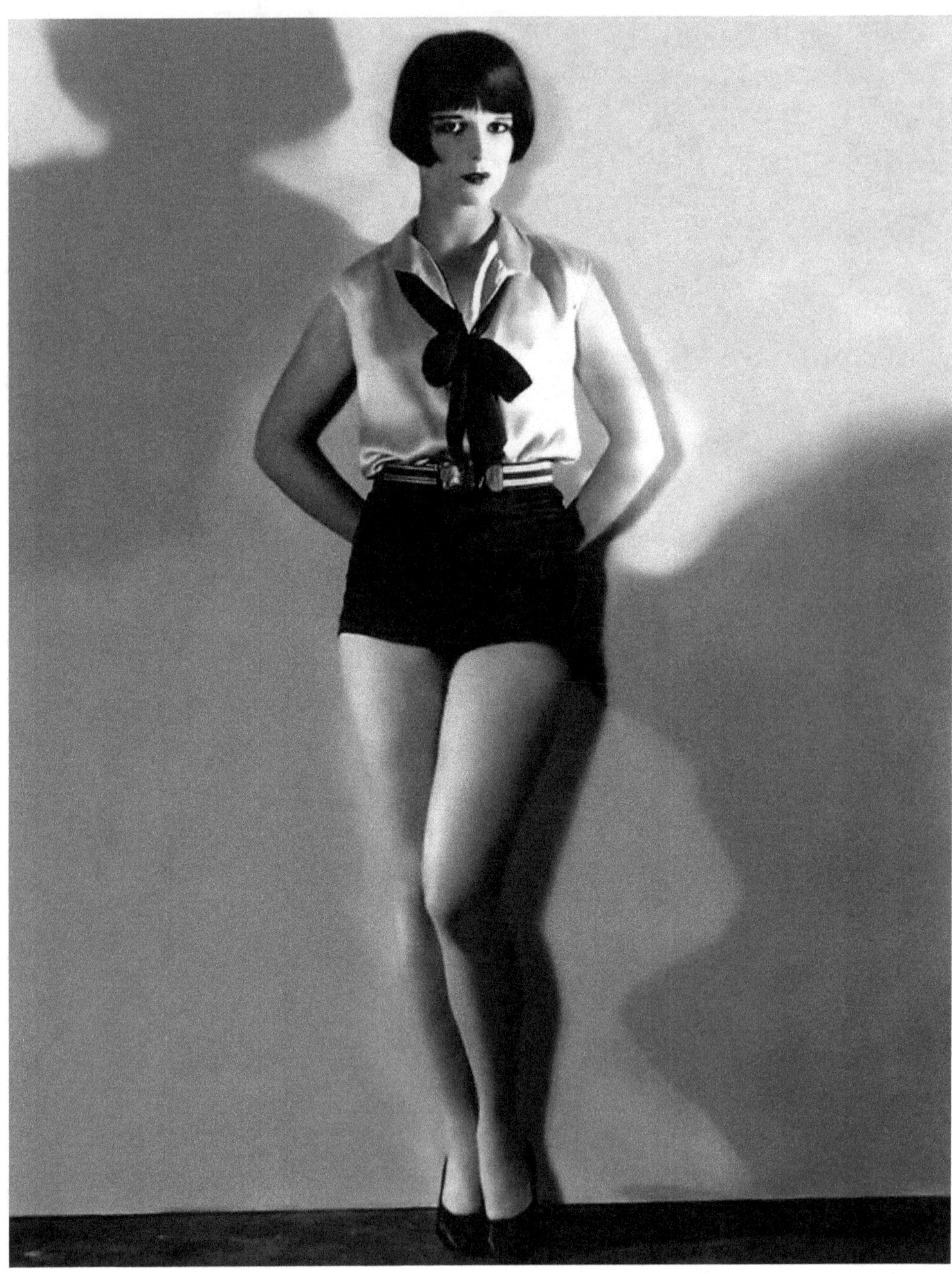

Image 36: Publicity photo, ca. 1927.

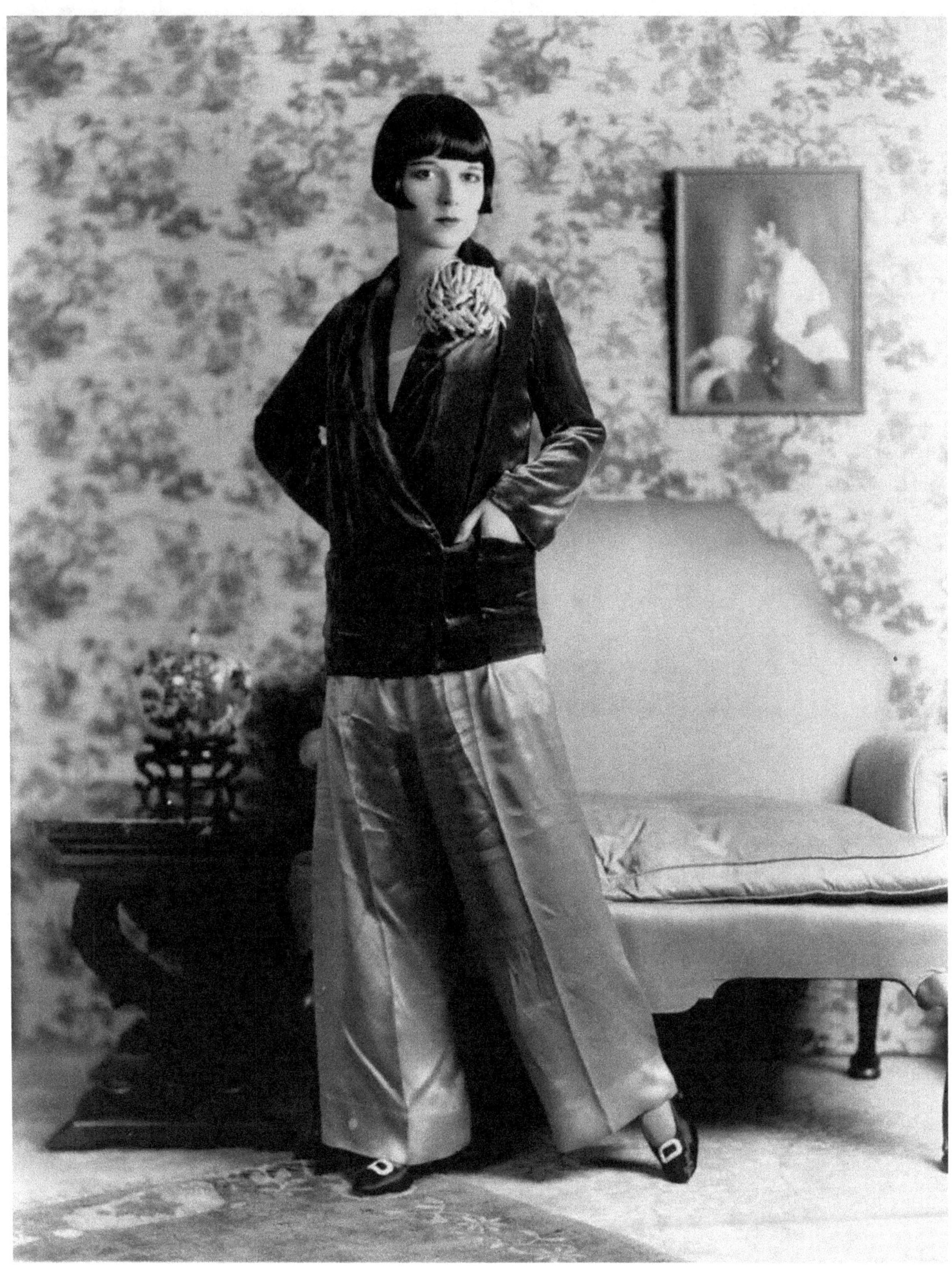

Image 37: Publicity photo, ca. 1927.

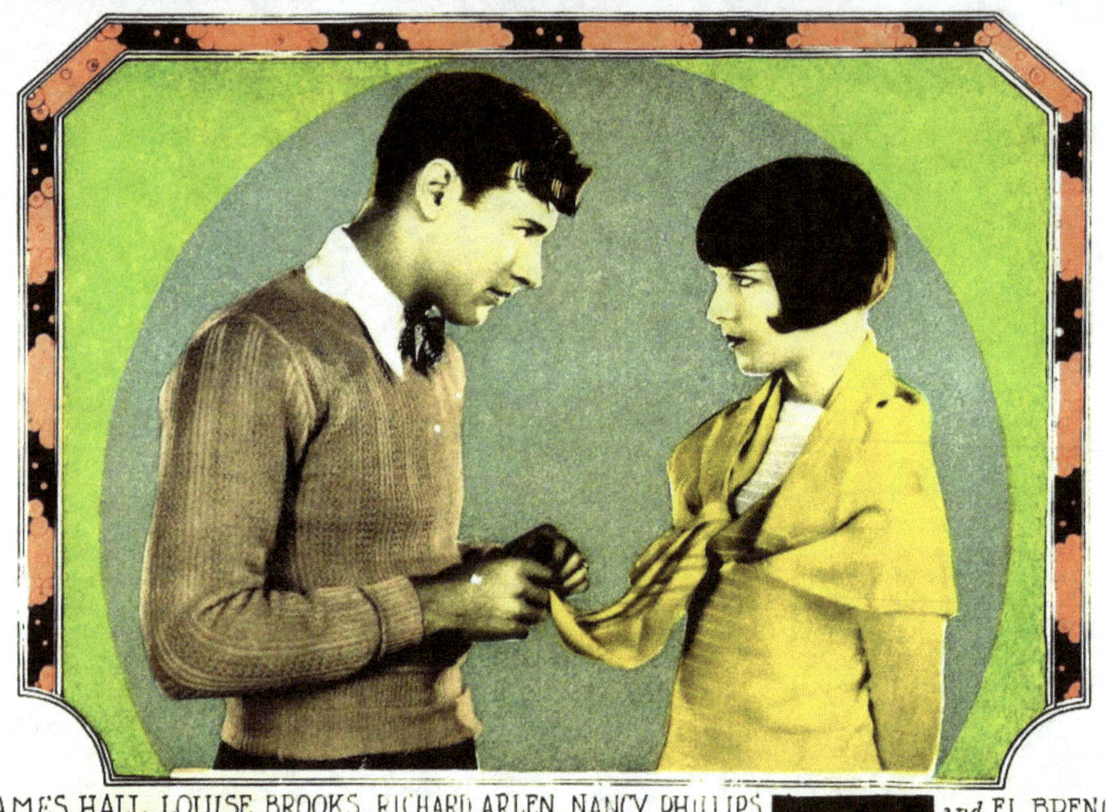

Image 38: Lobby card for *Rolled Stockings*, 1927.

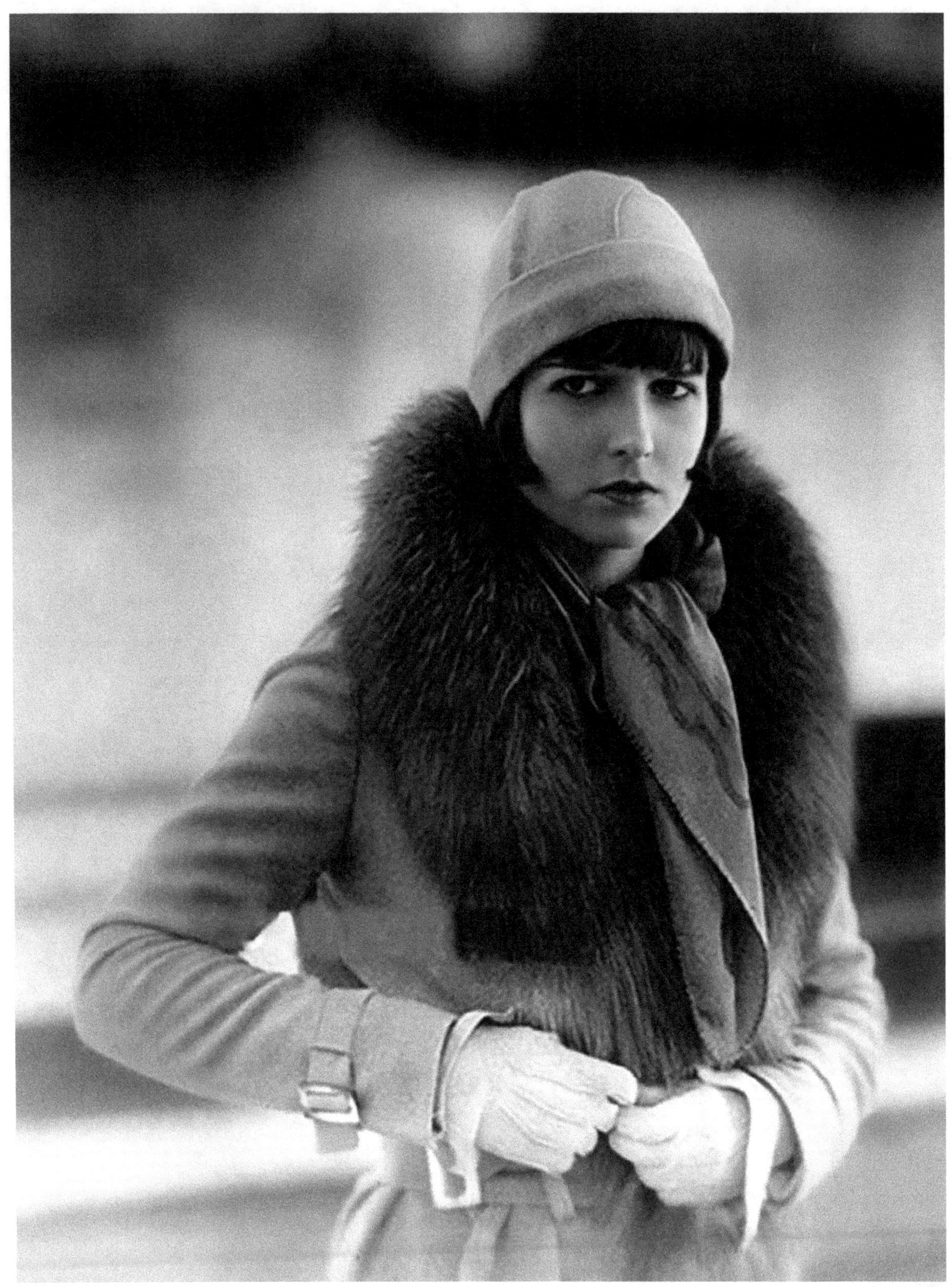

Image 39: *Rolled Stockings*, 1927.

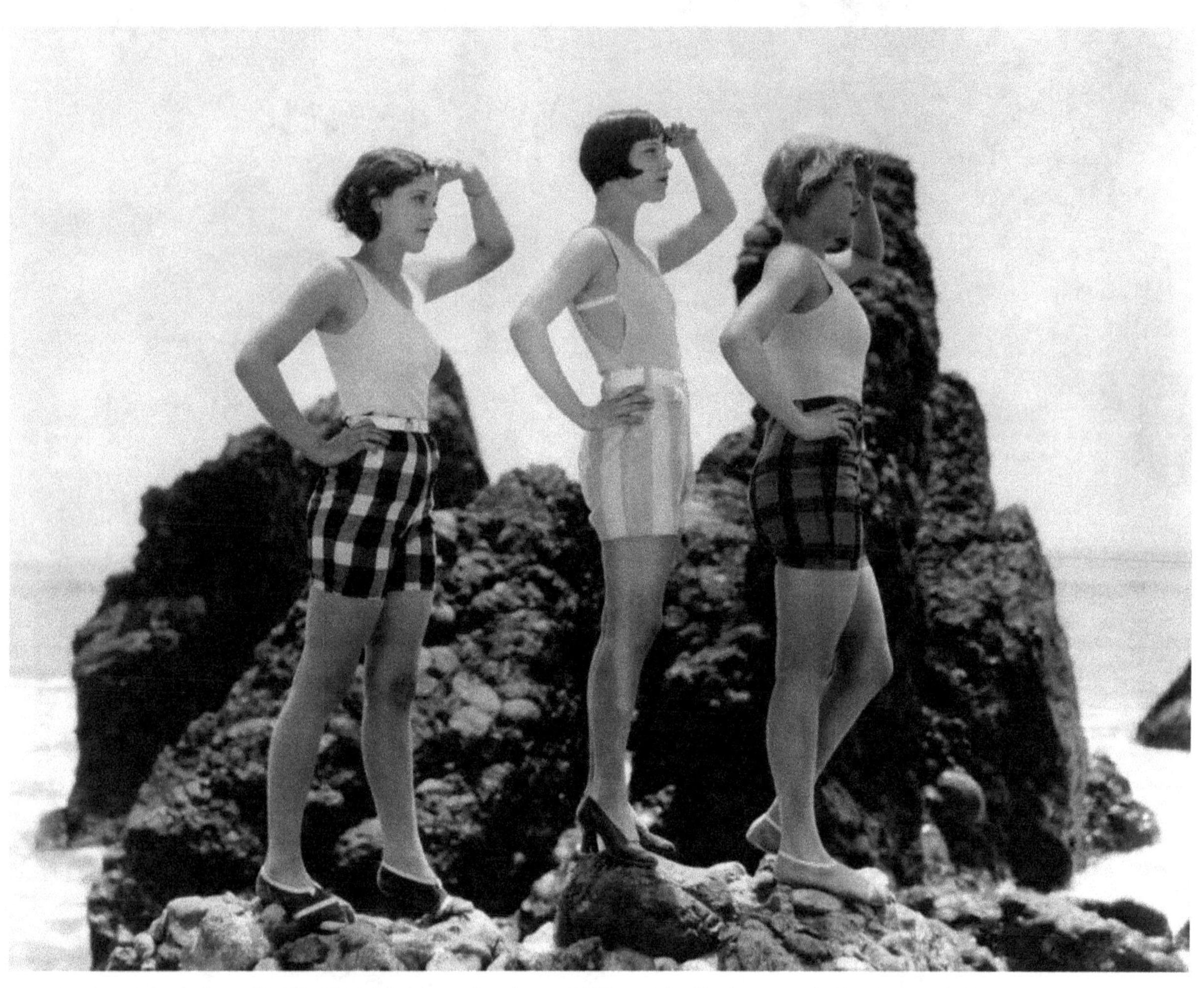

Image 40: From left, Sally Blane, Brooks, and Nancy Phillips, all of whom appeared in *Rolled Stockings*, 1927.

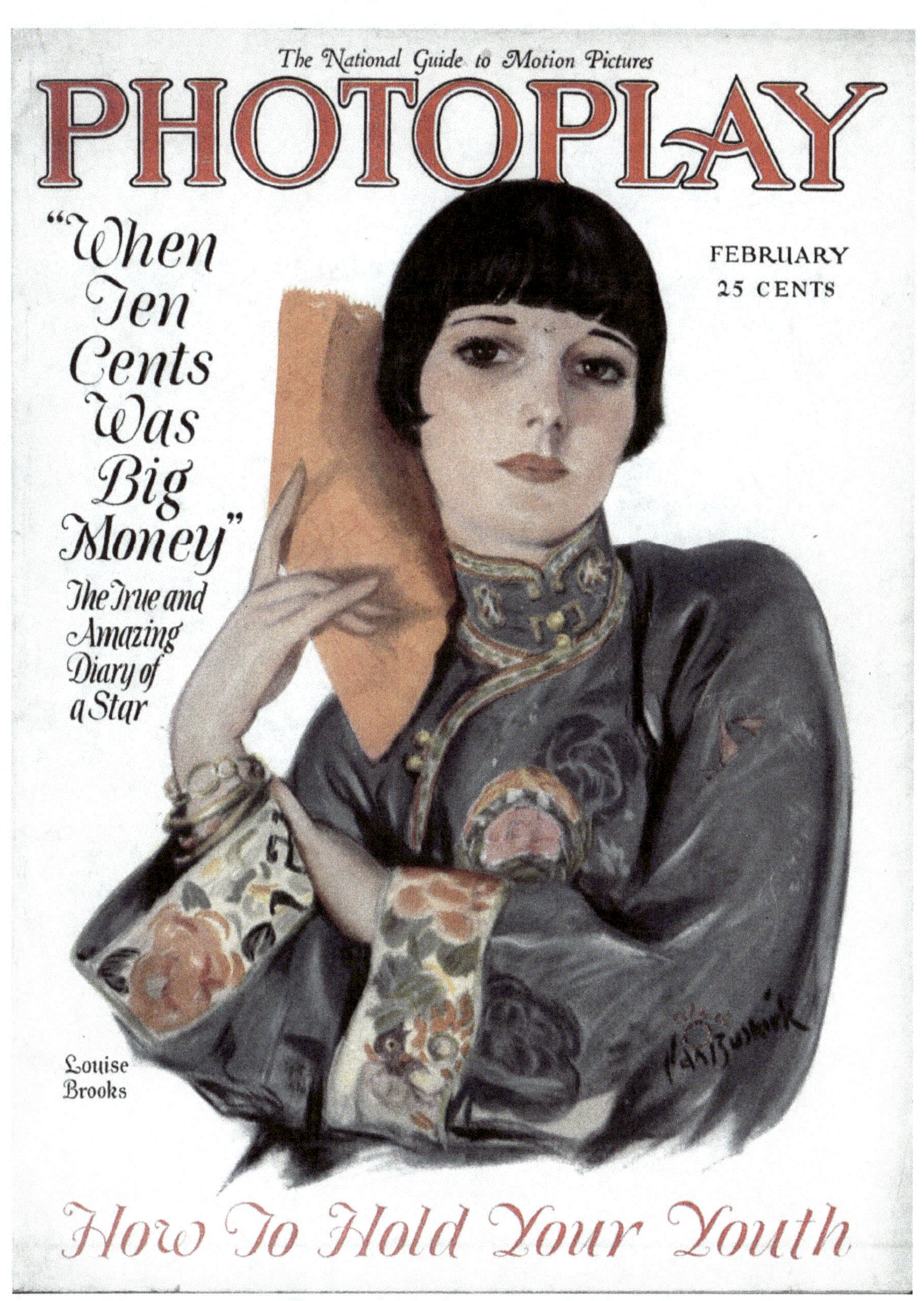

Image 41: Fan magazine cover, 1927.

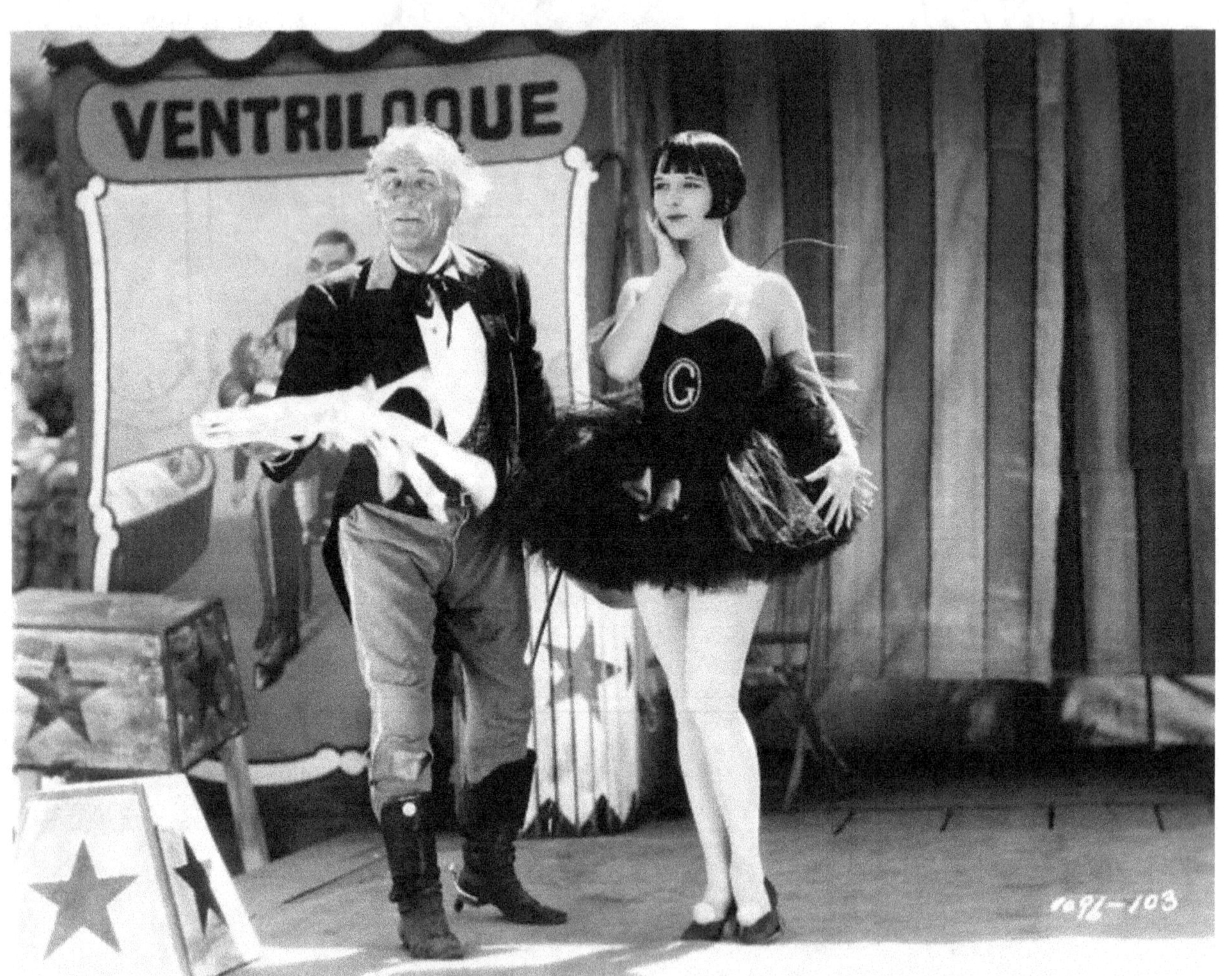

Image 42: *Now We're in the Air,* 1927.

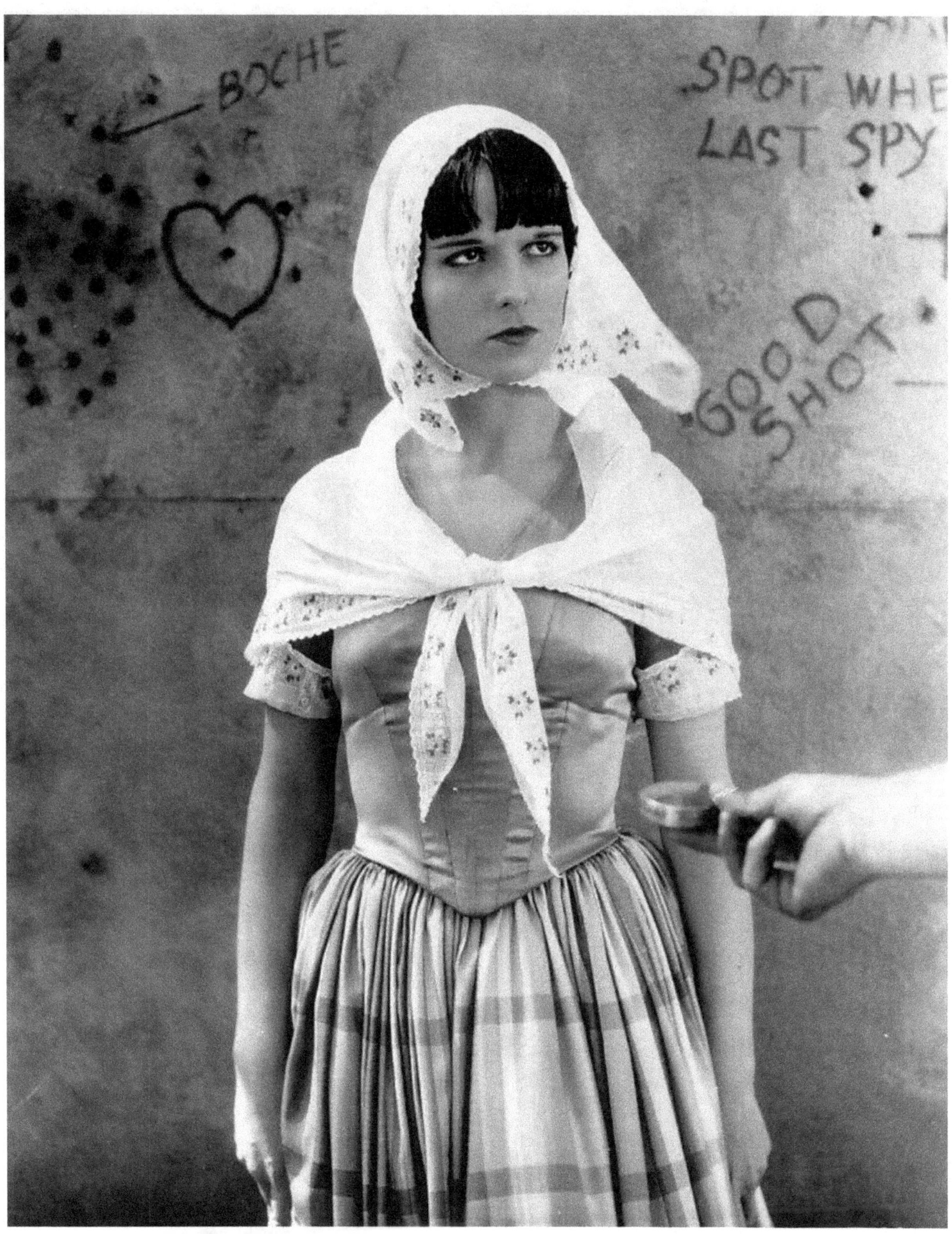

Image 43: *Now We're in the Air,* 1927.

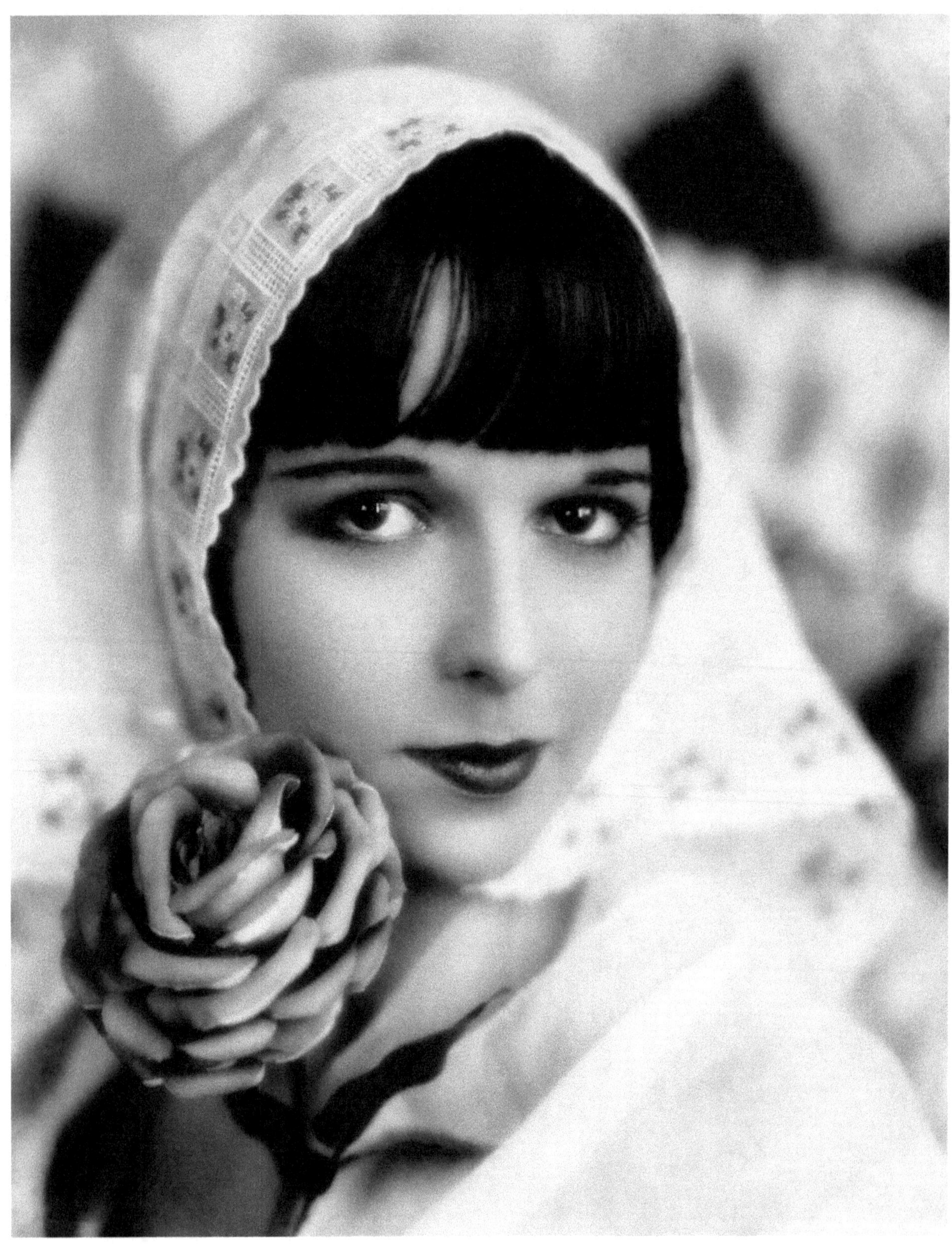

Image 44: *Now We're in the Air*, 1927.

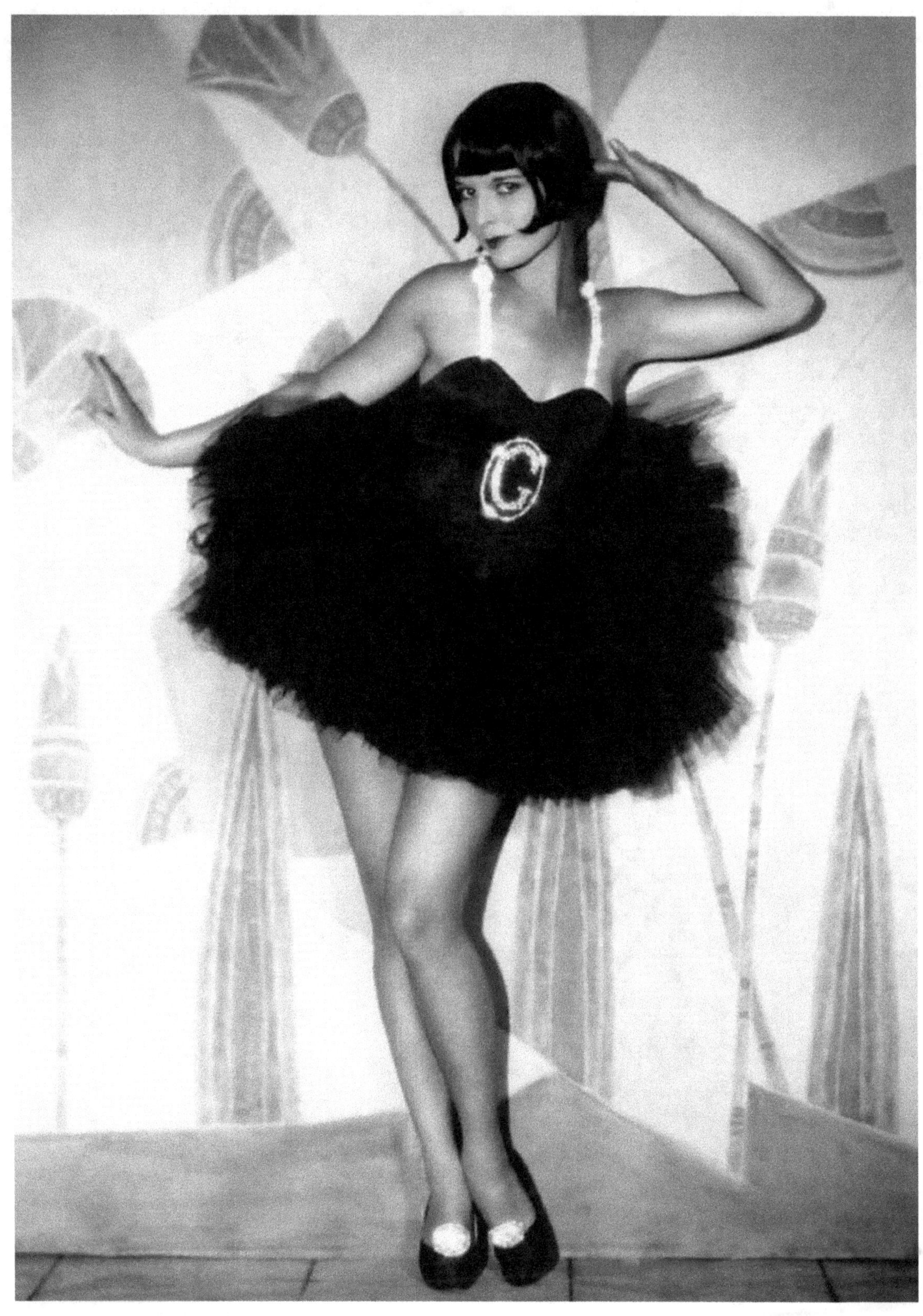

Image 45: *Now We're in the Air*, 1927.

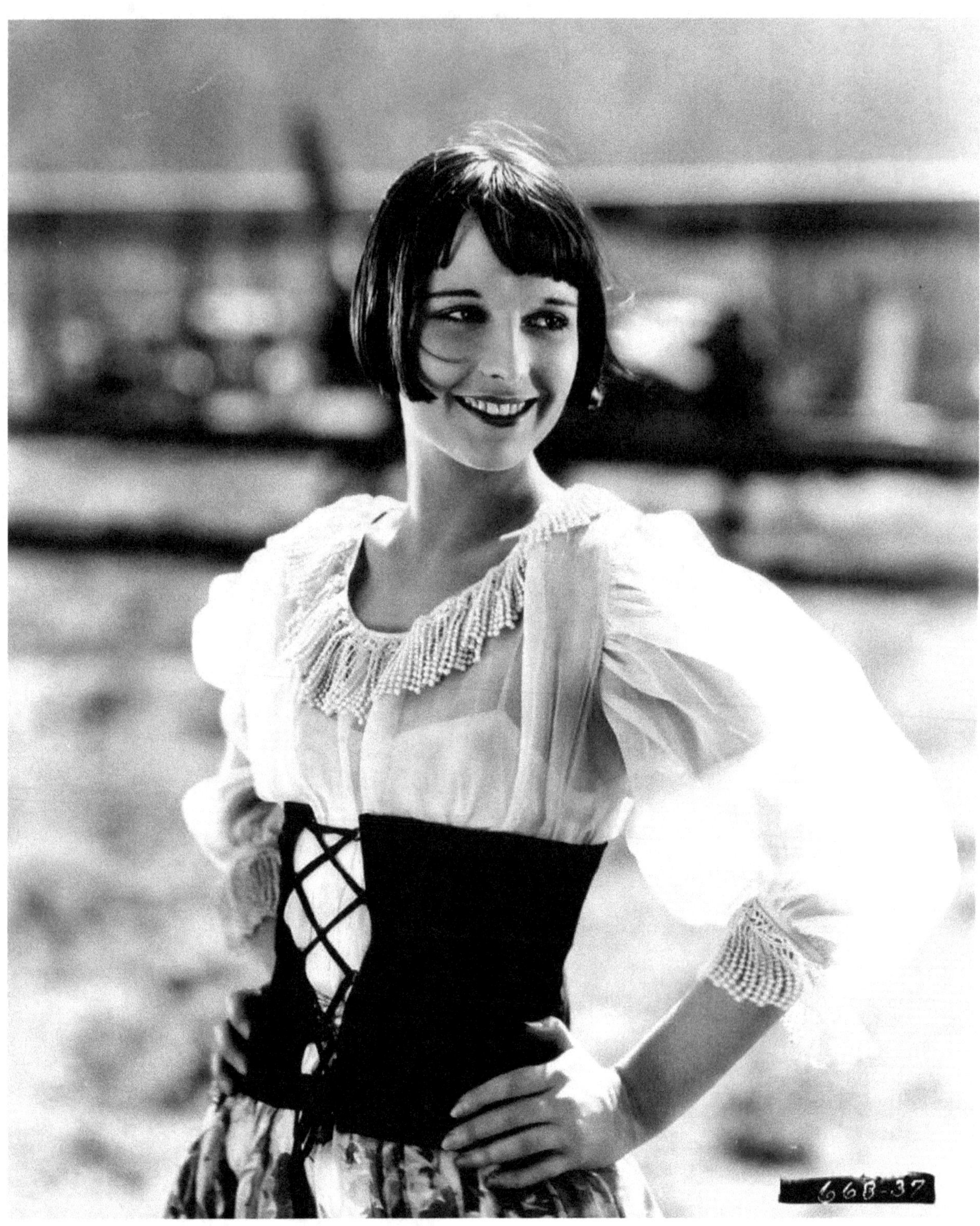

Image 46: *Now We're in the Air*, 1927.

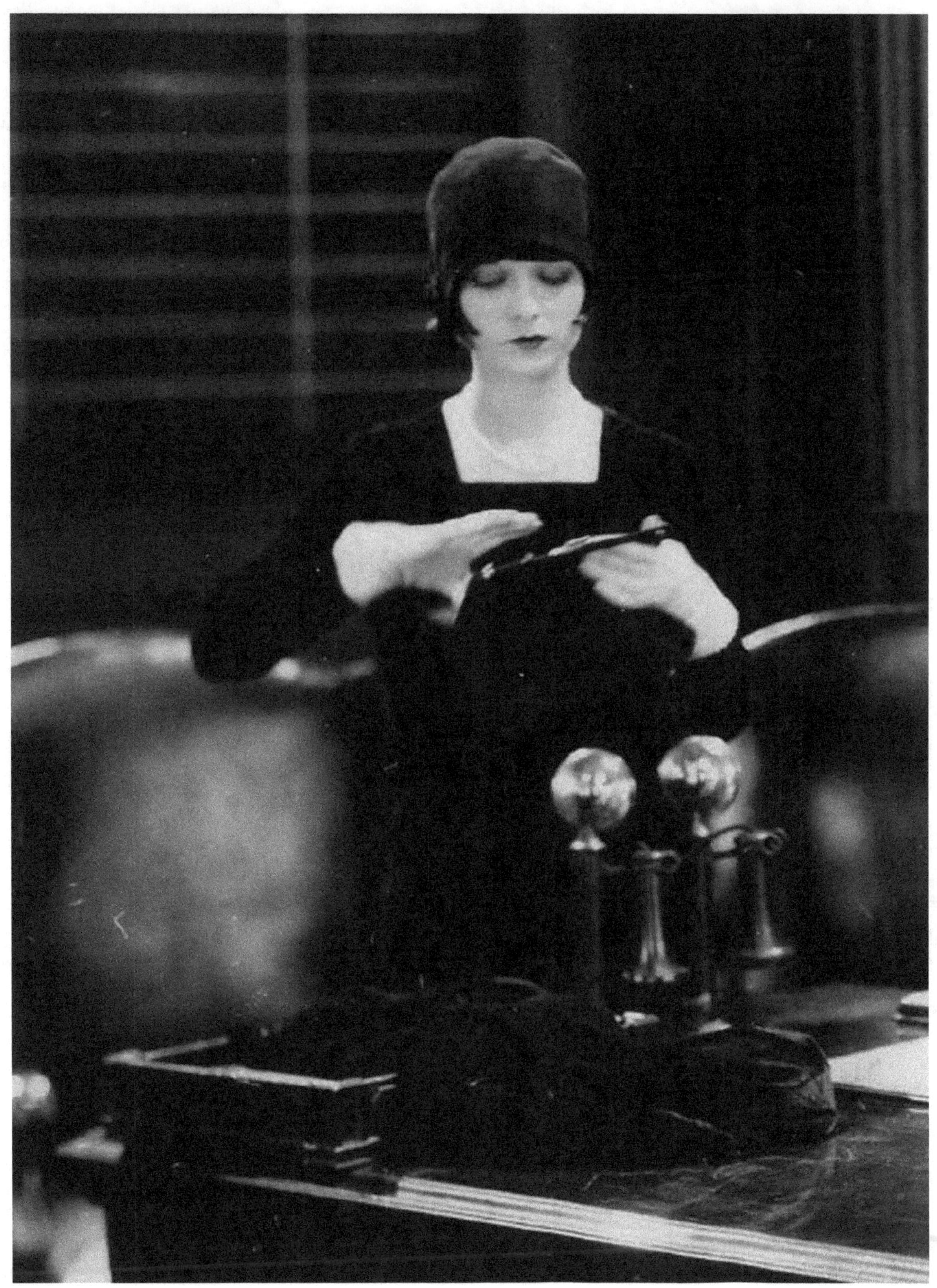

Image 47: *The City Gone Wild*, 1927.

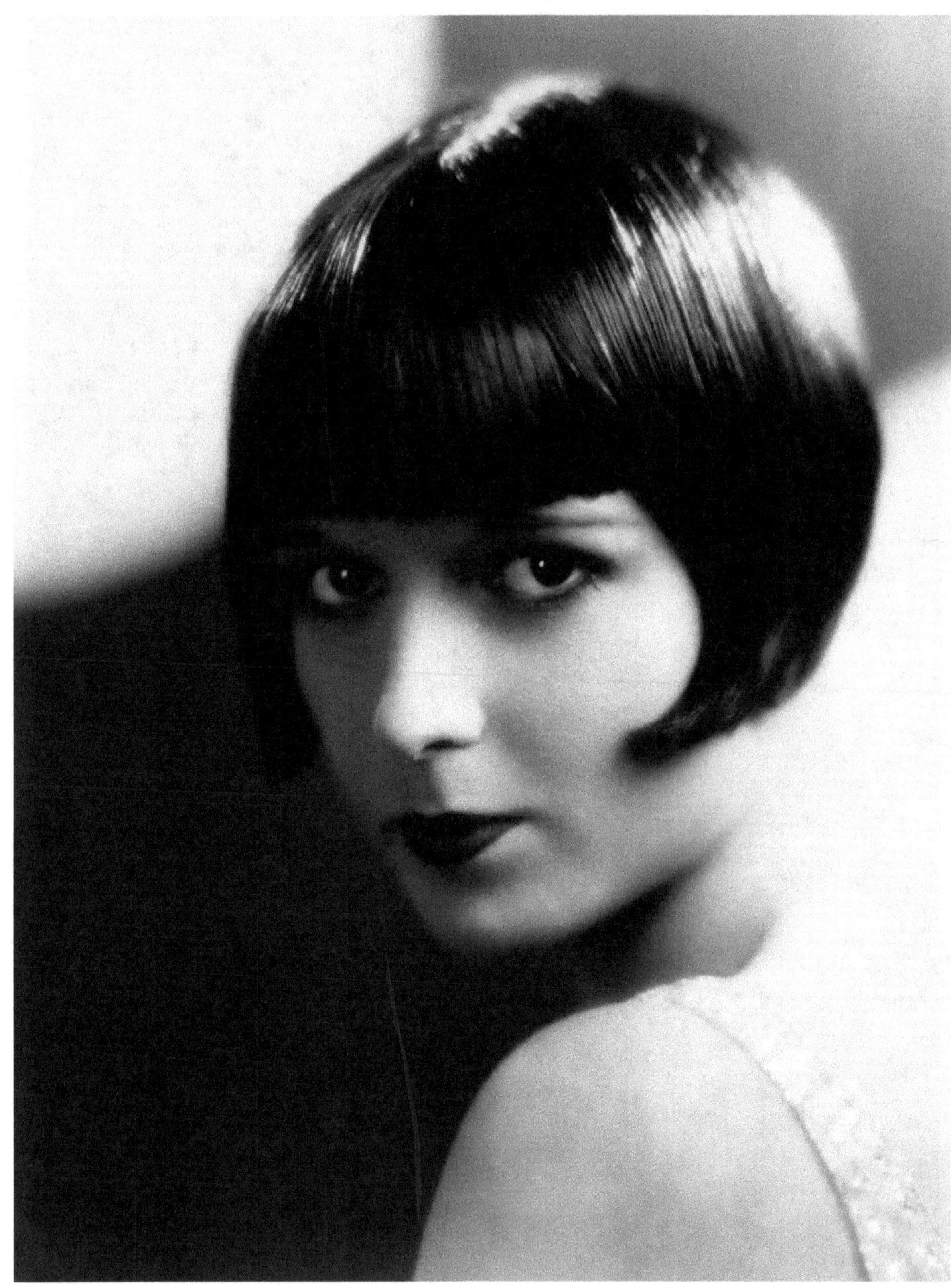

Image 48: Promotional photo, ca. 1927.

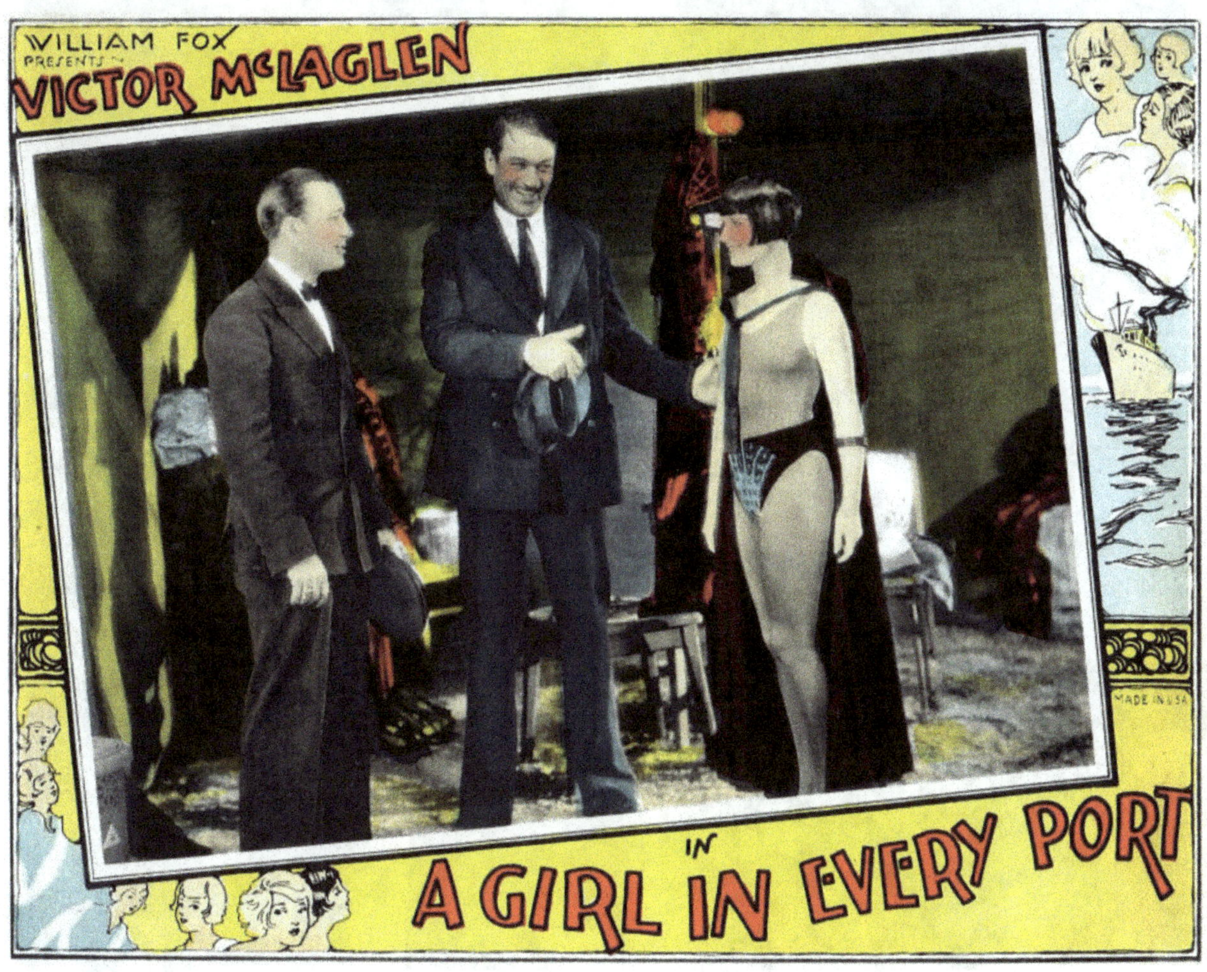

Image 49: Lobby card for *A Girl in Every Port*, 1927.

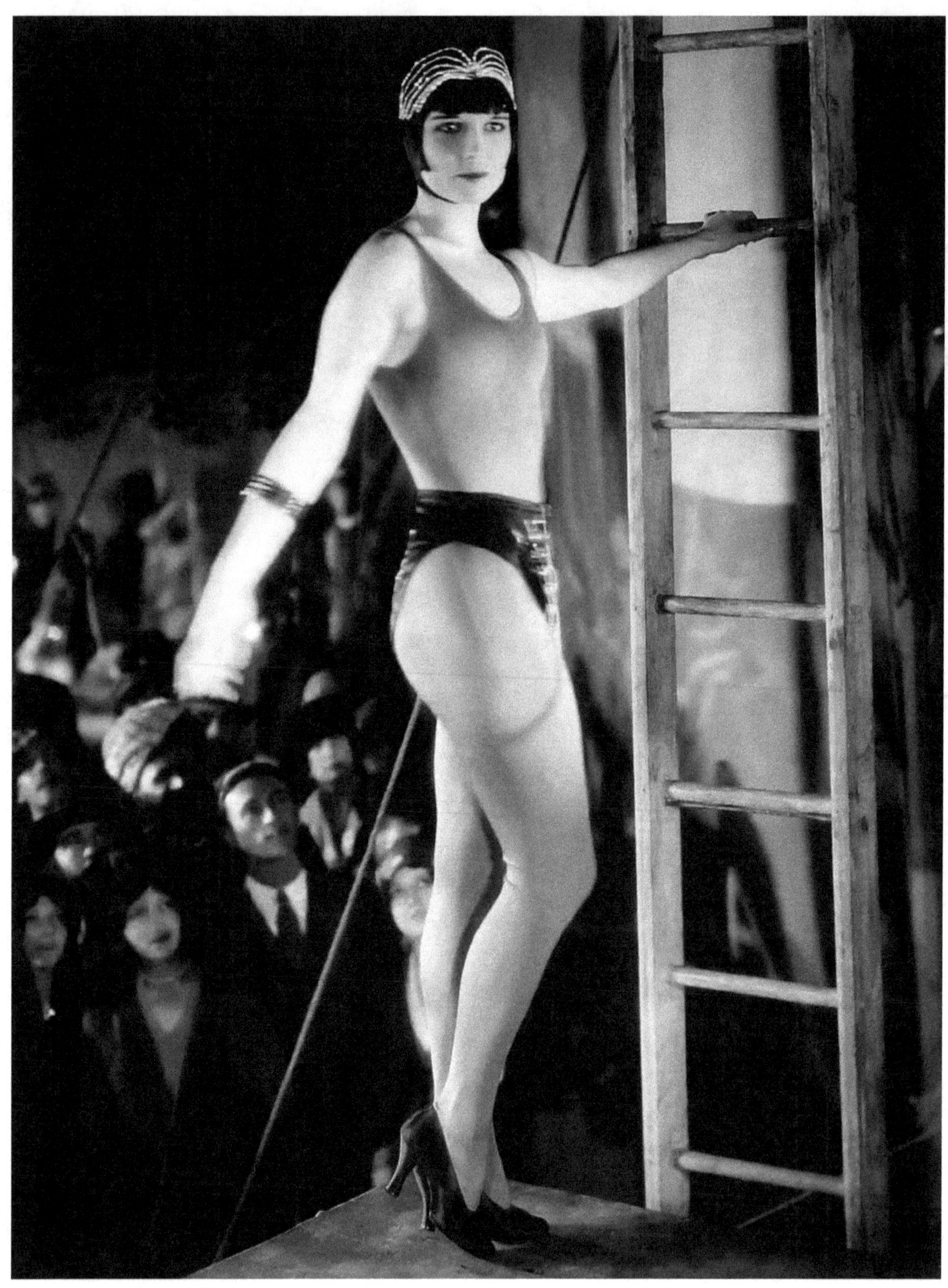

Image 50: *A Girl in Every Port*, 1927.

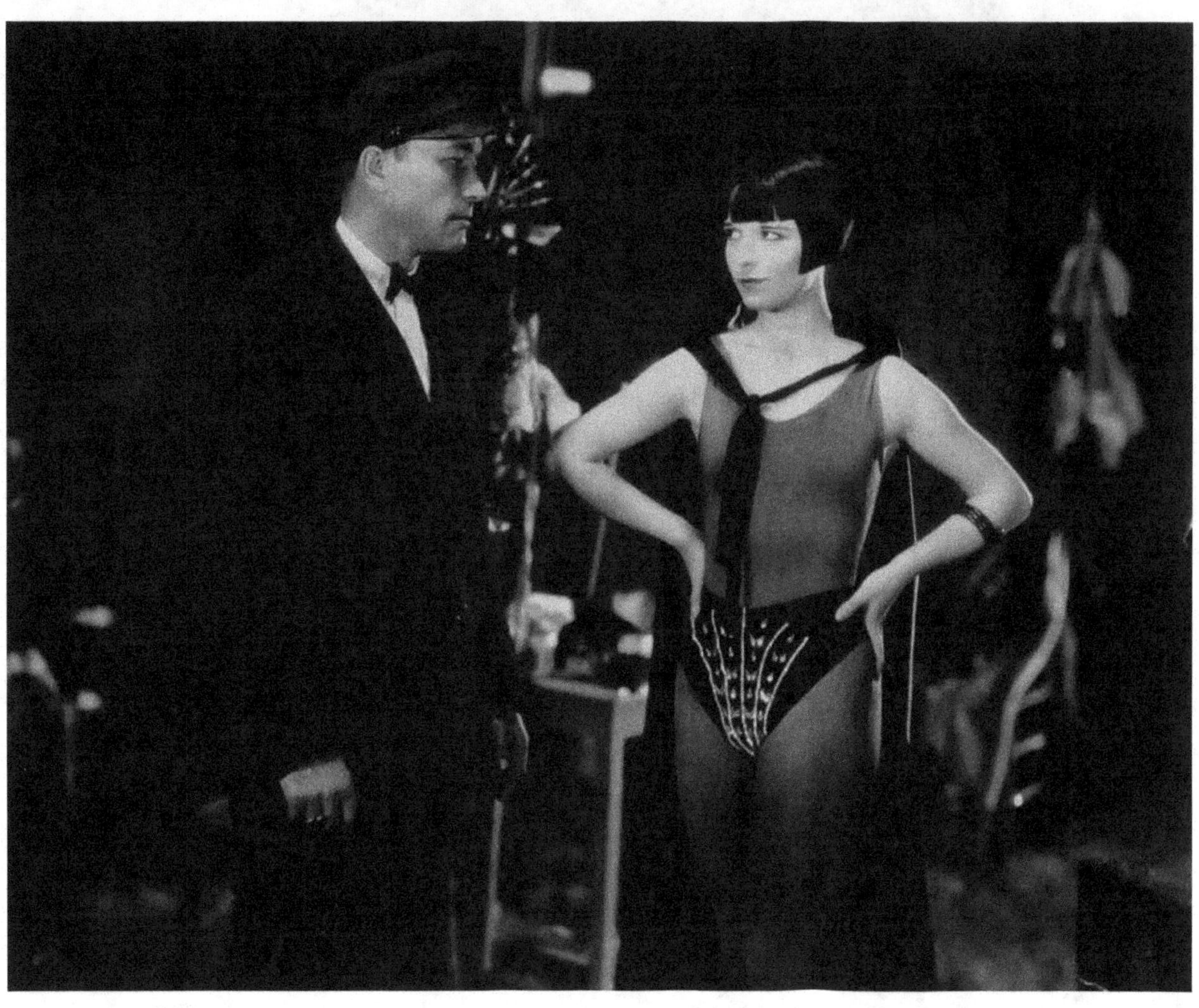

Image 51: *A Girl in Every Port*, 1927.

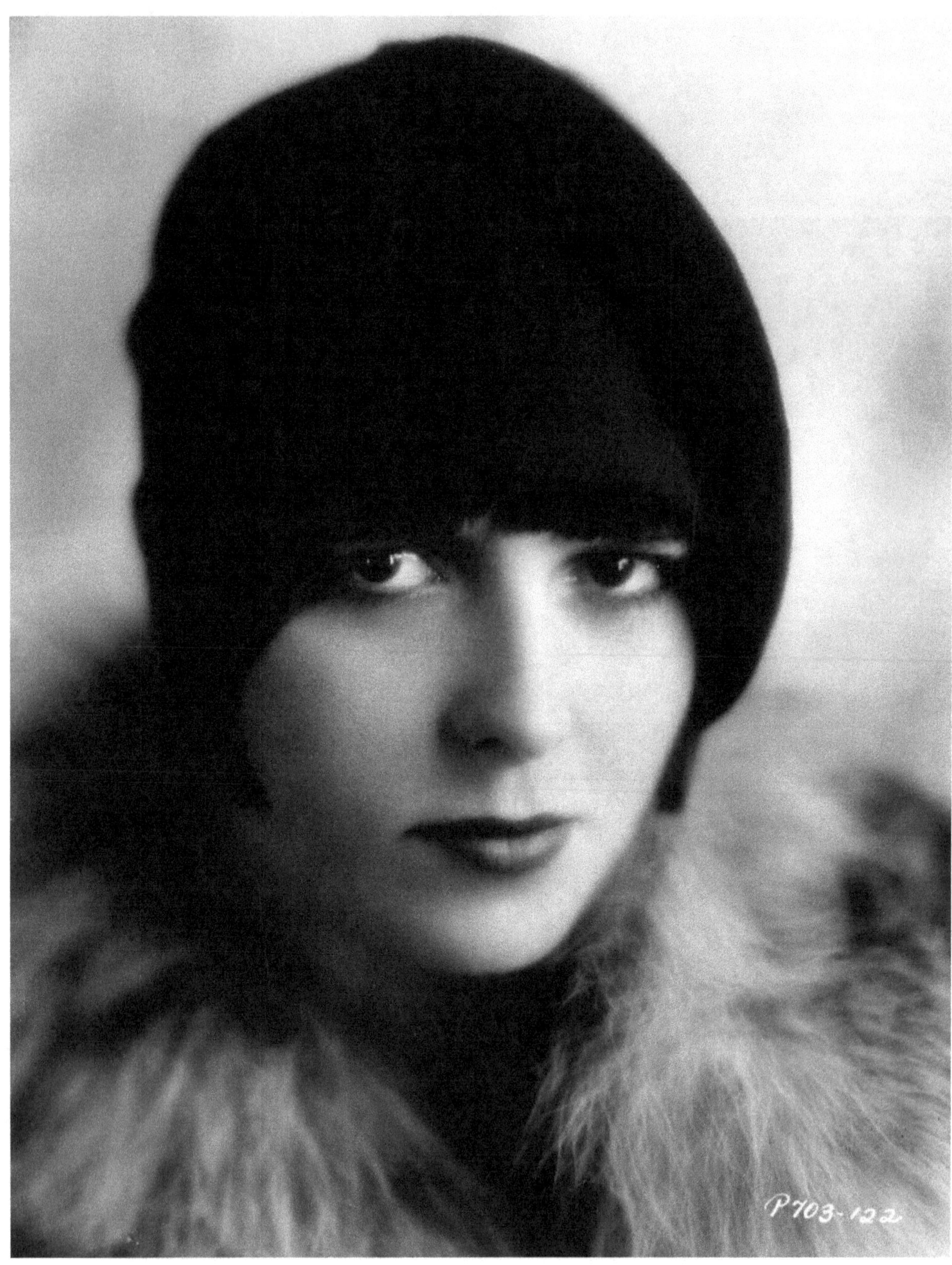

Image 52: Publicity photo, ca. 1927.

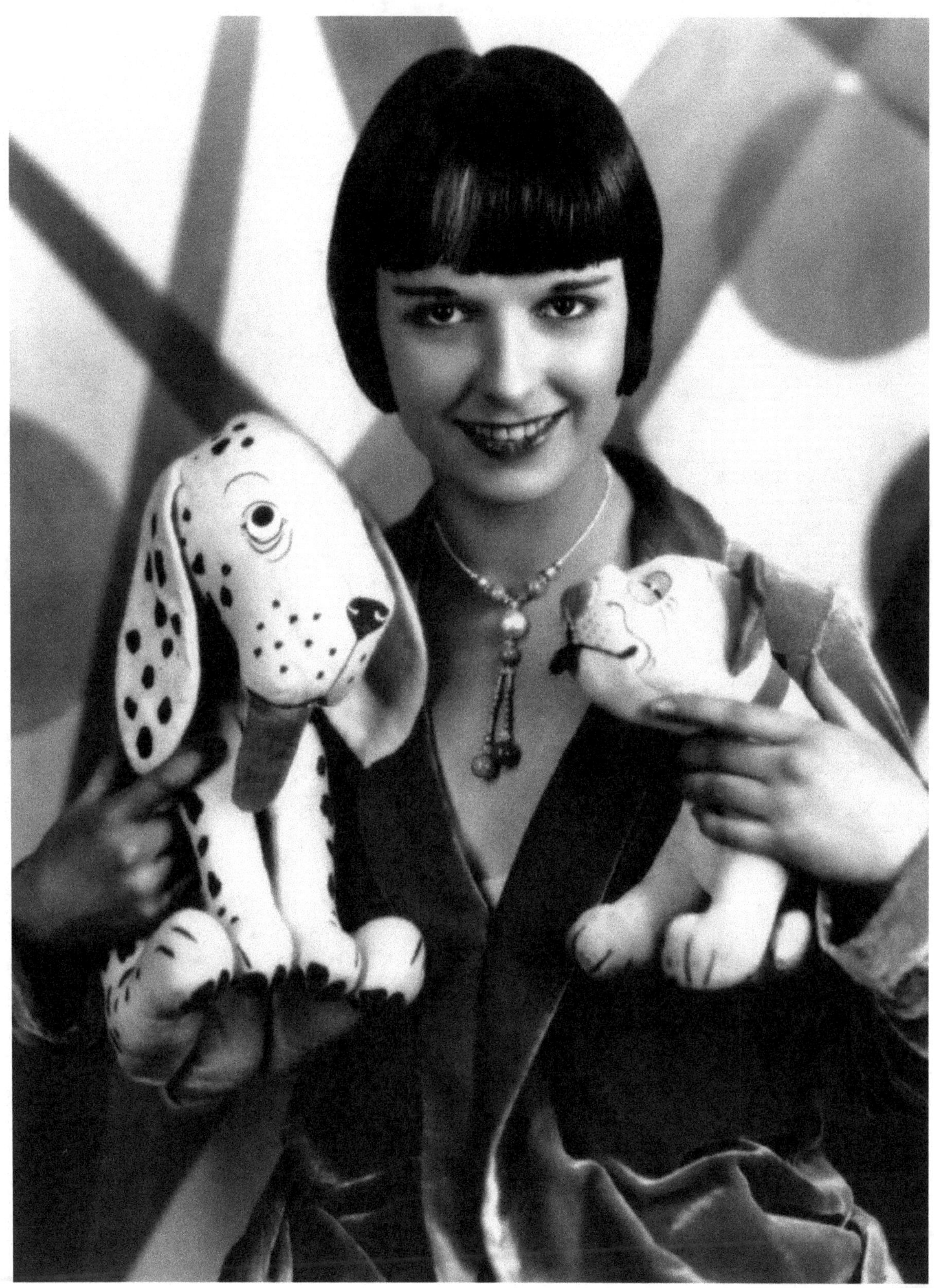

Image 53: Publicity photo, ca. 1927.

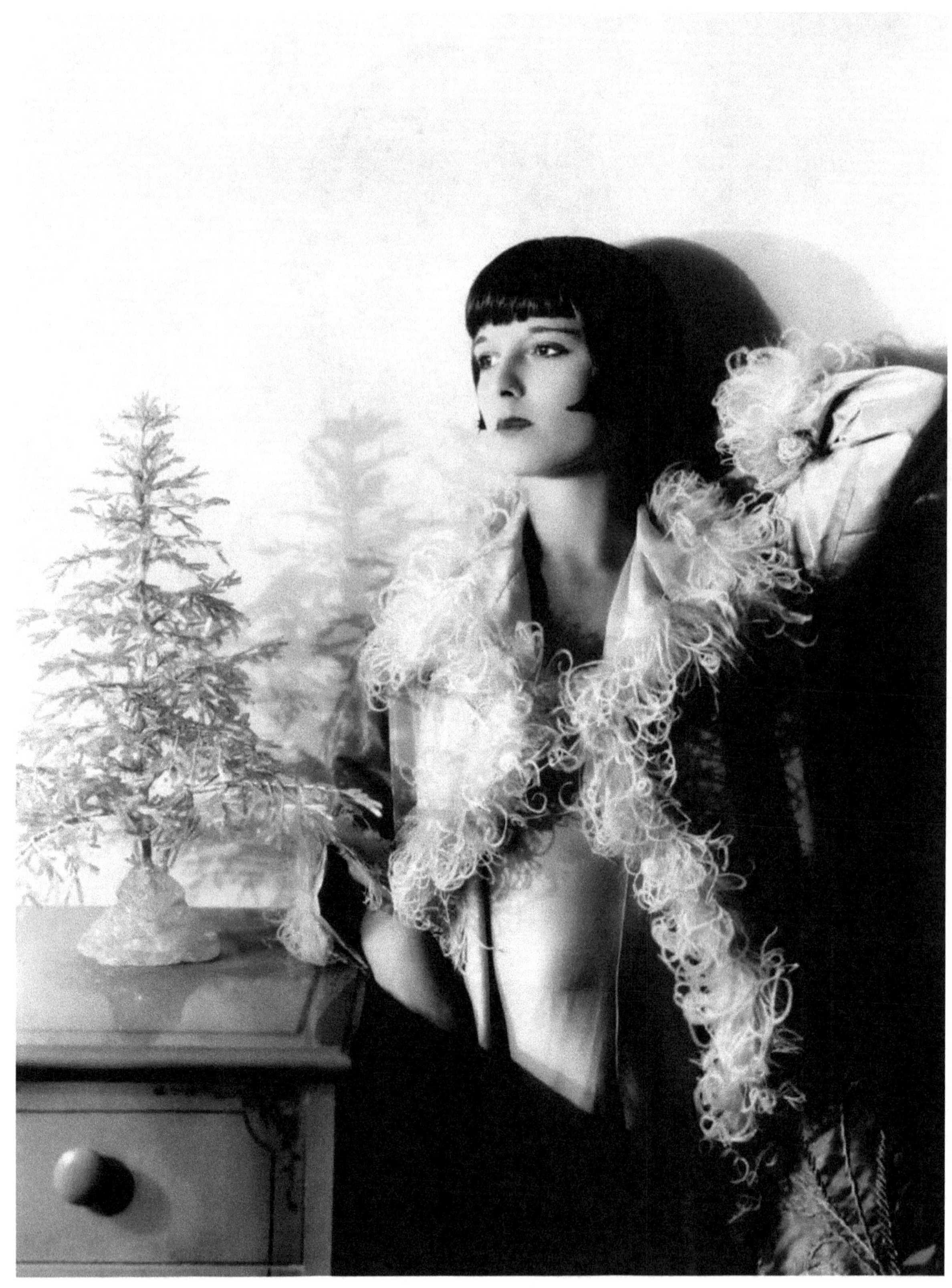

Image 54: Publicity photo, ca. 1927.

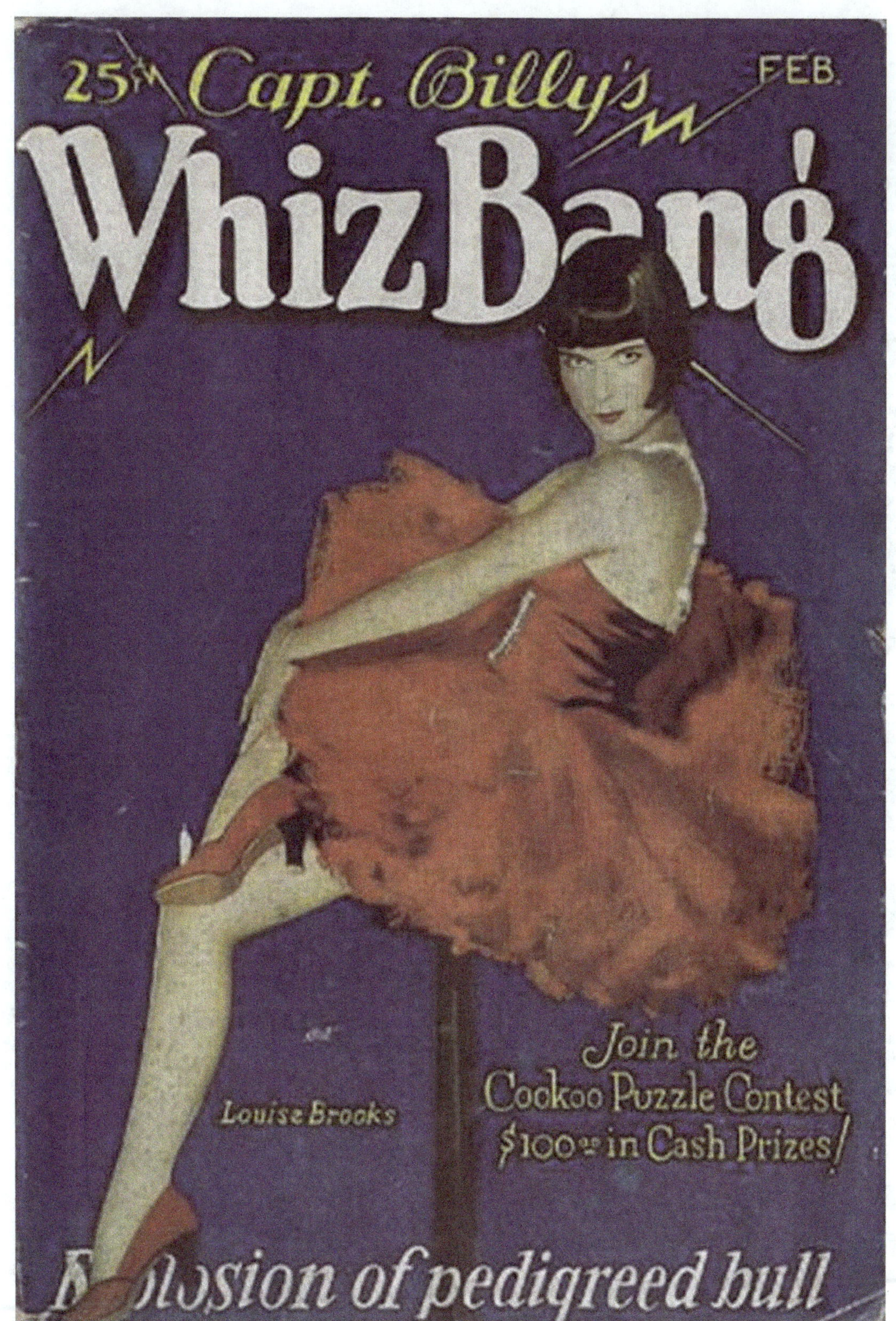

Image 55: Cover of fan magazine, 1928

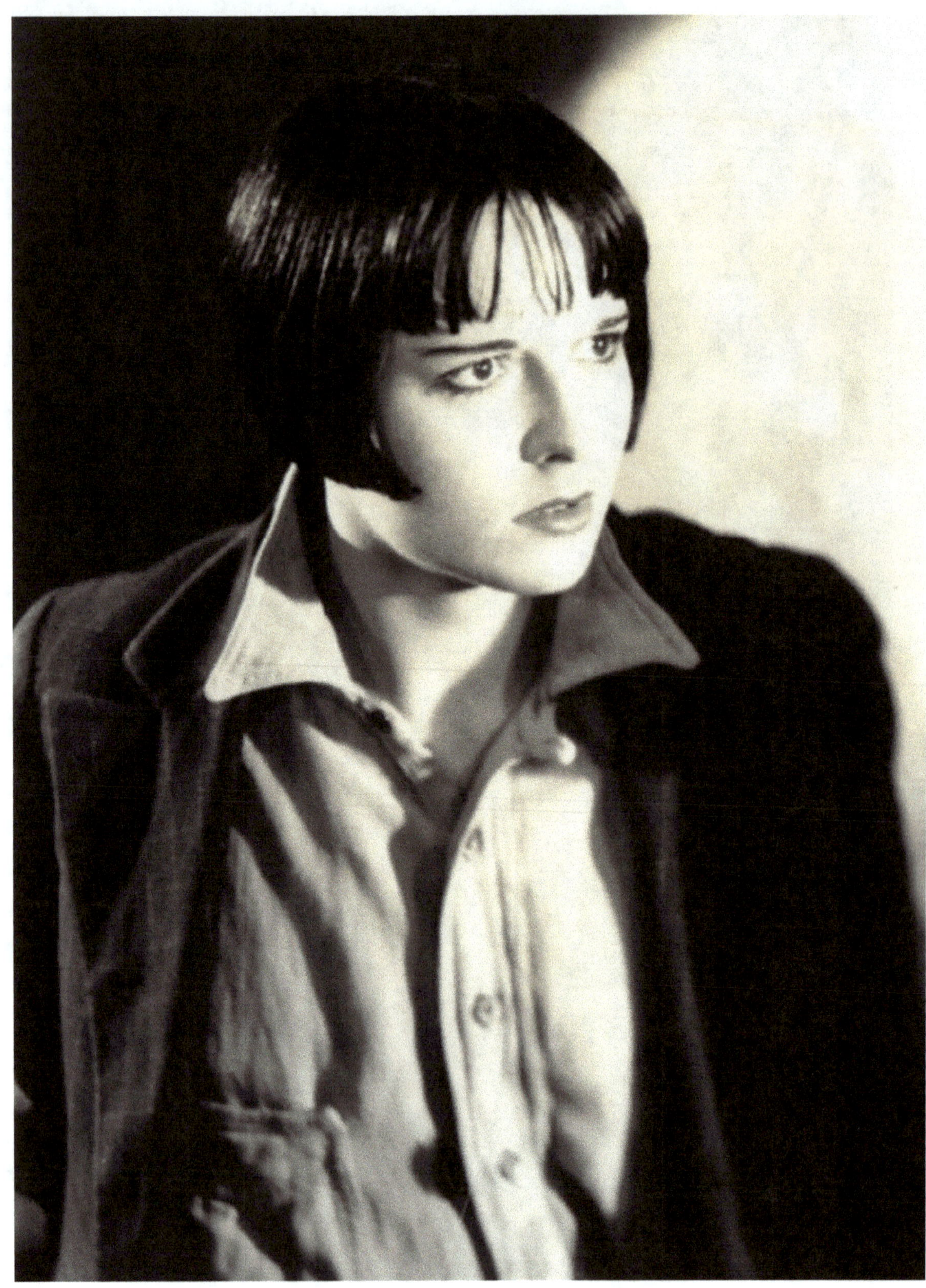

Image 56: *Beggars of Life*, 1928.

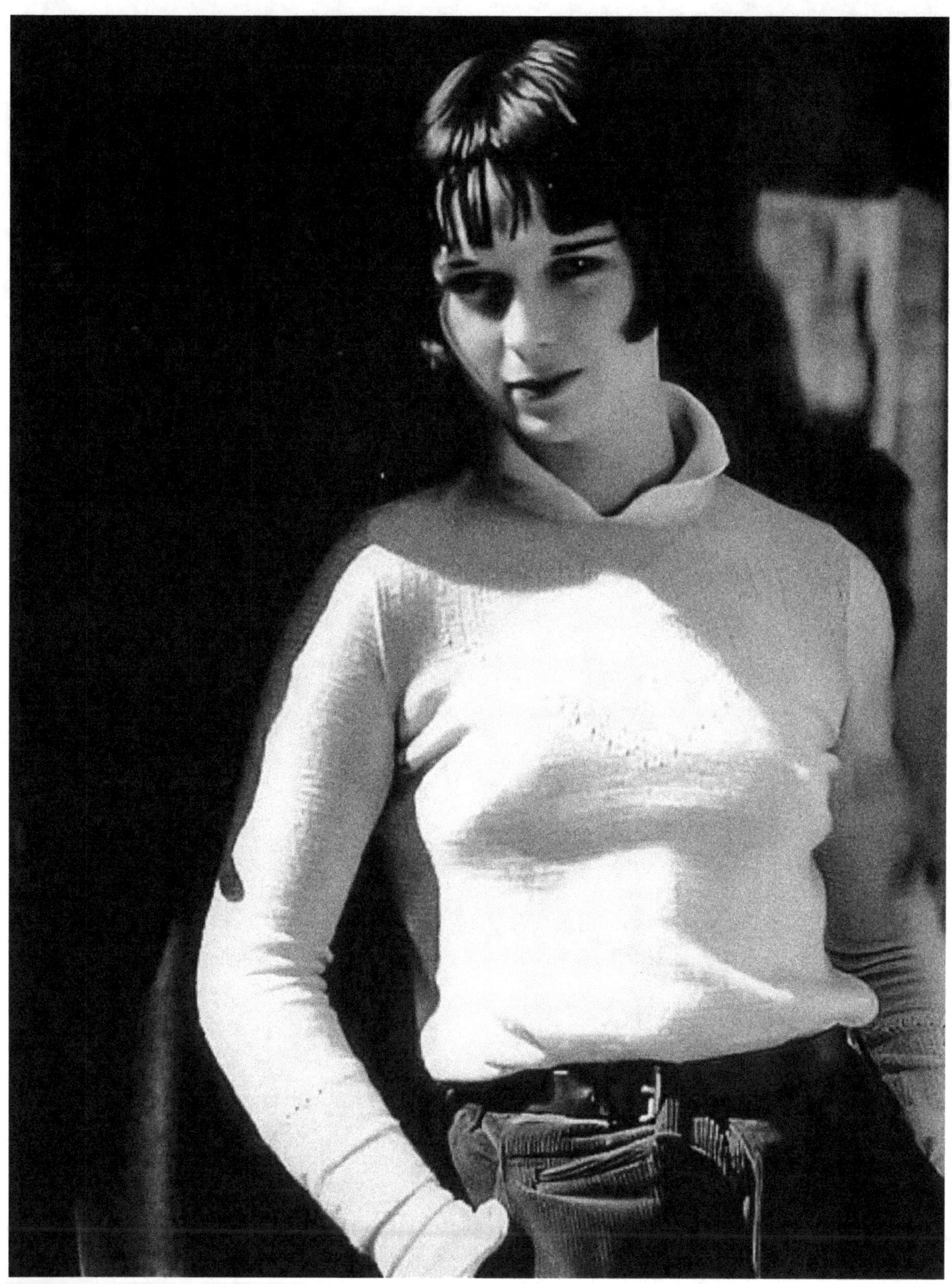

Image 57: *Beggars of Life*, 1928.

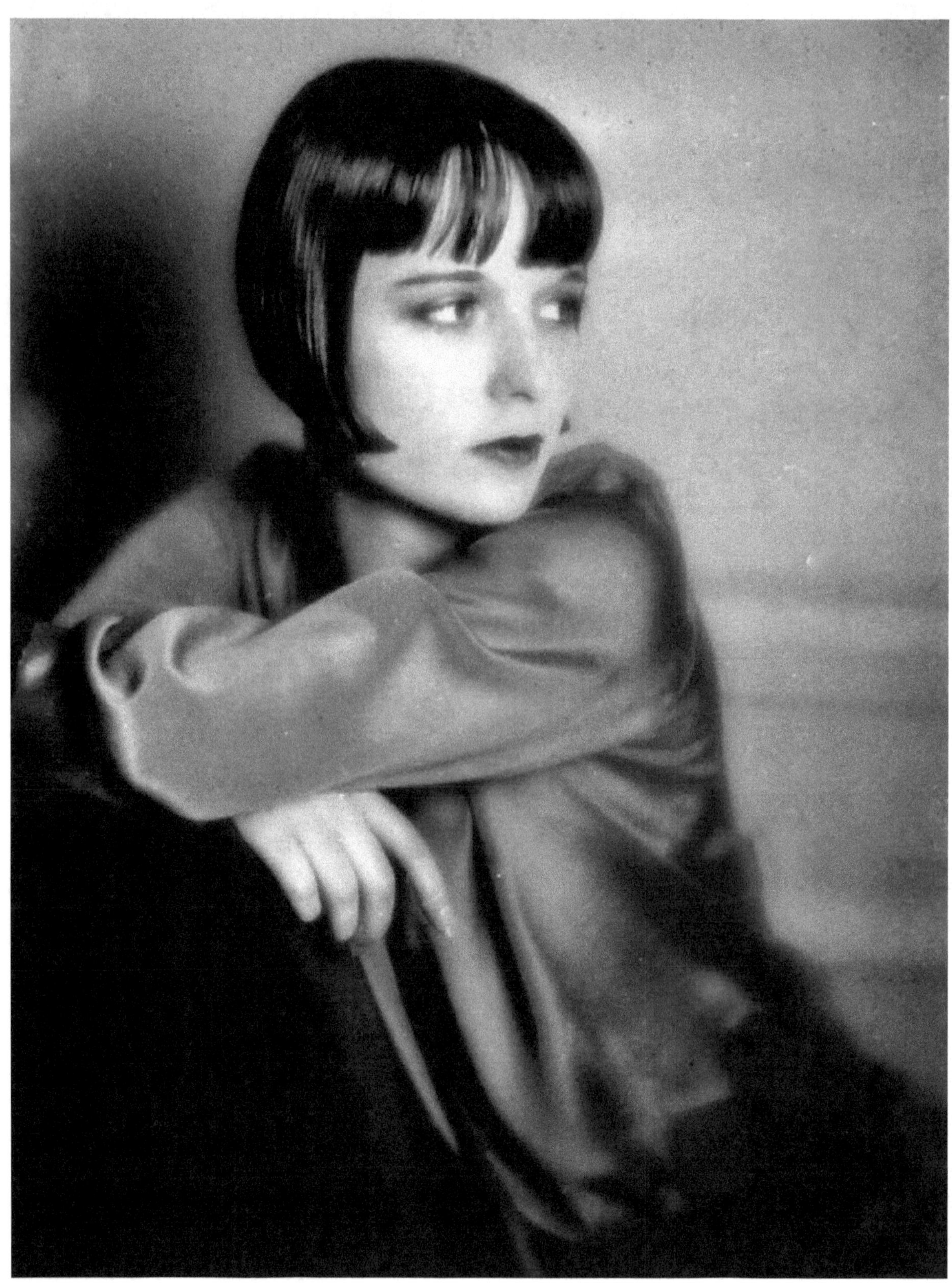

Image 58: Promotional photo, ca. 1928.

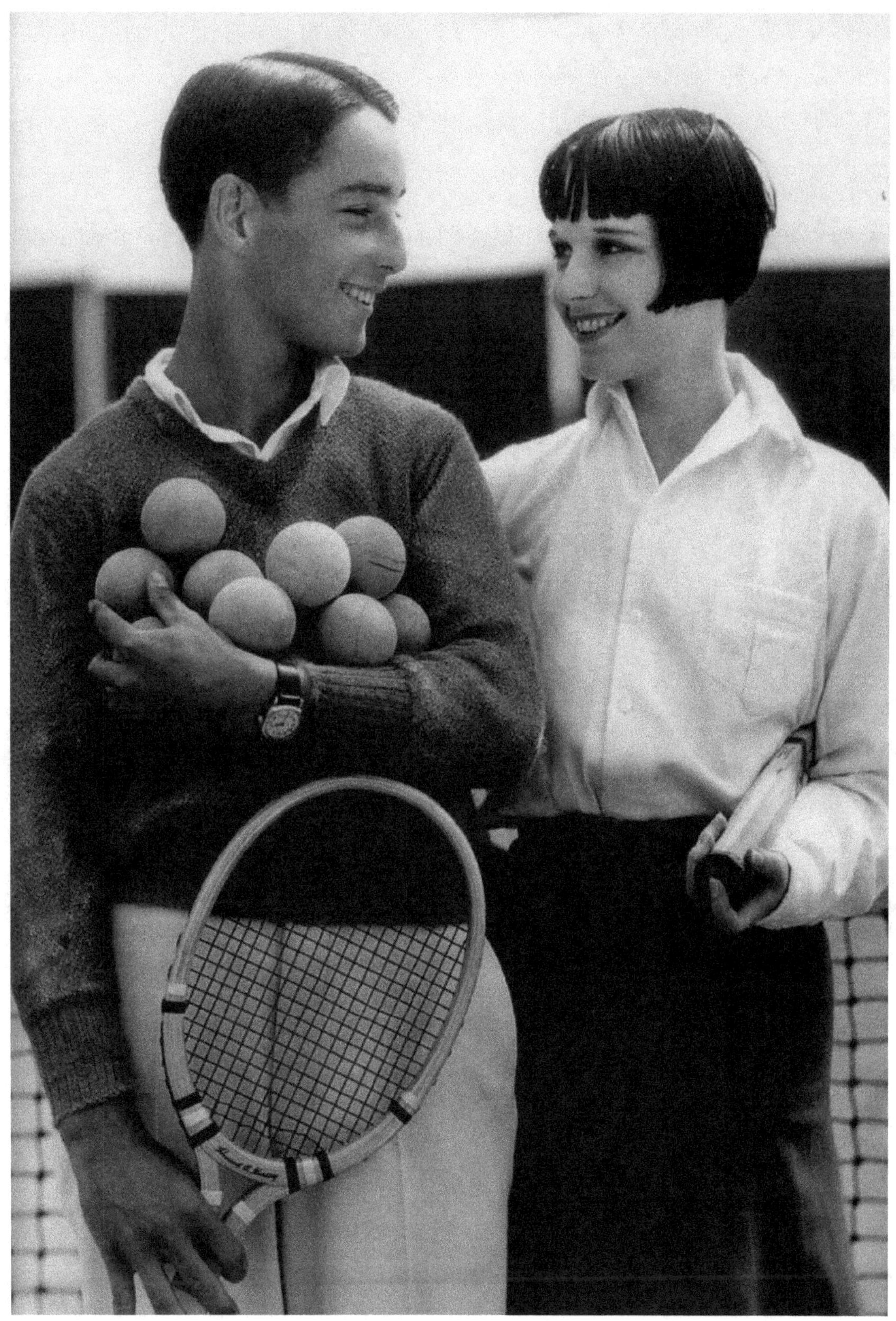

Image 59: With brother Theodore Roscoe Brooks, 1928.

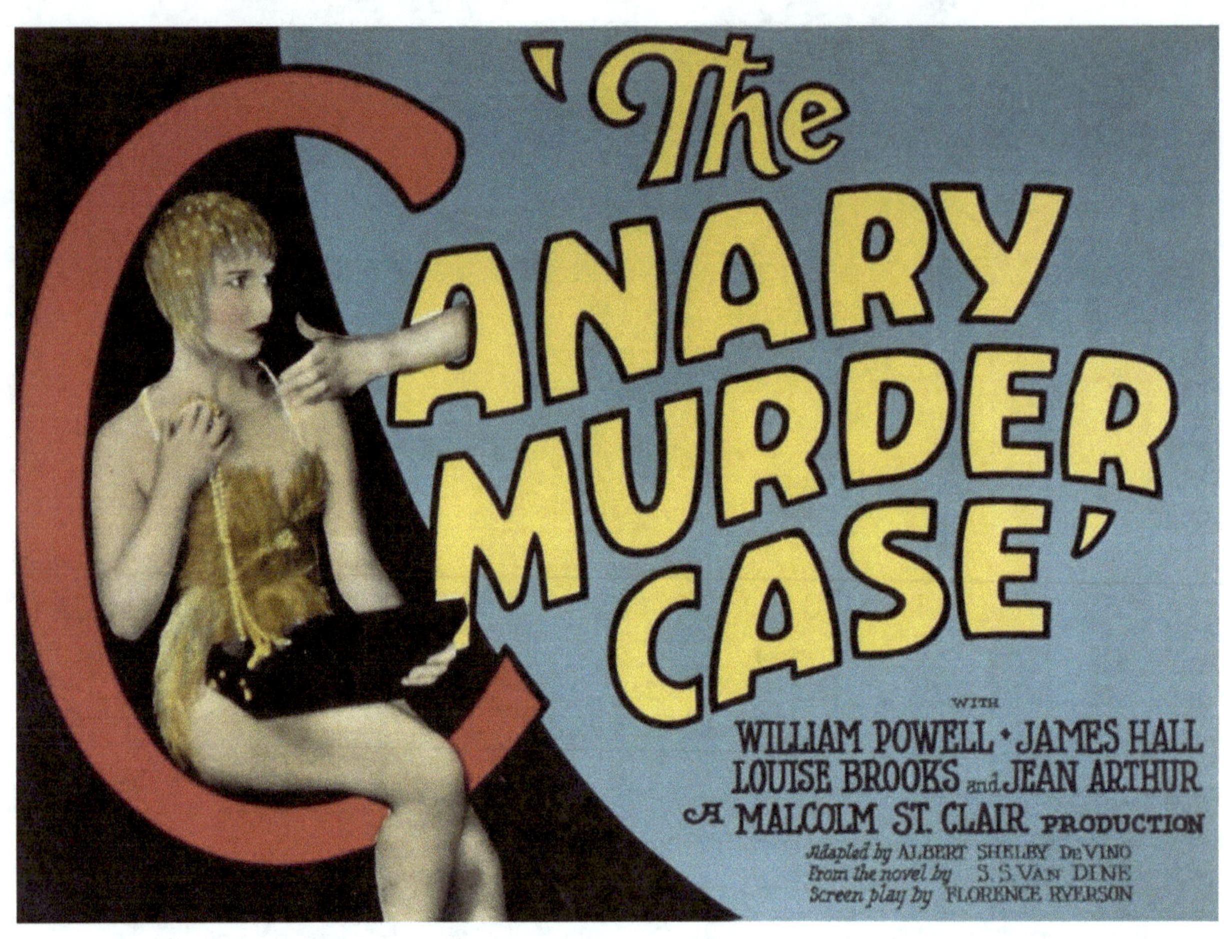

Image 60: Lobby card for *The Canary Murder Case,* 1929.

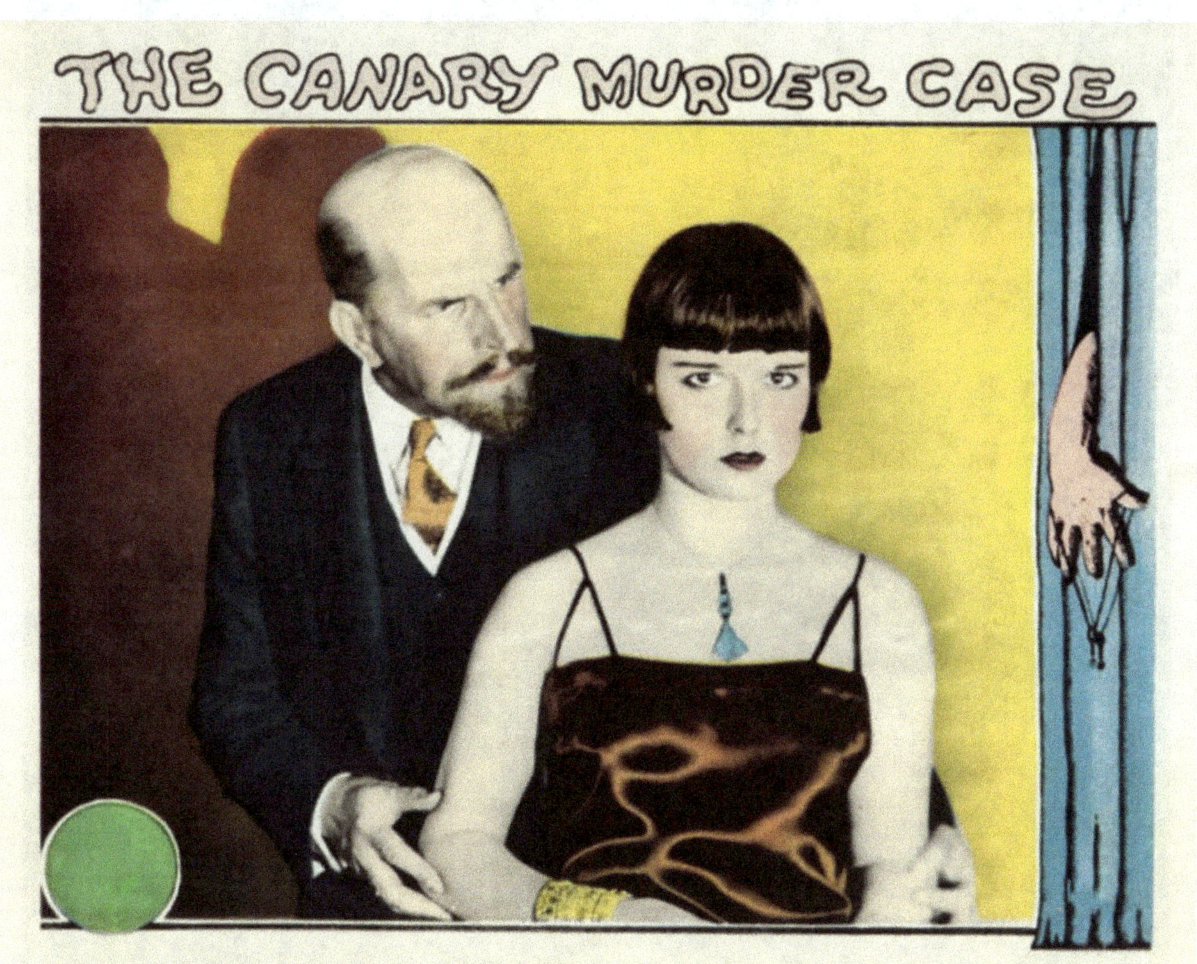

Image 61: Lobby card for *The Canary Murder Case,* 1929.

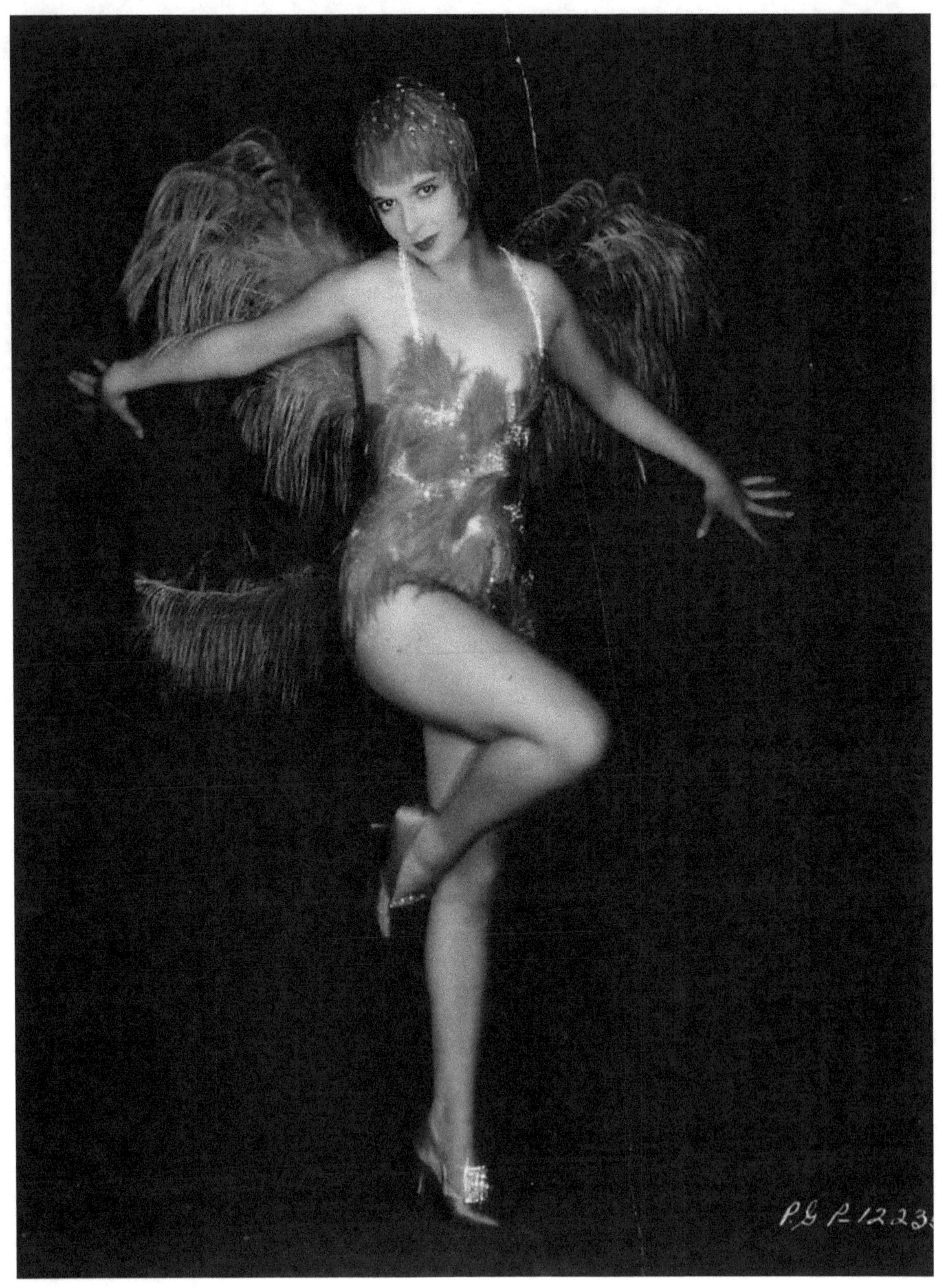

Image 62: *The Canary Murder Case*, 1929.

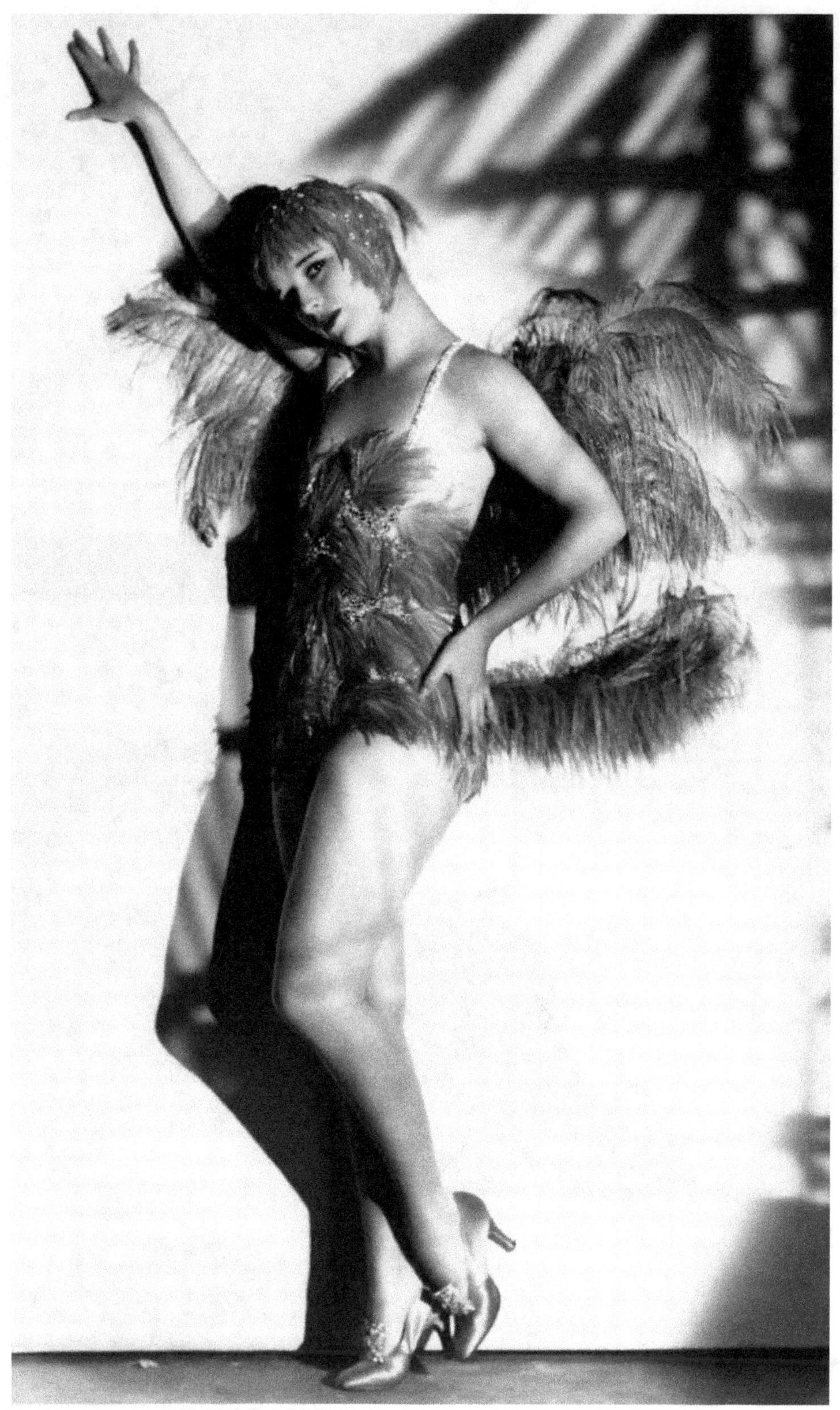

Image 63: *The Canary Murder Case*, 1929.

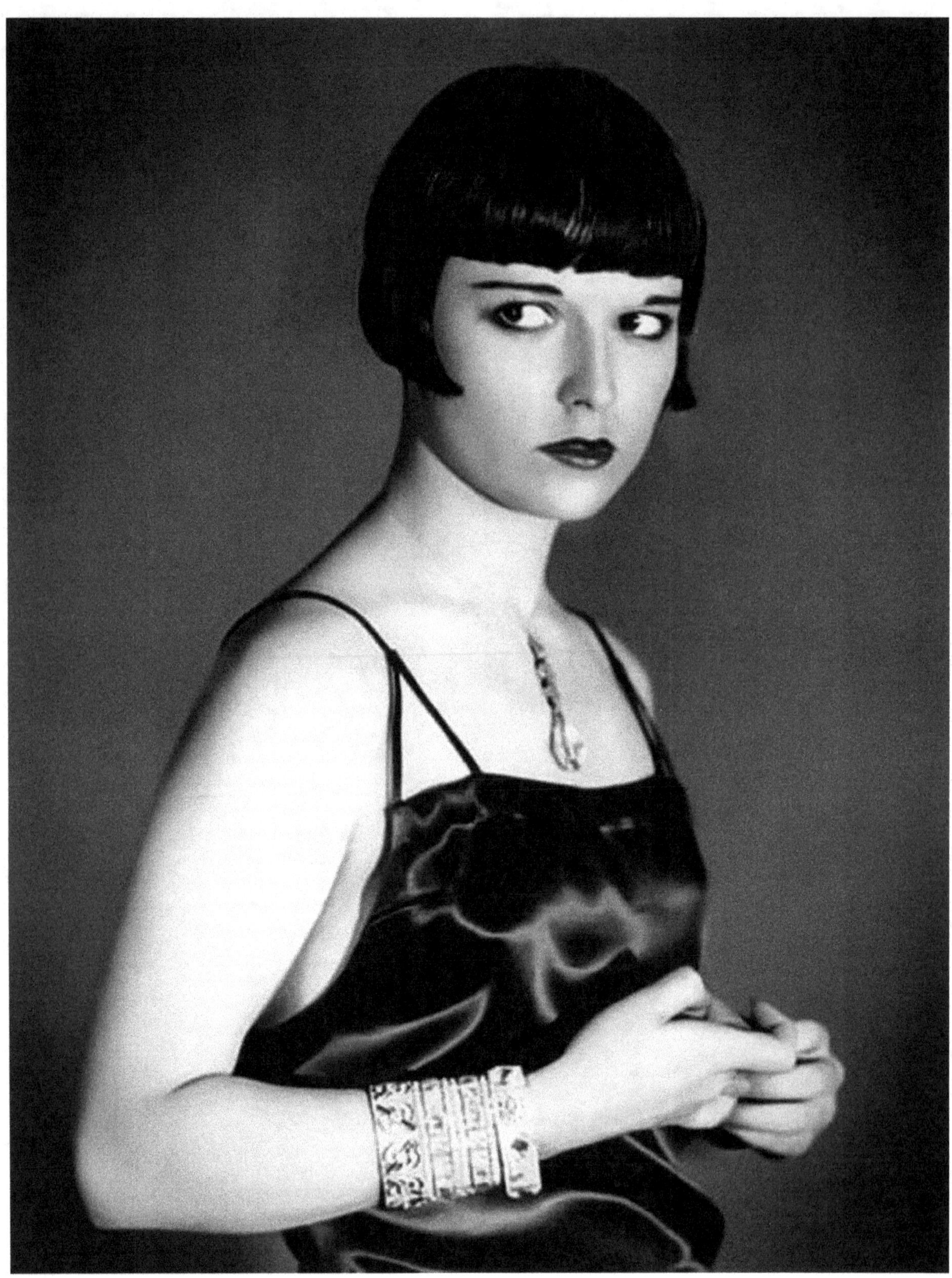

Image 64: *The Canary Murder Case*, 1929.

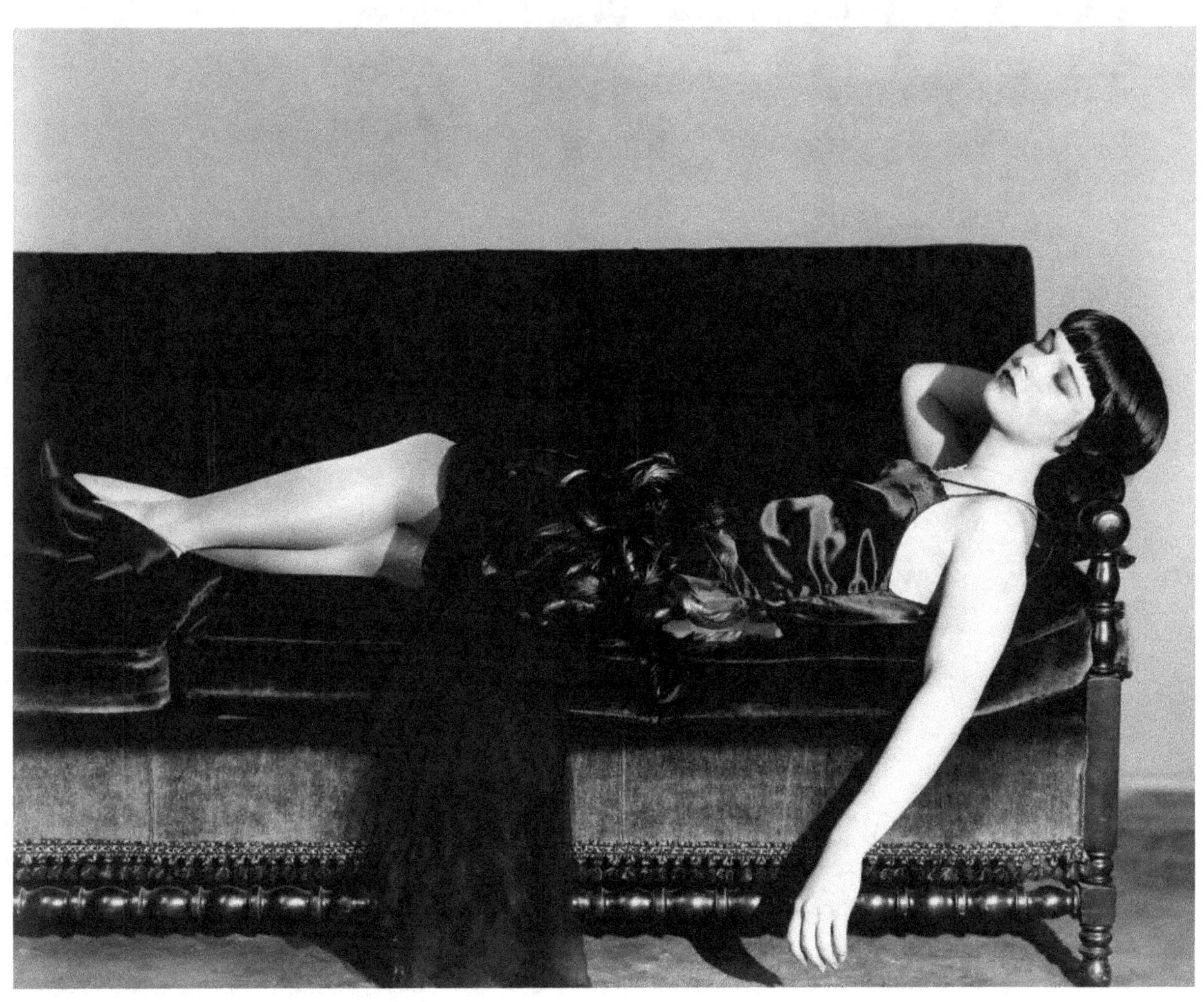

Image 65: *The Canary Murder Case*, 1929.

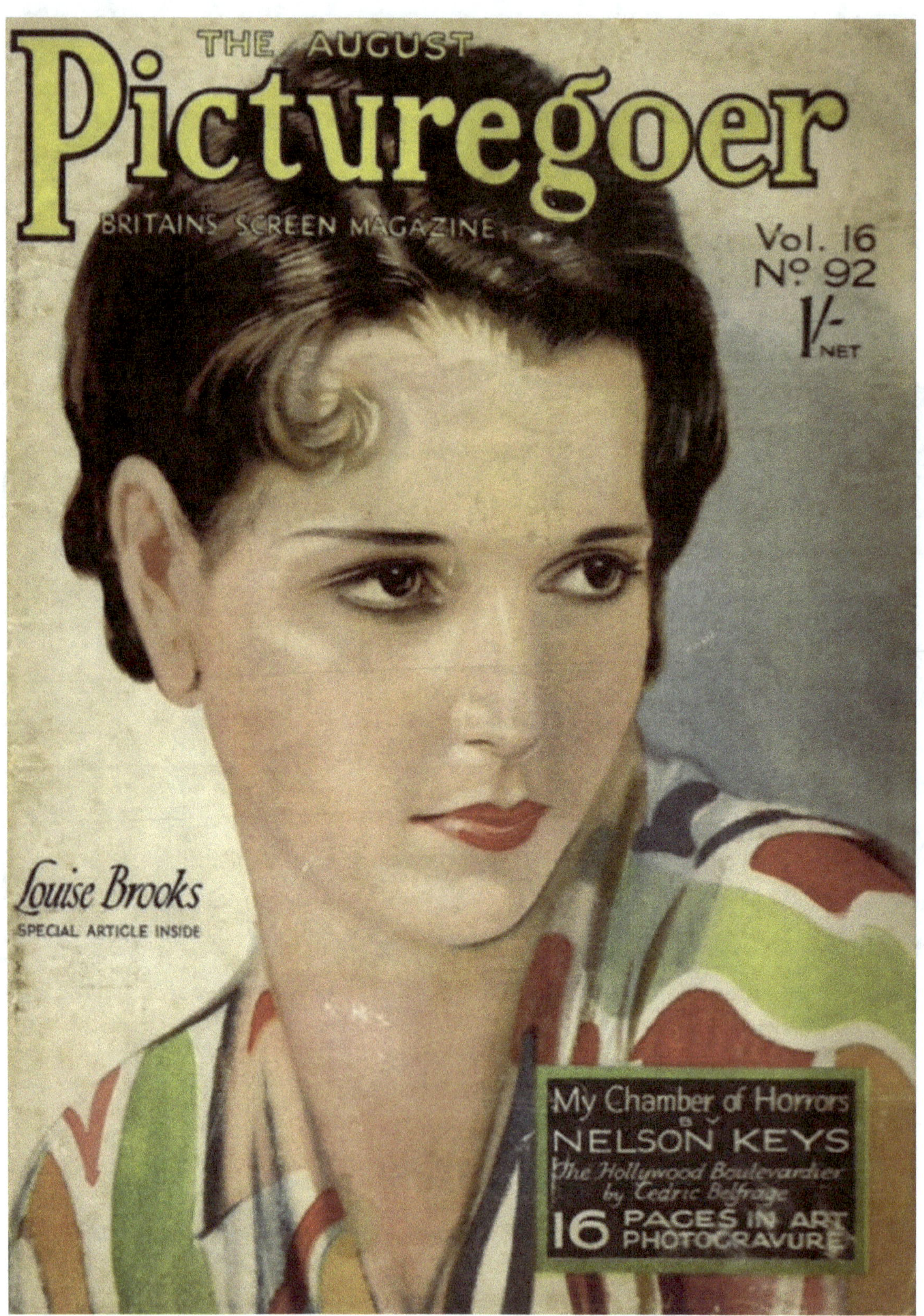

Image 66: Fan magazine cover, 1928.

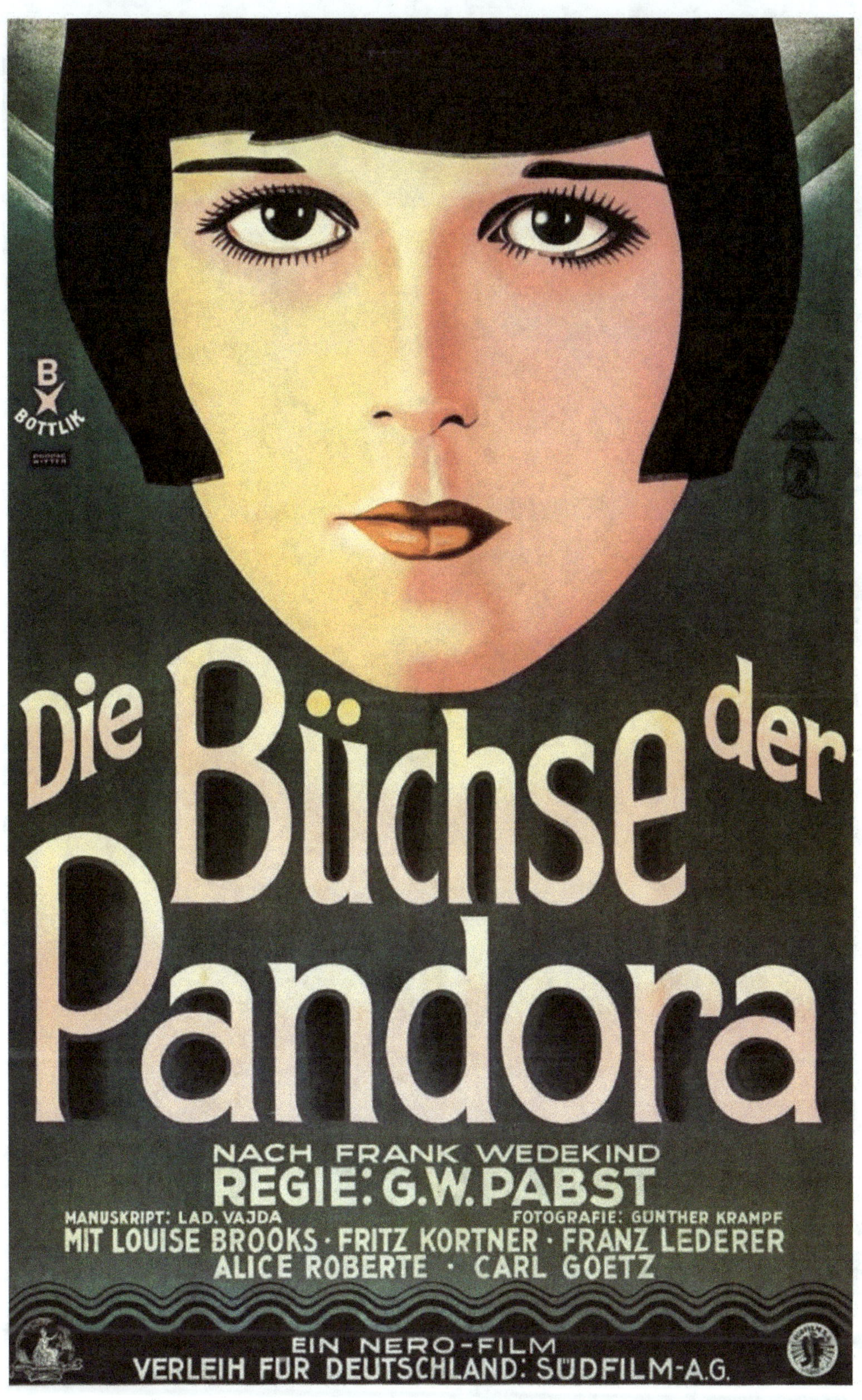

Image 67: German poster for *Pandora's Box*, 1929.

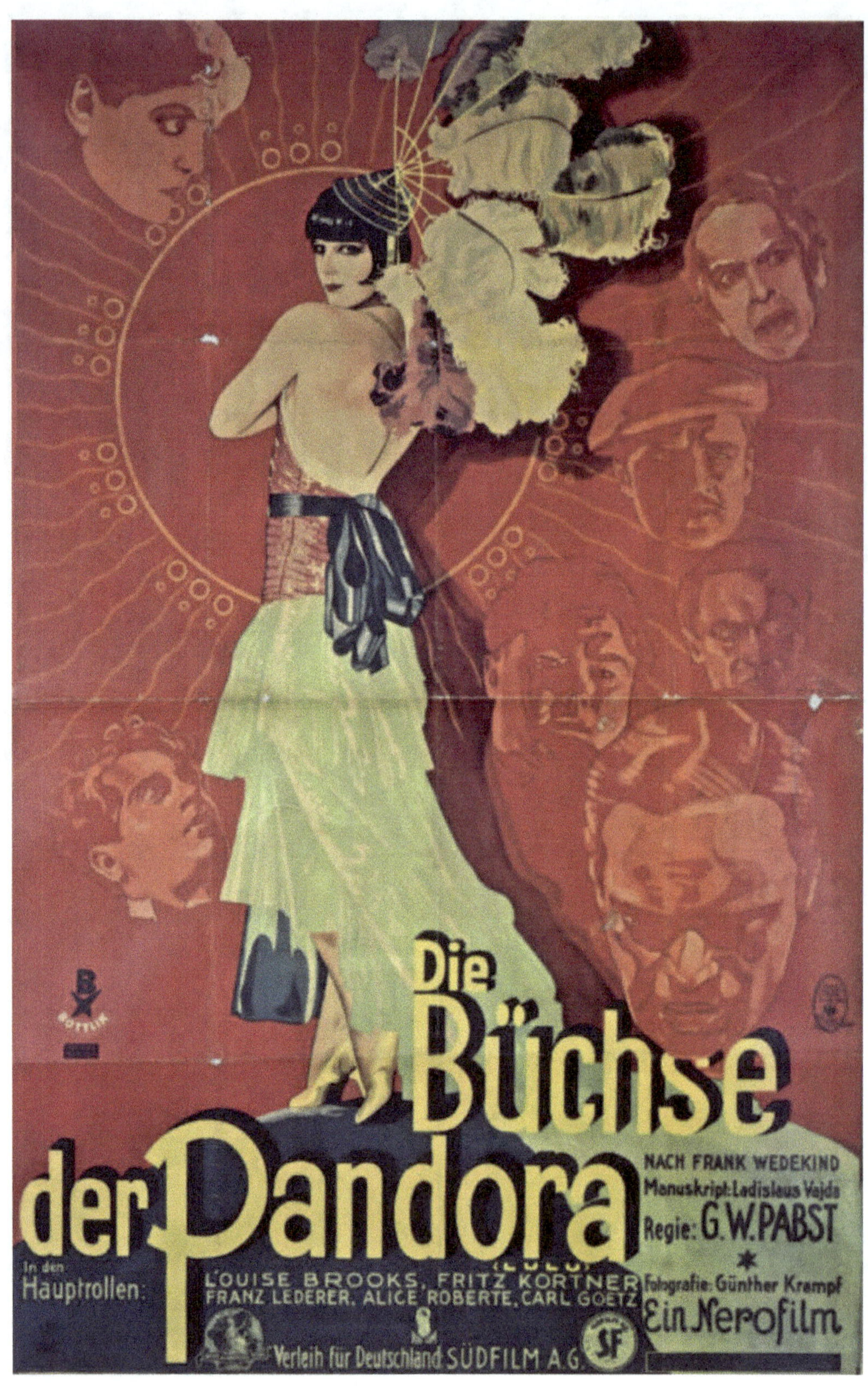

Image 68: German poster for *Pandora's Box*, 1929.

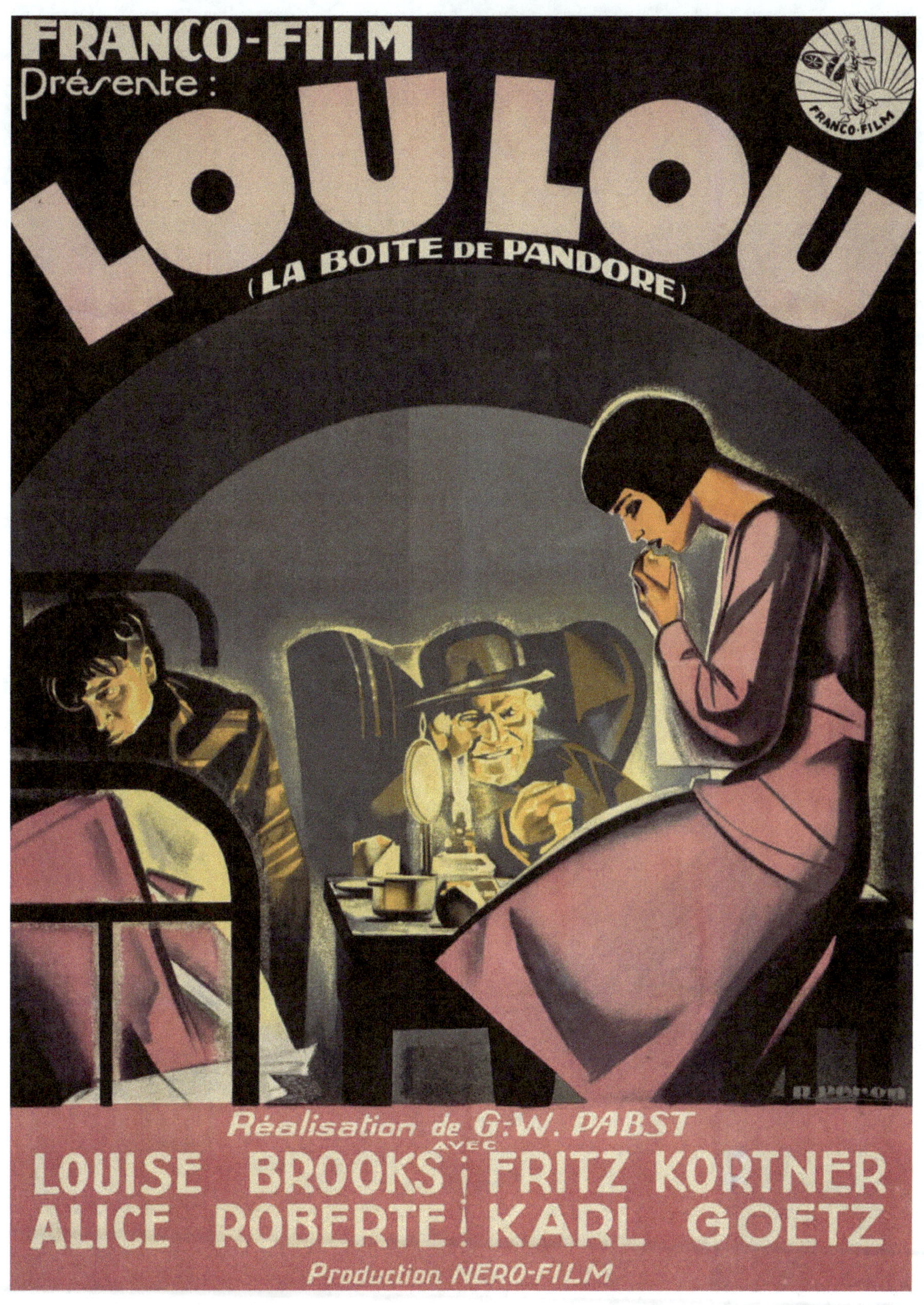

Image 69: French poster for *Pandora's Box*, 1929.

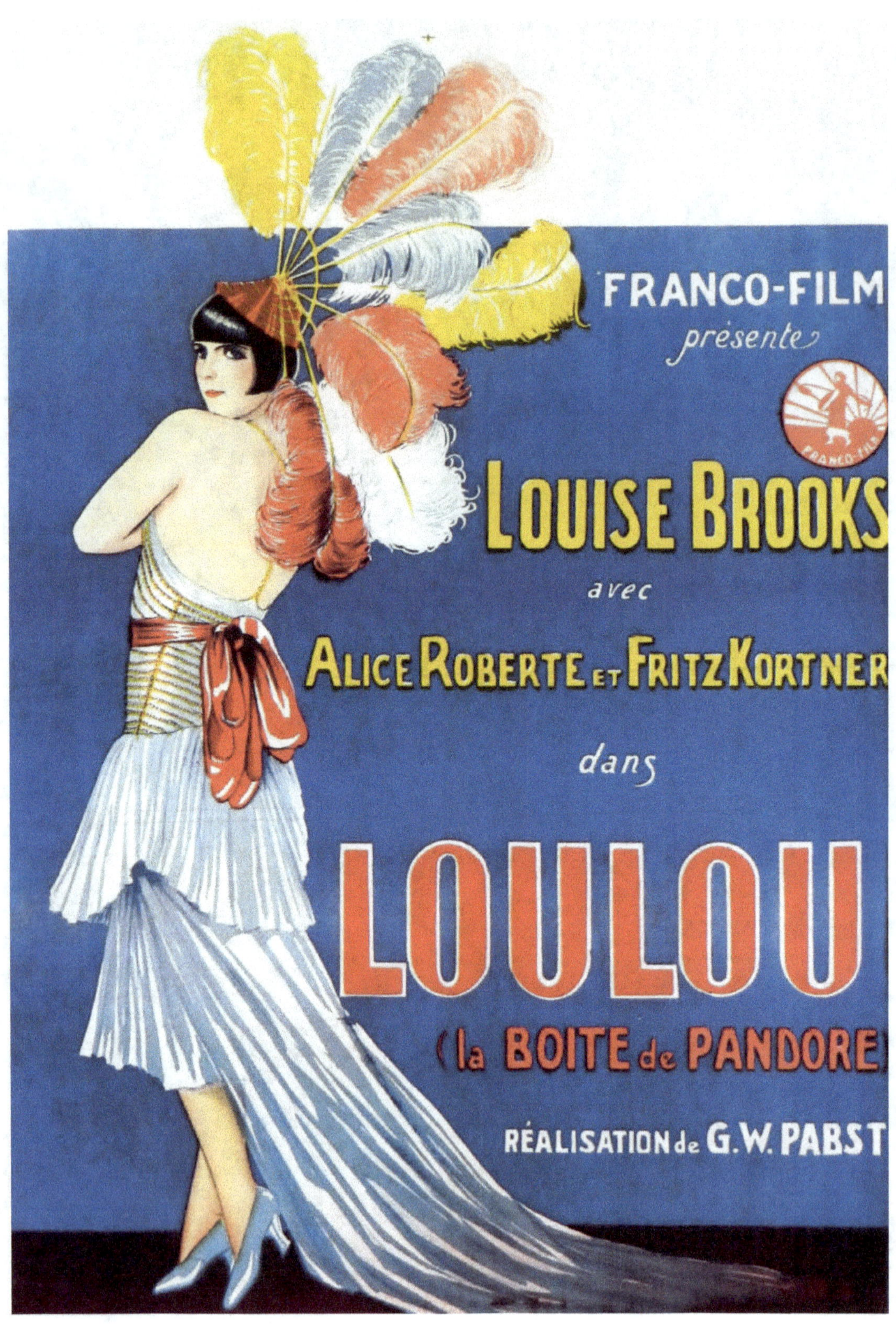

Image 70: Belgian poster for *Pandora's Box*, 1929.

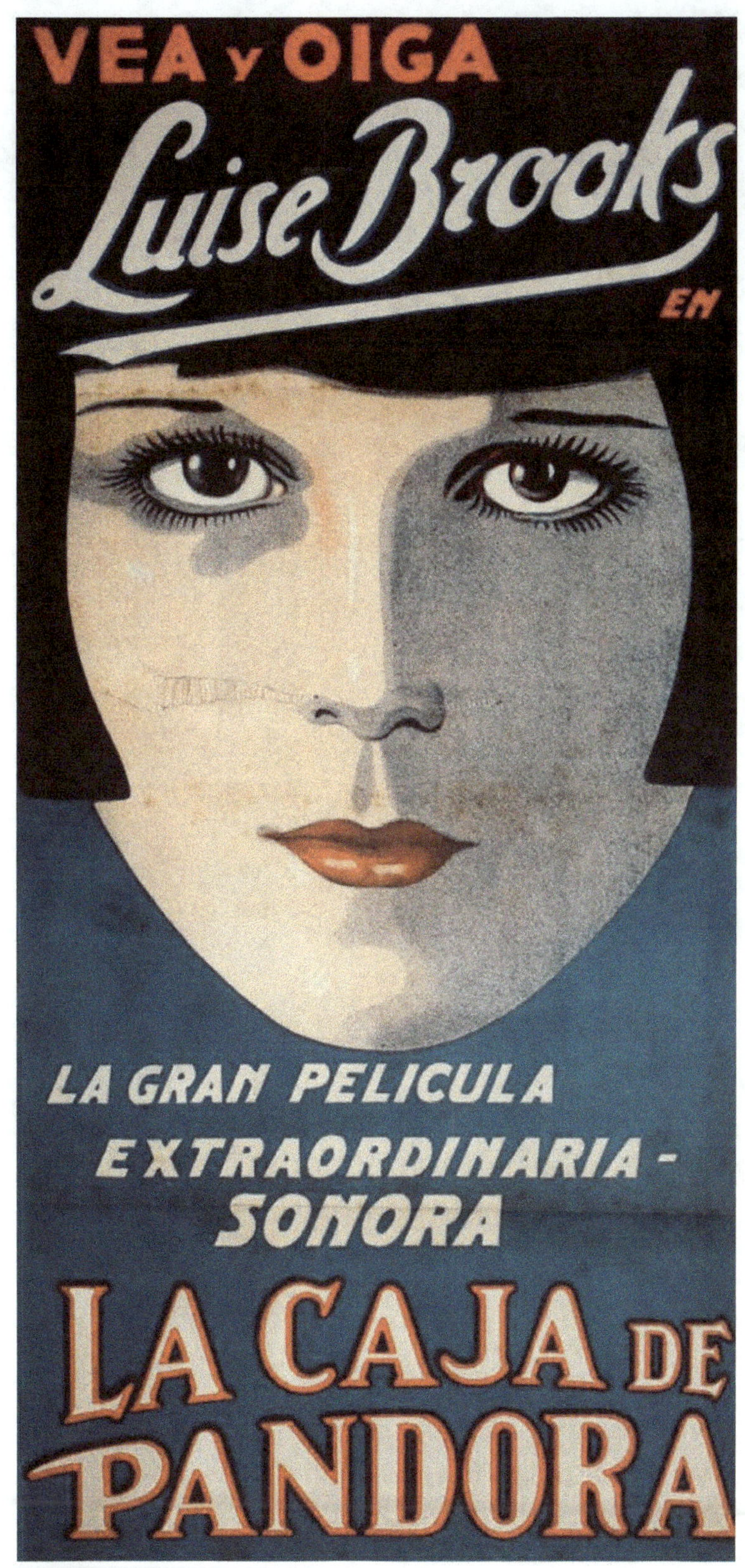

Image 71: Argentinian poster for *Pandora's Box*, 1929.

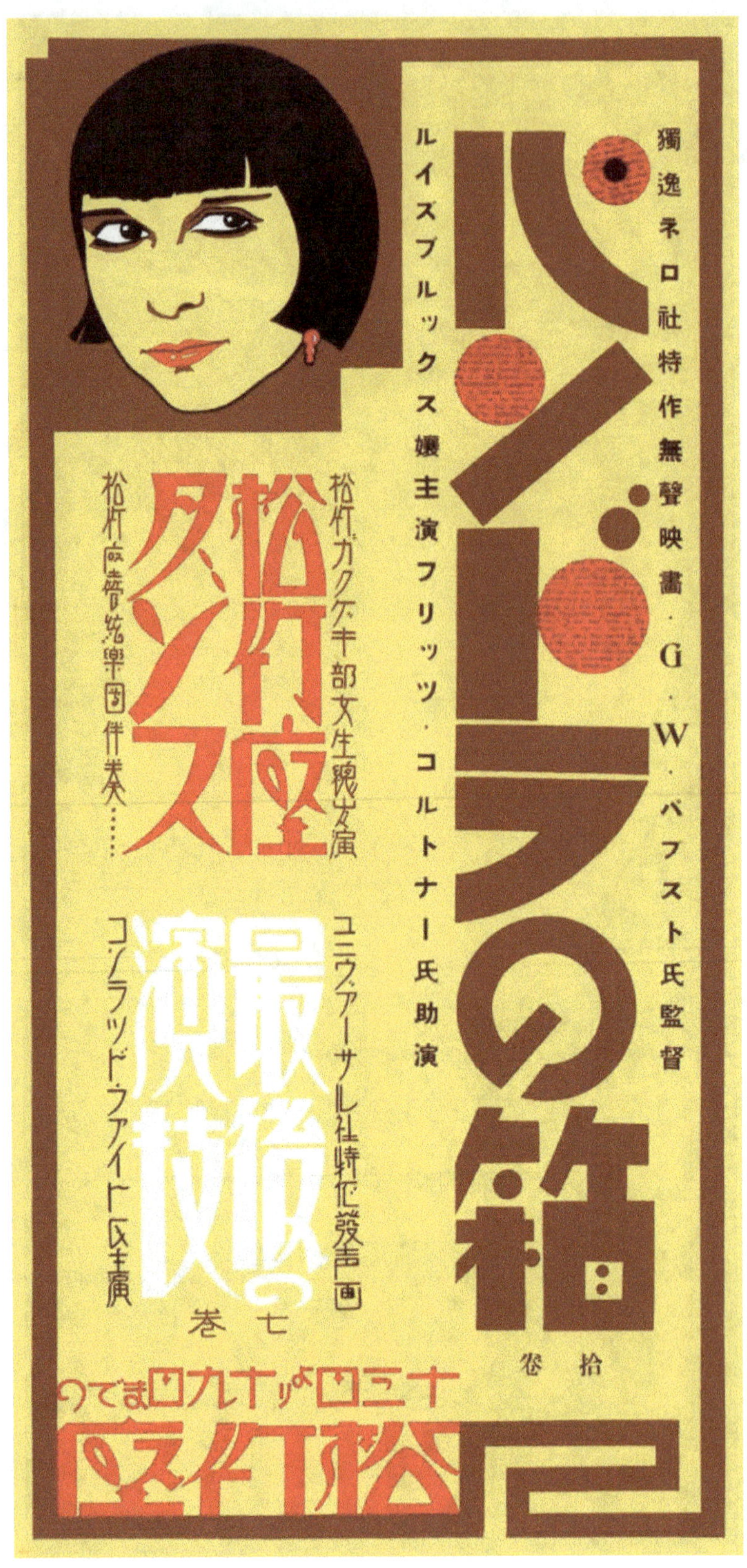

Image 72: Japanese poster for *Pandora's Box*, ca. 1929.

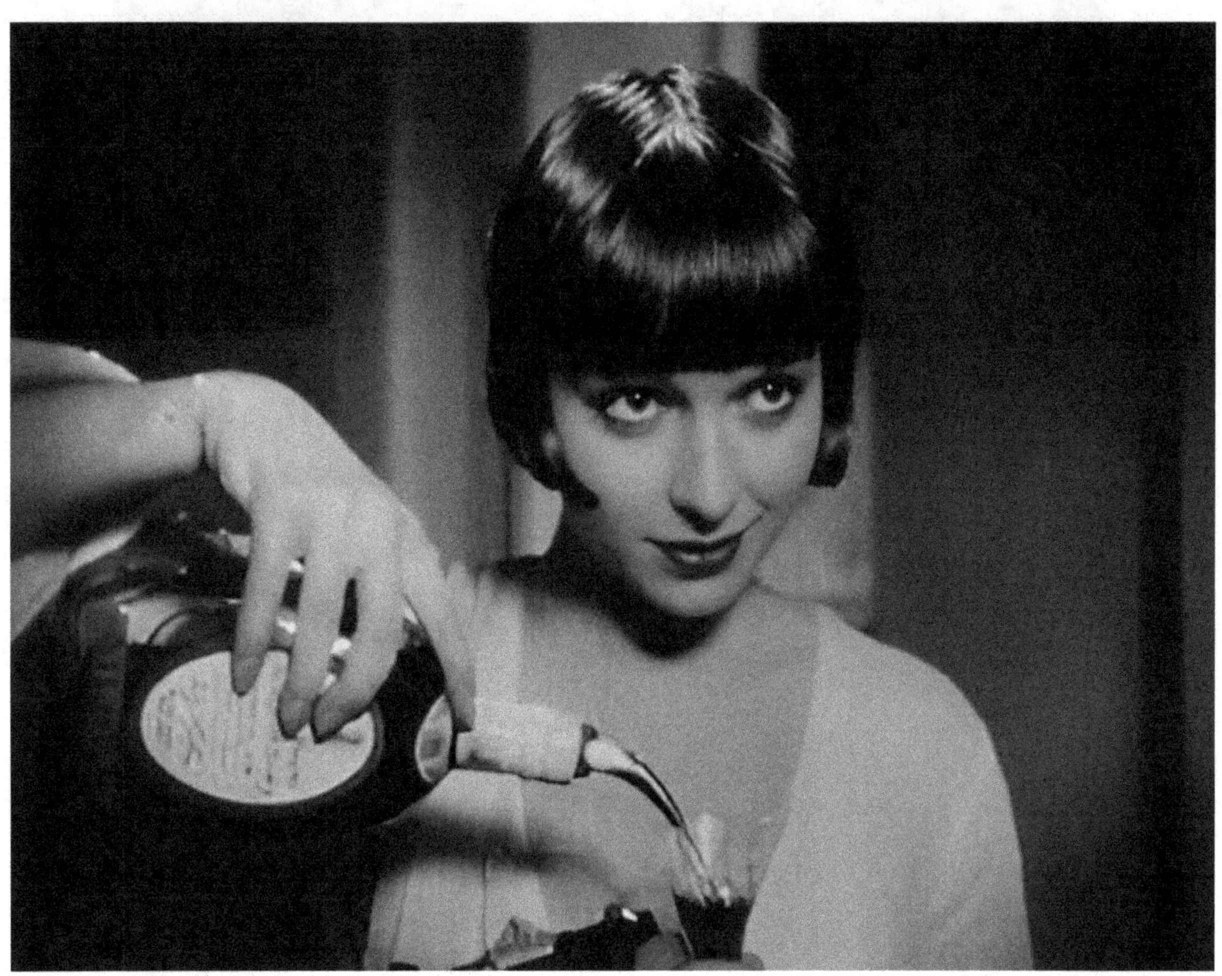

Image 73: *Pandora's Box,* 1929.

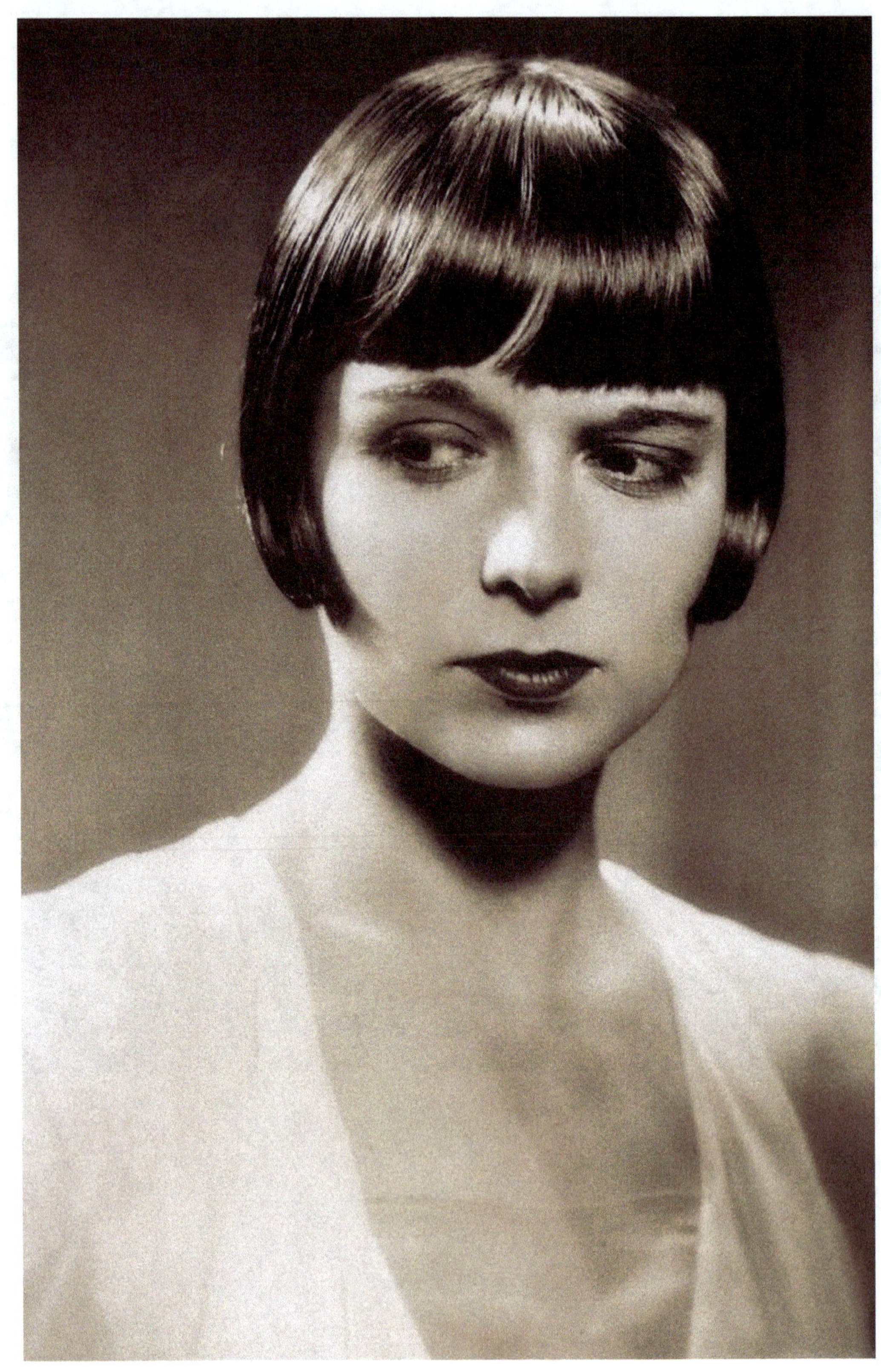

Image 74: *Pandora's Box*, 1929.

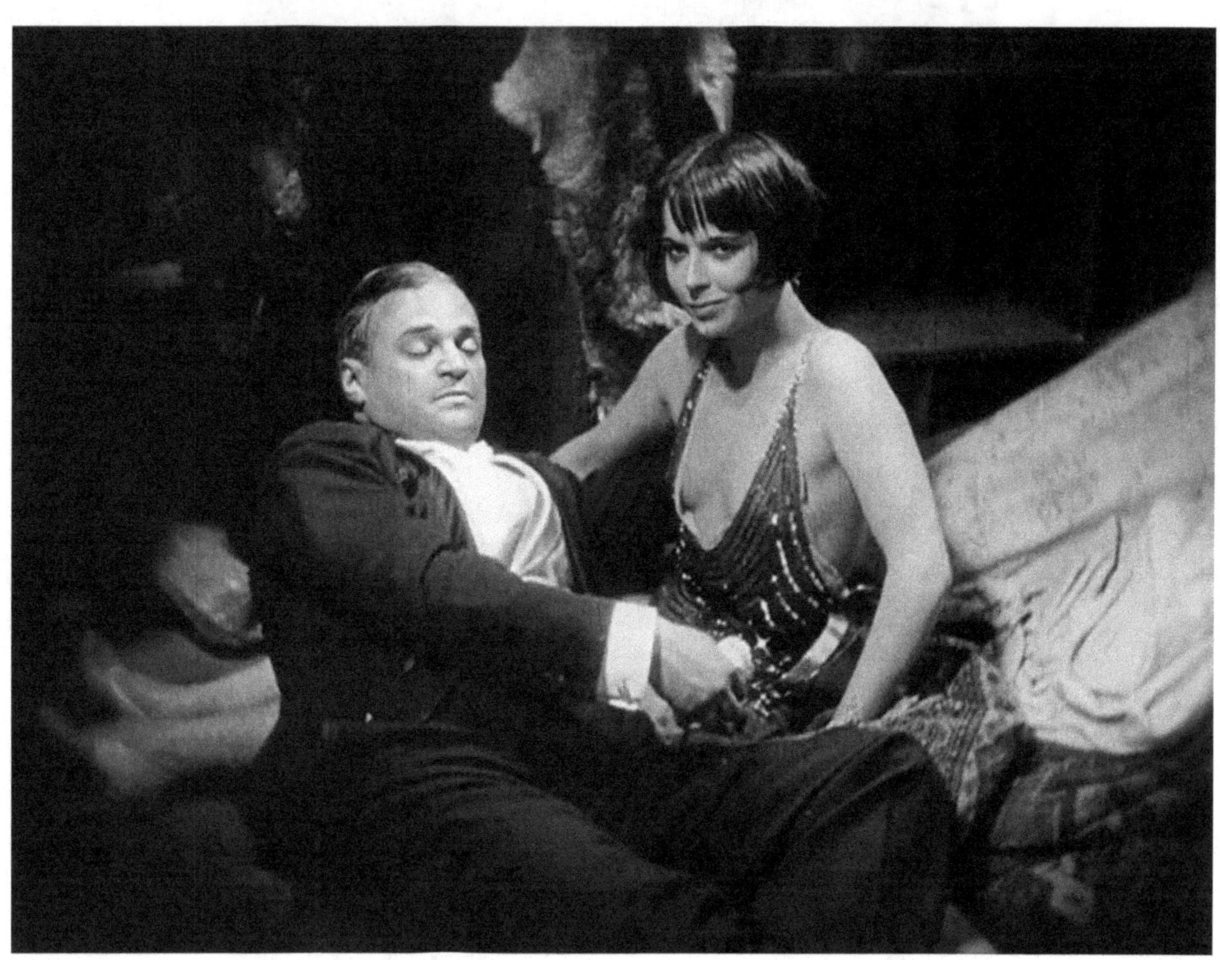

Image 75: *Pandora's Box*, 1929.

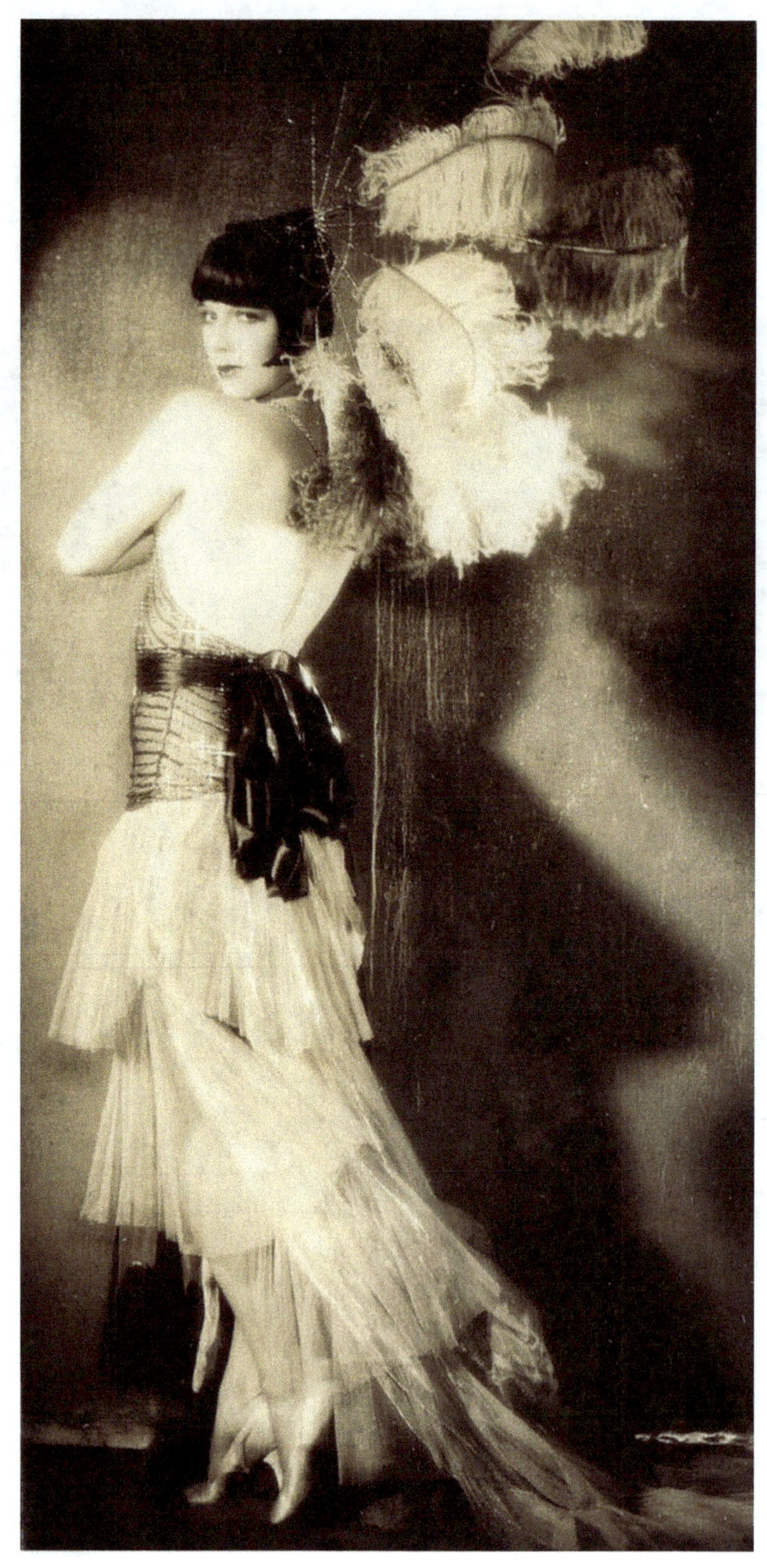

Image 76: *Pandora's Box*, 1929.

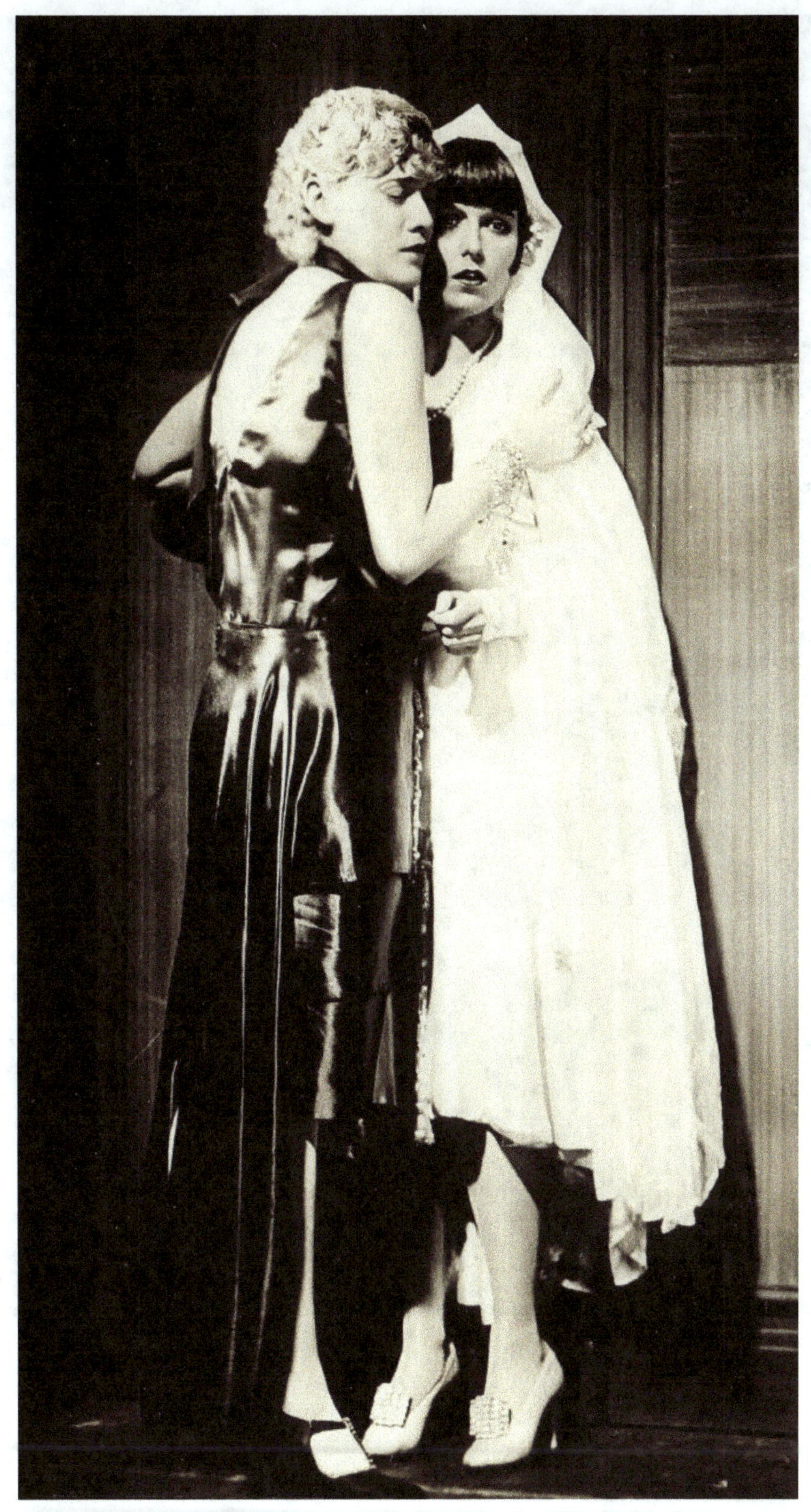

Image 77: *Pandora's Box*, 1929.

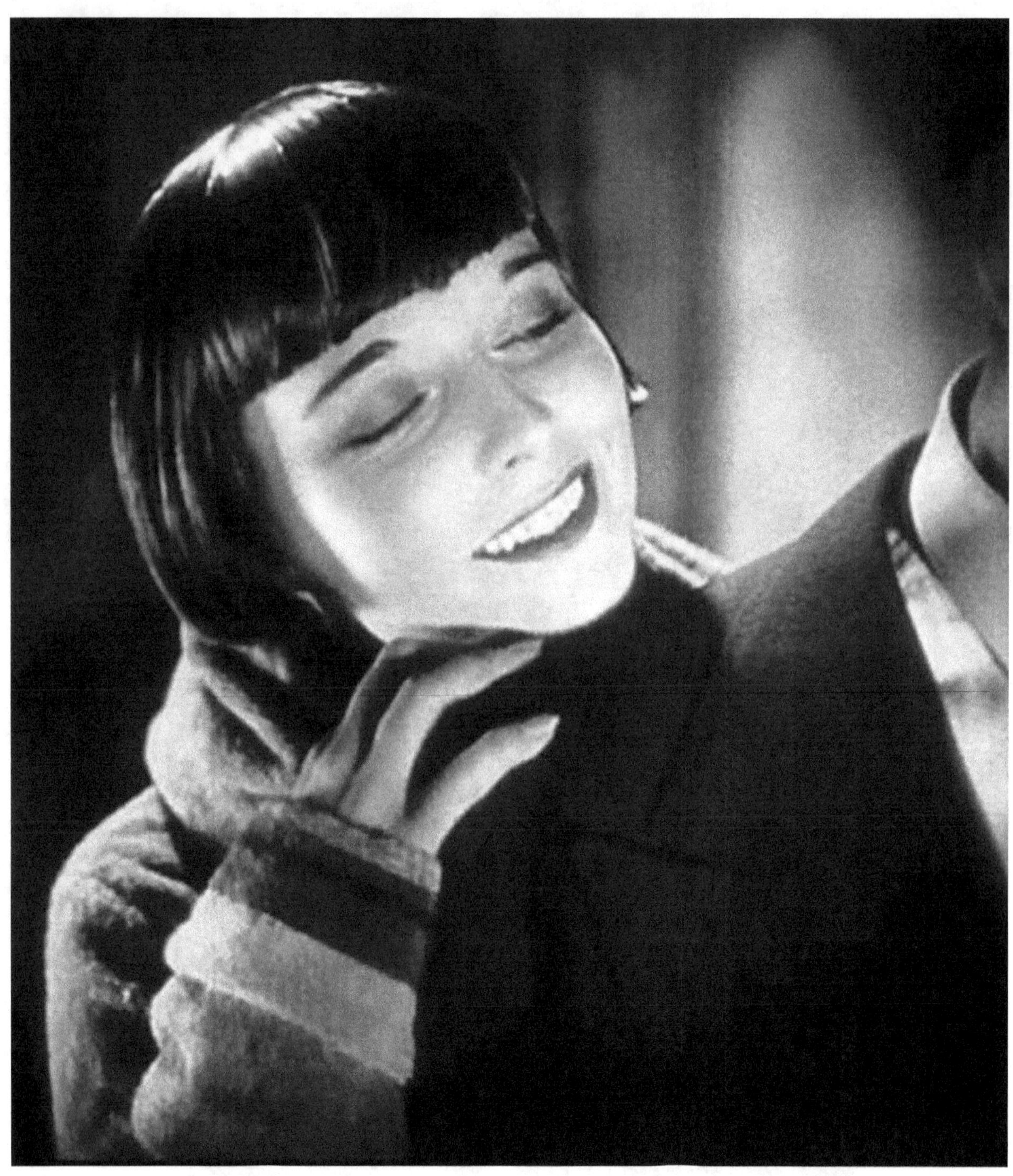

Image 78: *Pandora's Box*, 1929.

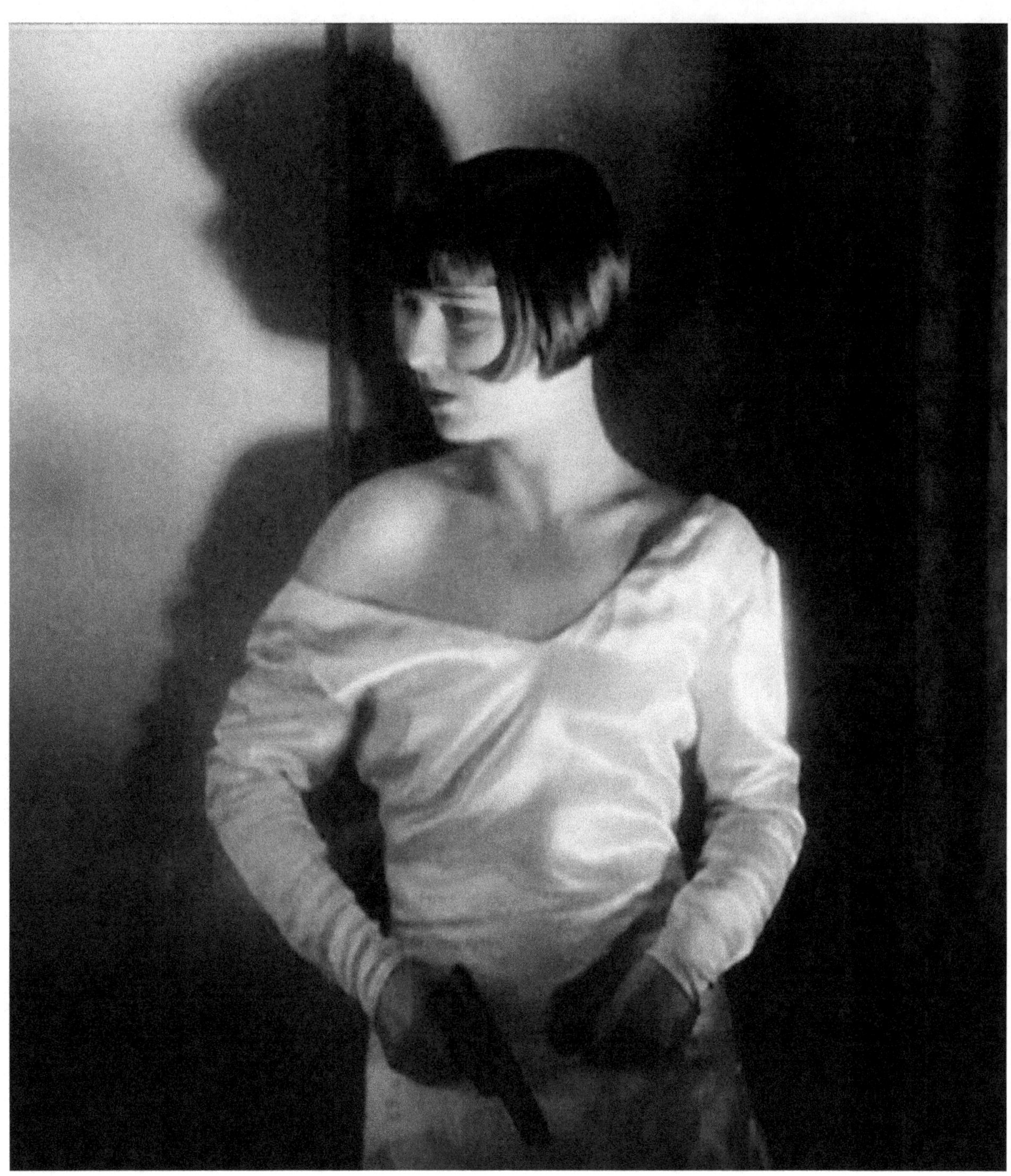

Image 79: *Pandora's Box*, 1929.

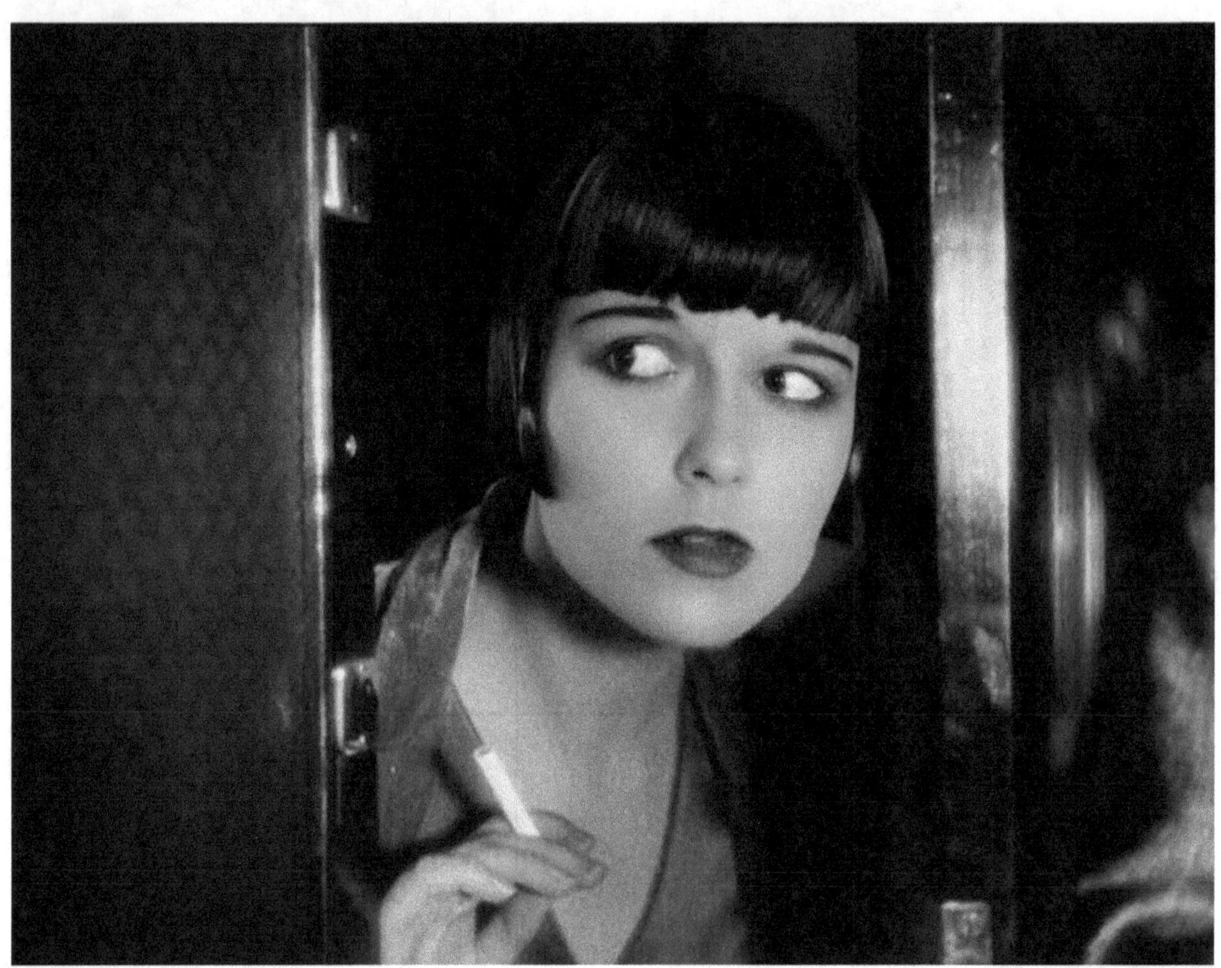

Image 80: *Pandora's Box*, 1929.

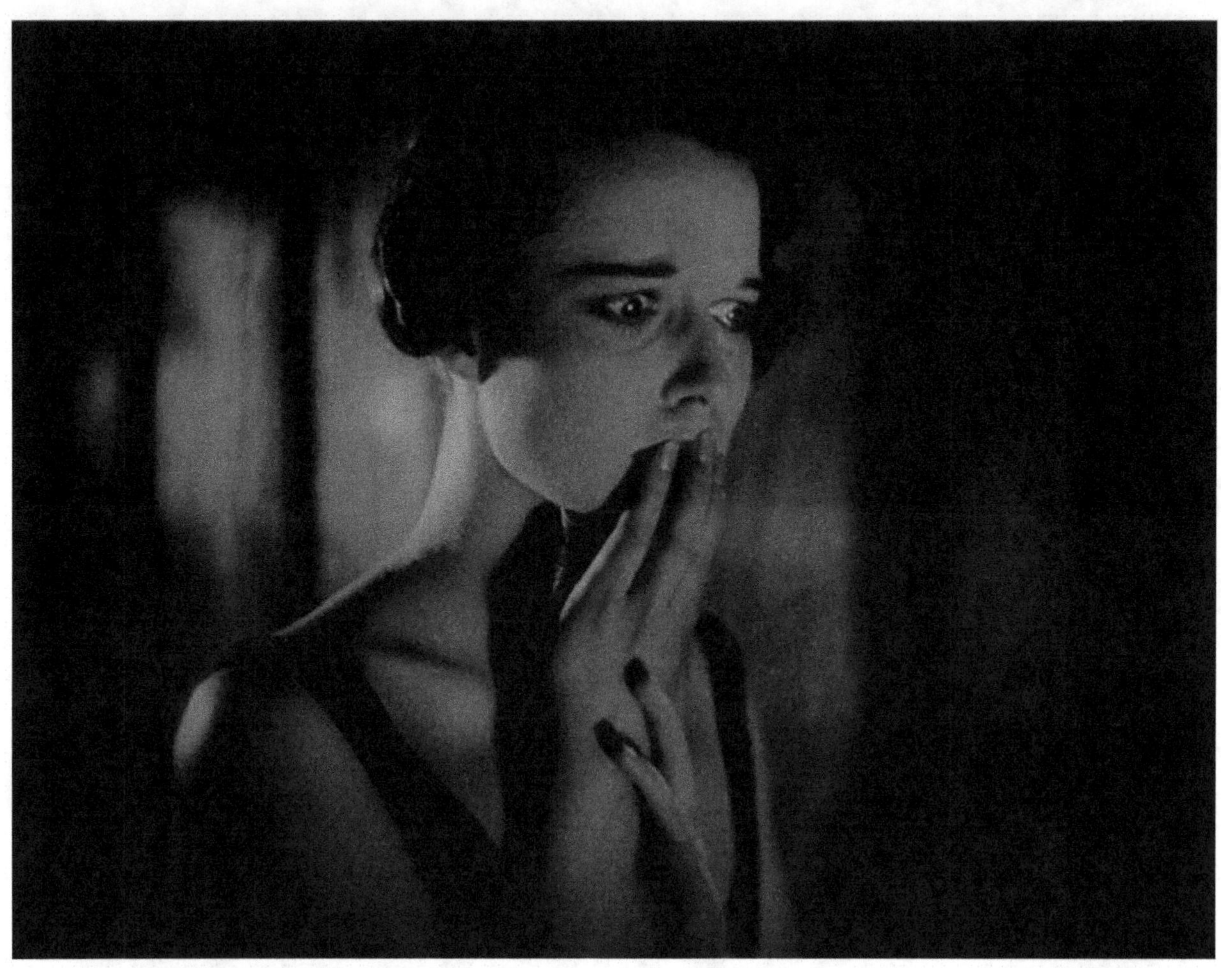

Image 81: *Pandora's Box*, 1929.

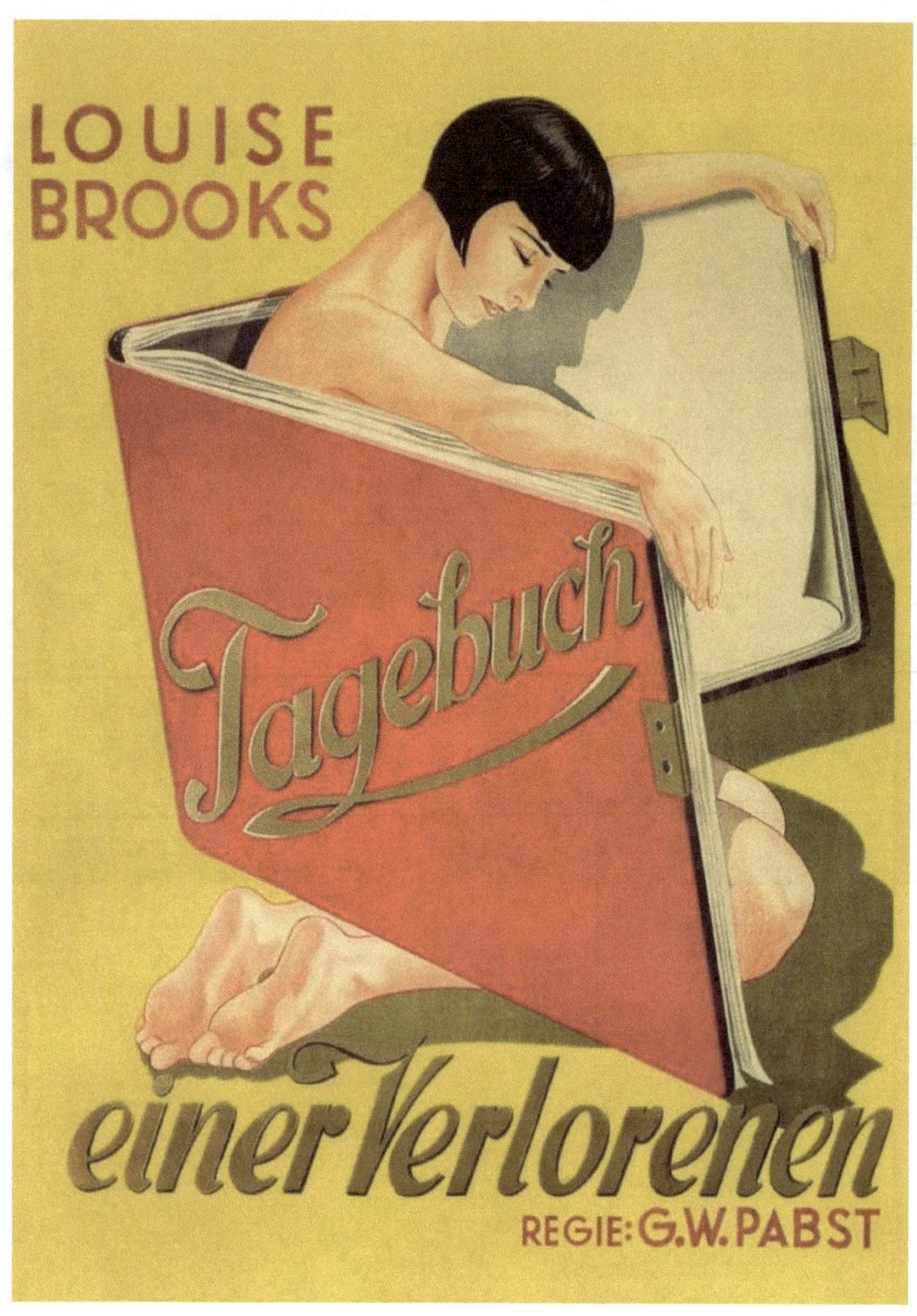

Image 82: German poster for *Diary of a Lost Girl*, 1929.

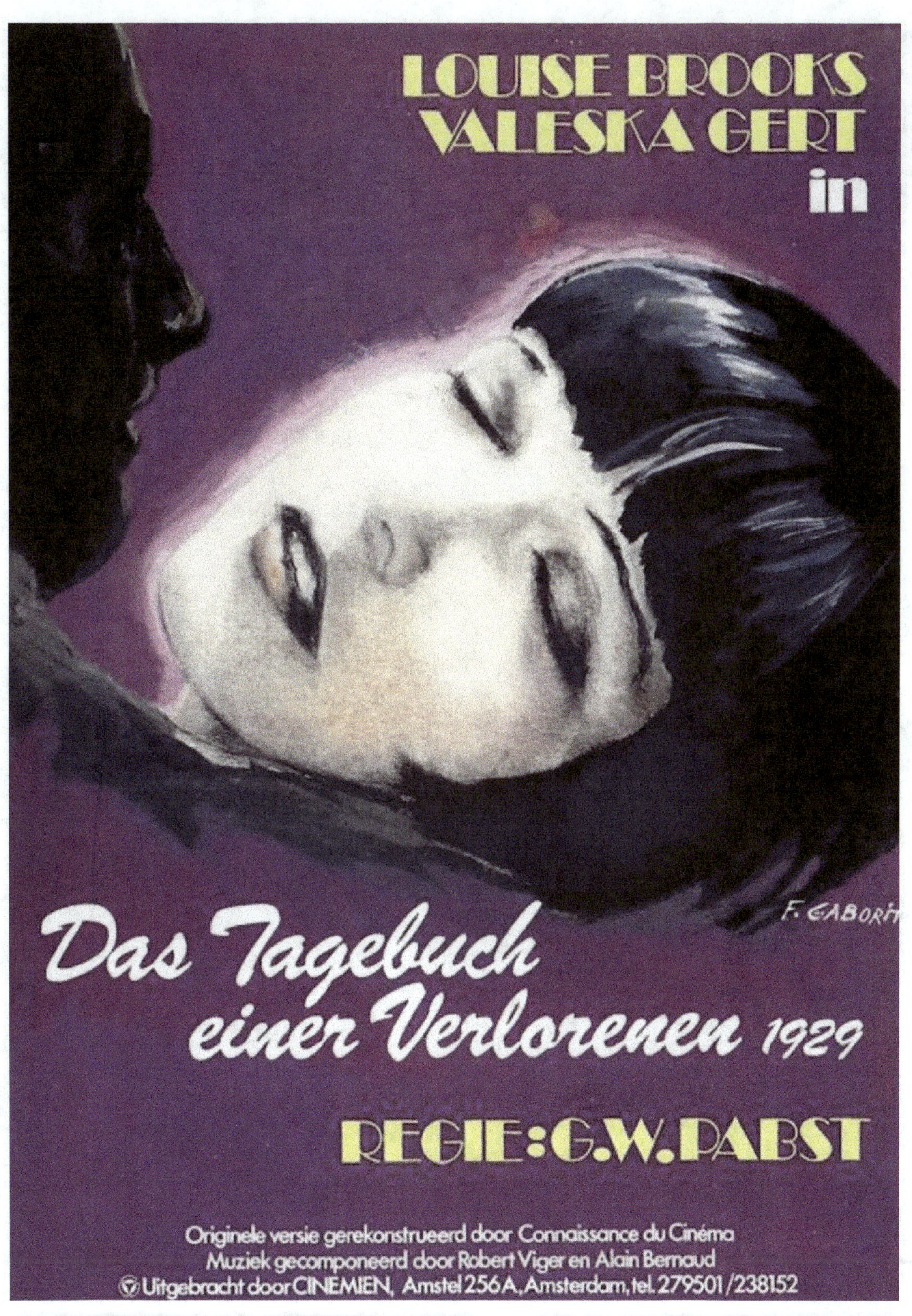

Image 83: German poster for *Diary of a Lost Girl,* 1929.

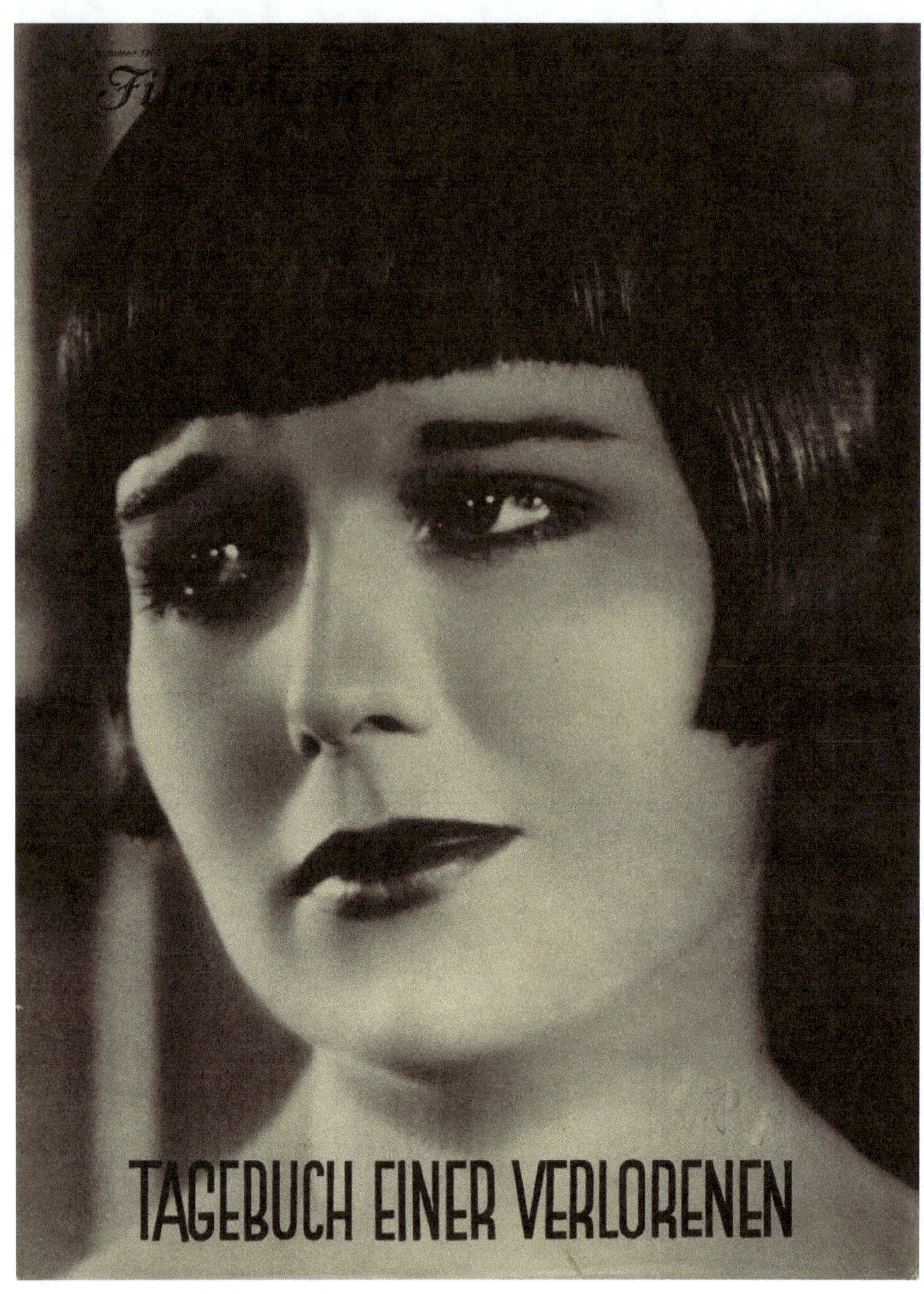

Image 84: Program fo *Diary of a Lost Girl*, 1929.

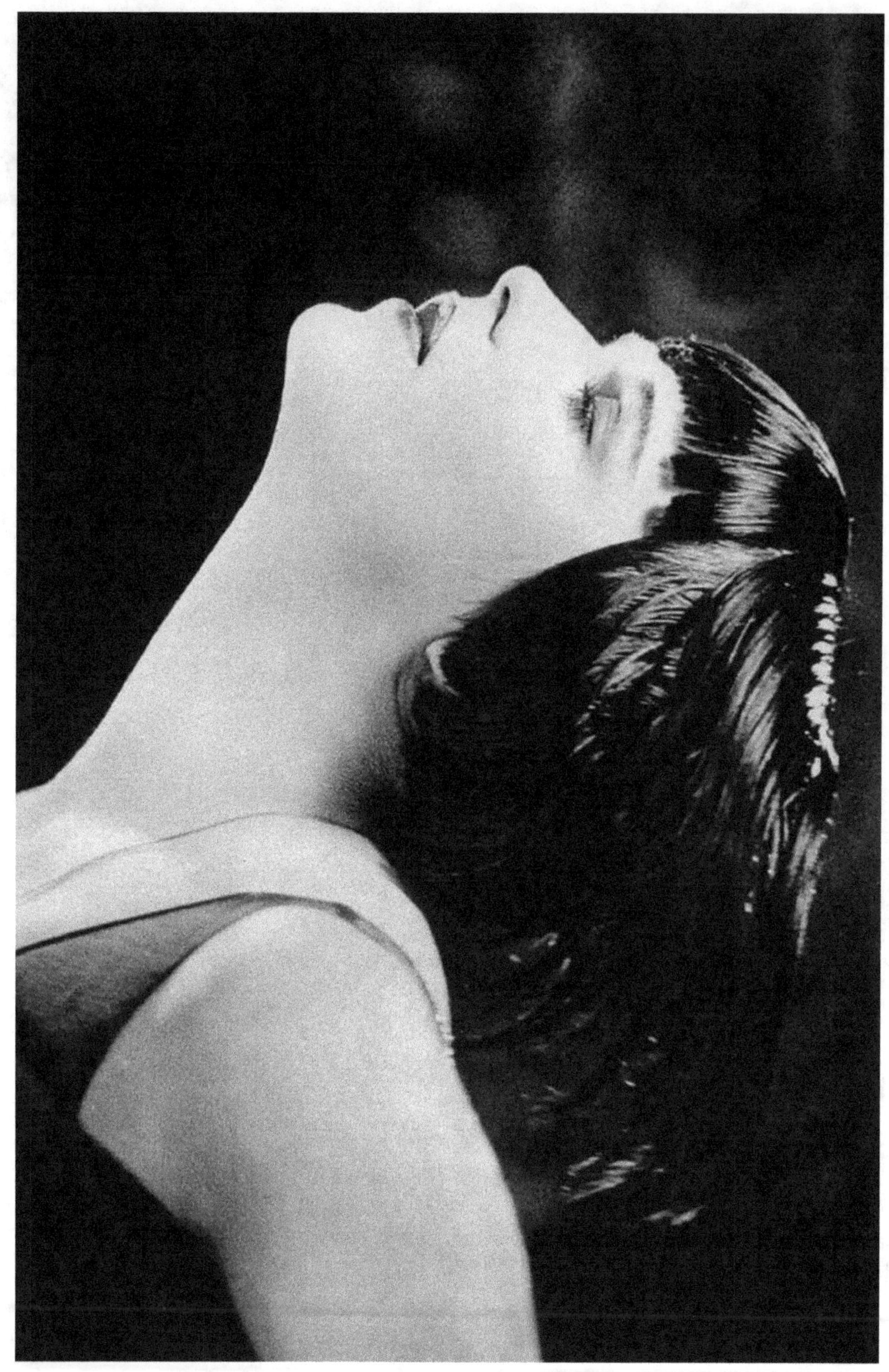

Image 85: *Diary of a Lost Girl*, 1929.

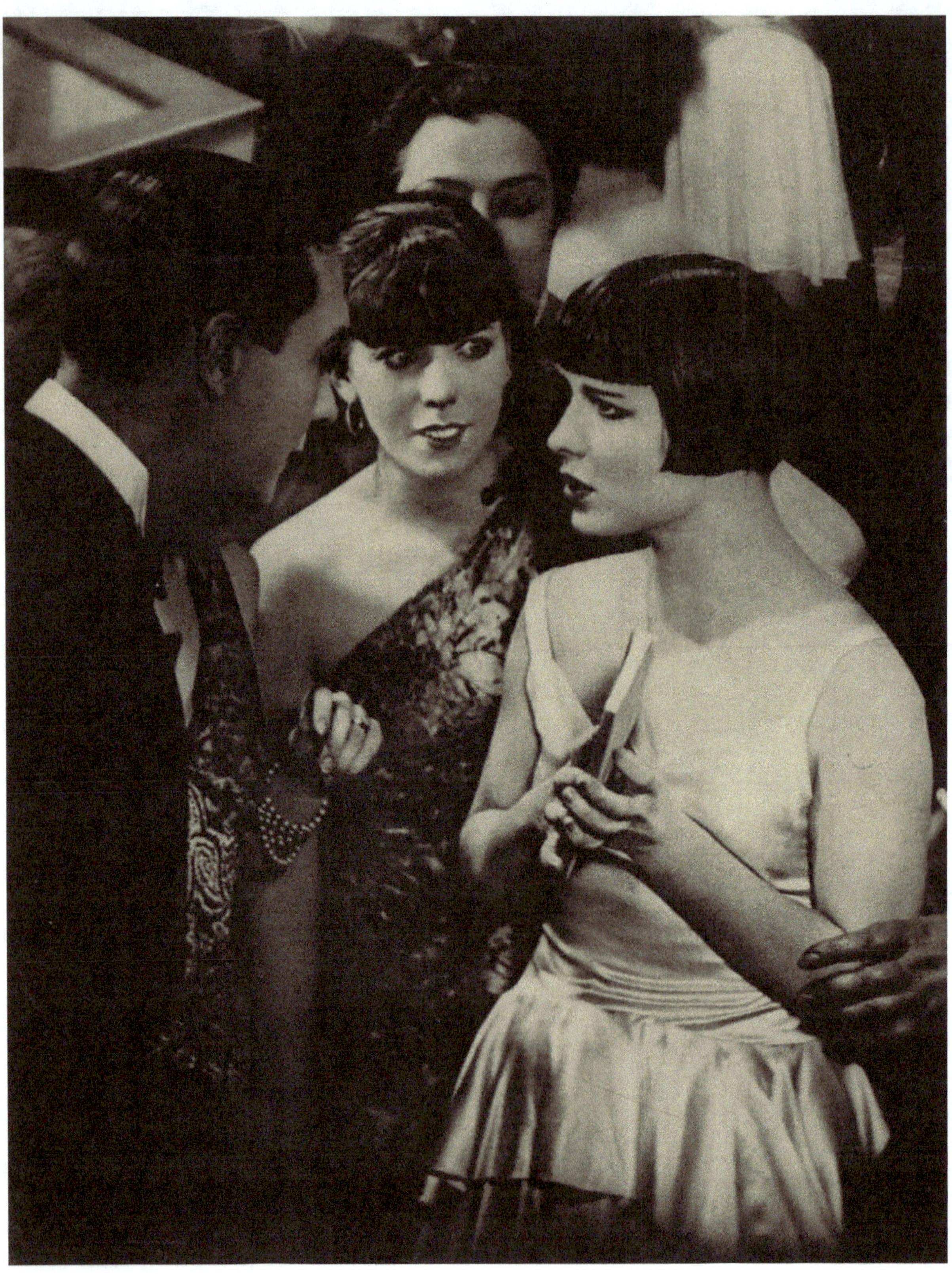

Image 86: *Diary of a Lost Girl*, 1929.

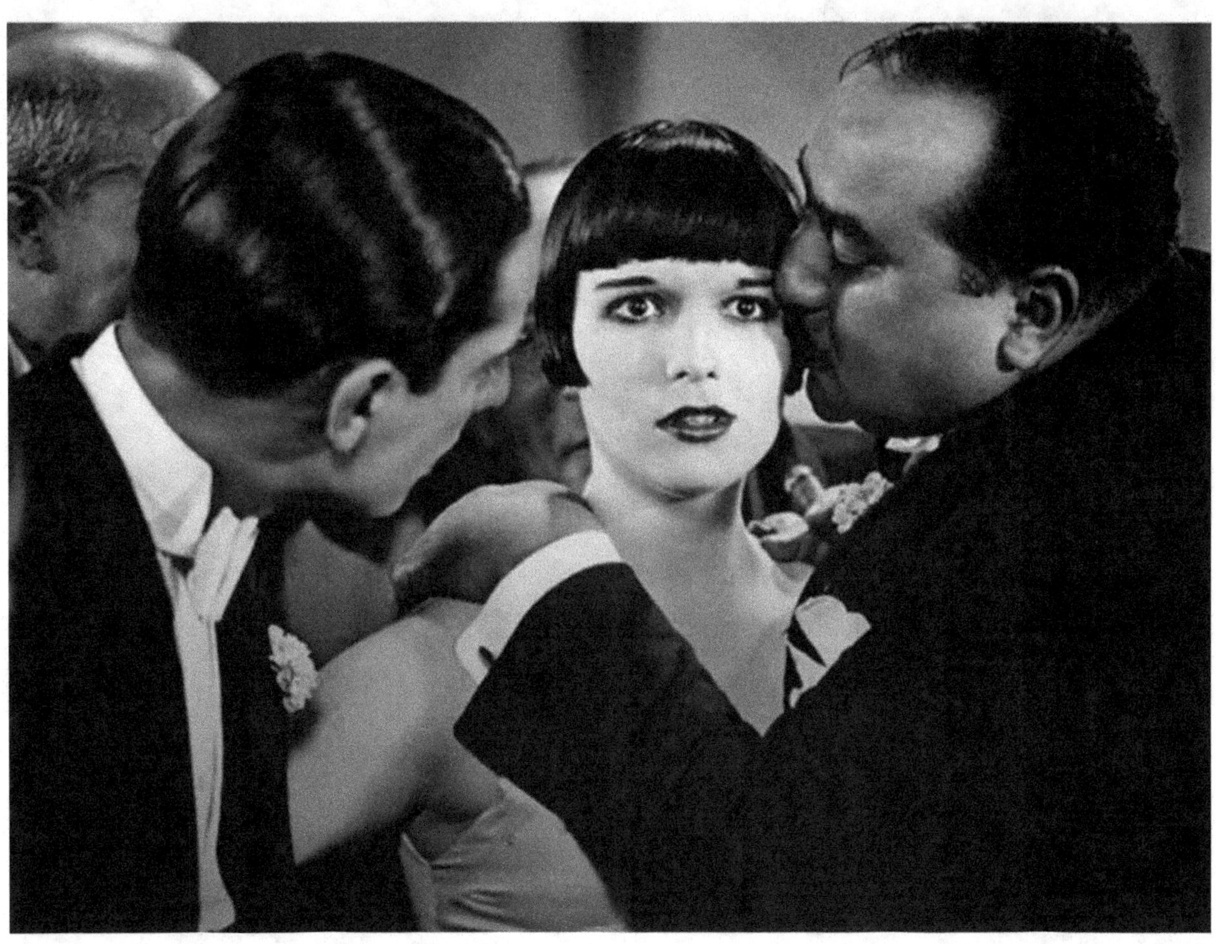

Image 87: *Diary of a Lost Girl*, 1929.

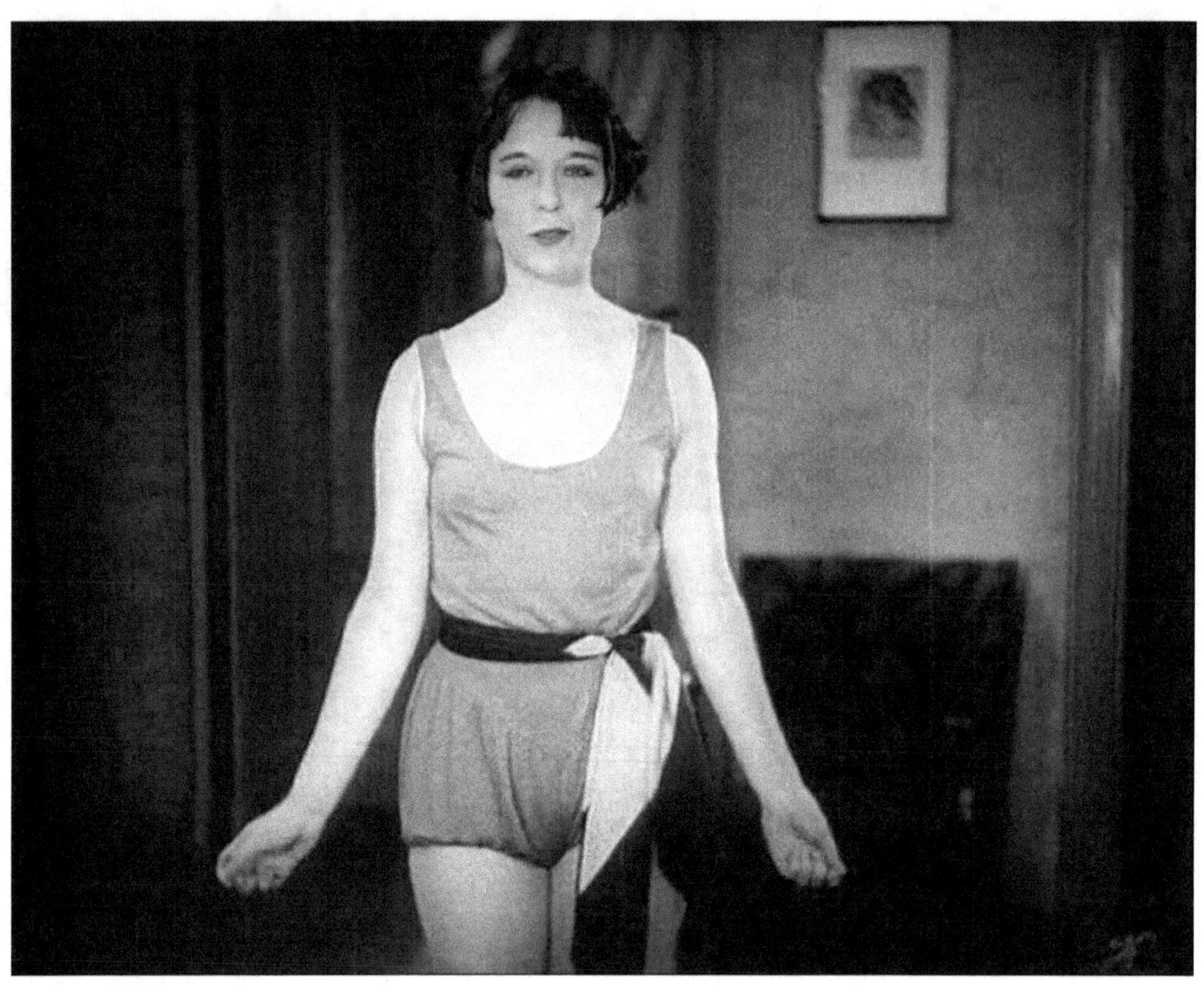

Image 88: *Diary of a Lost Girl*, 1929.

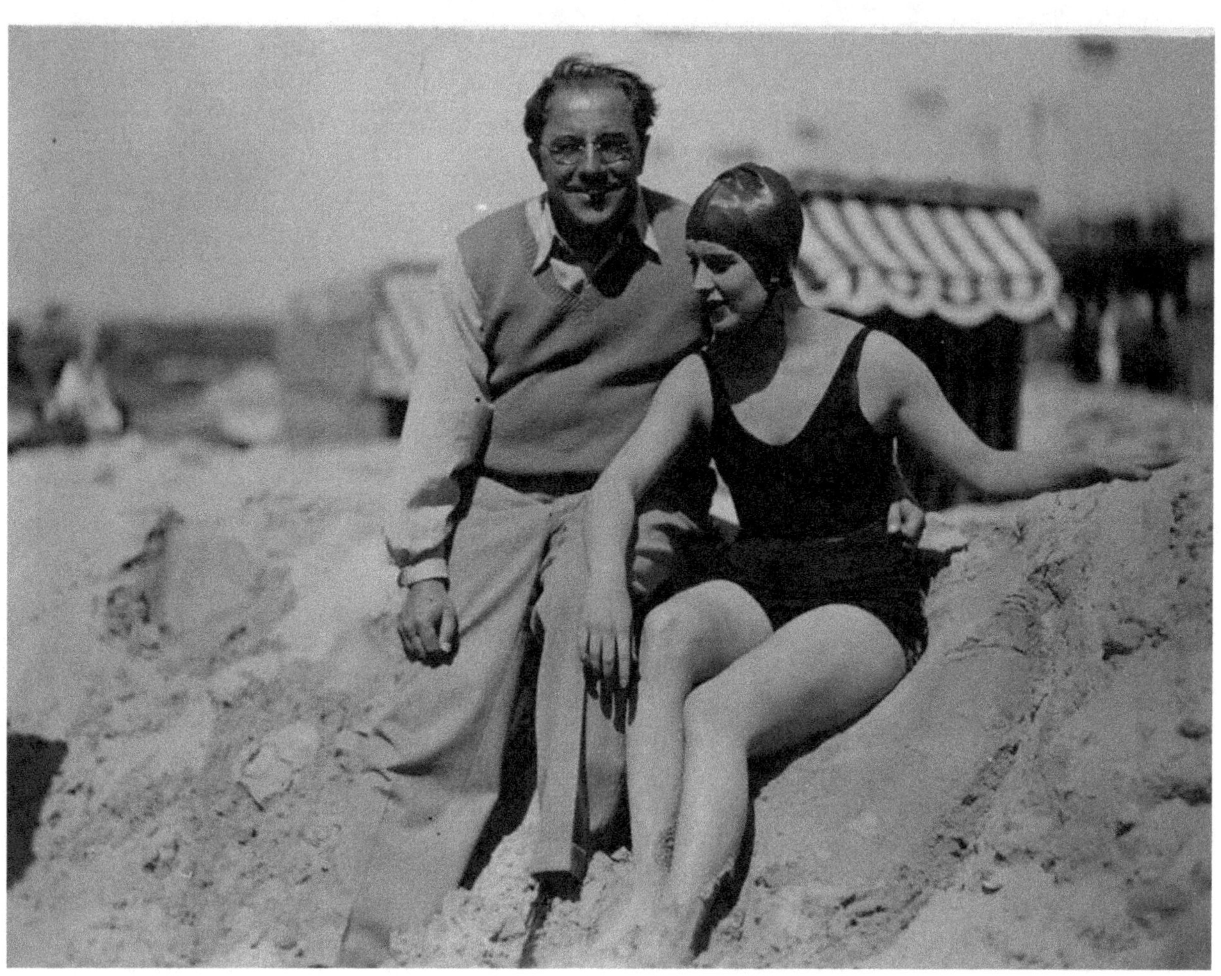

Image 89: With German director G.W. Pabst, 1929.

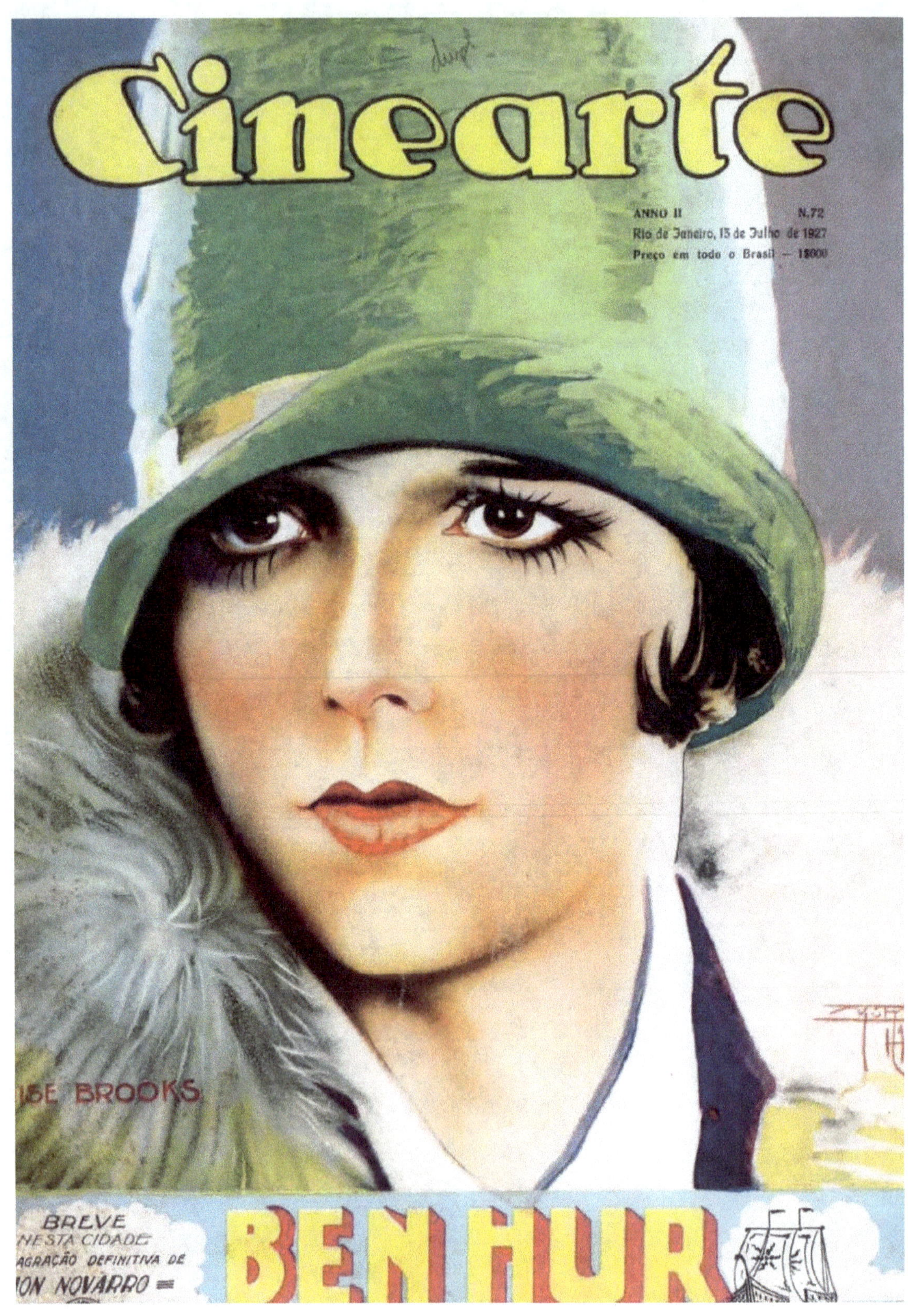

Image 90: Cover of Brazilian magazine, 1929.

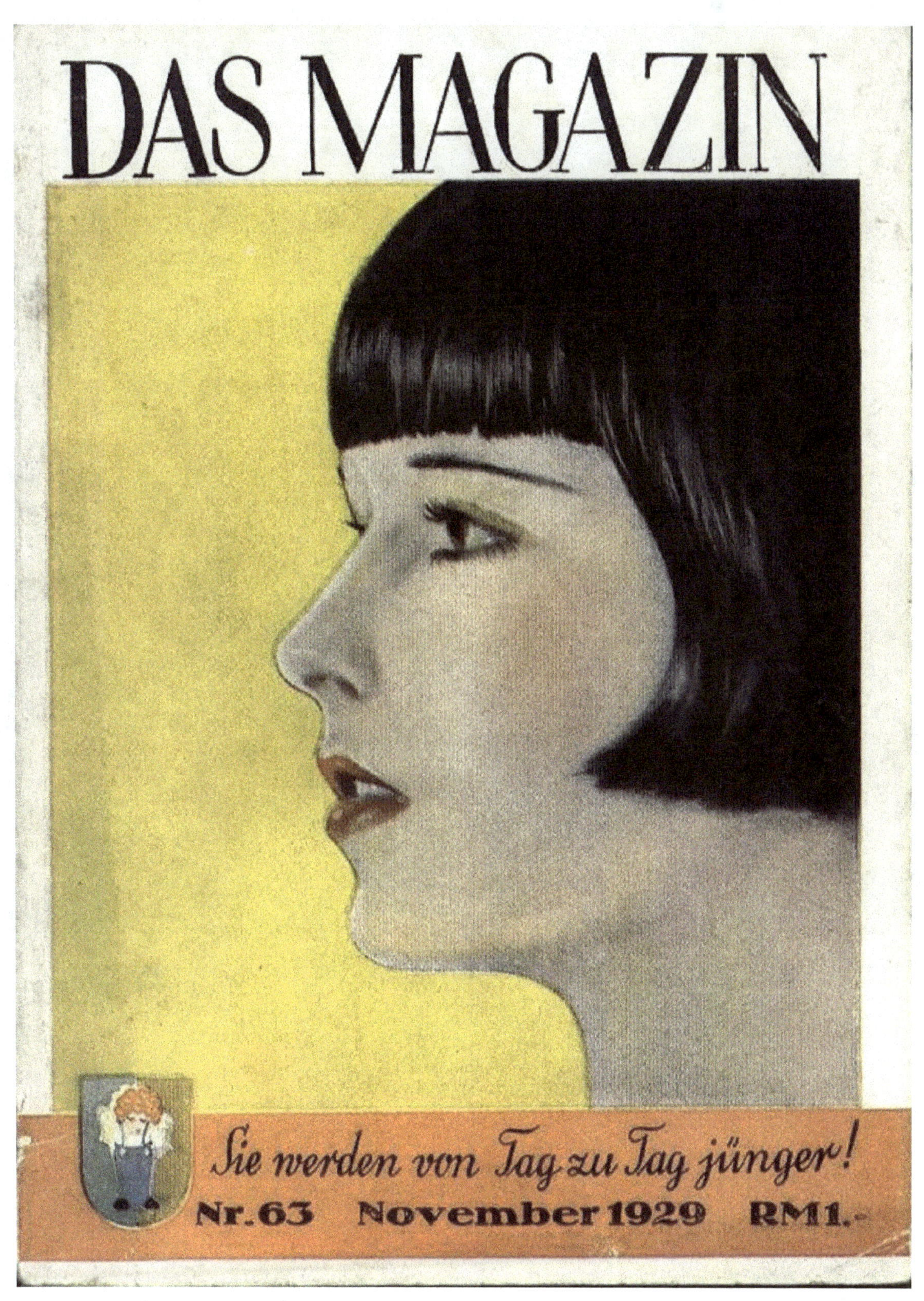

Image 91: Cover of German magazine, 1929.

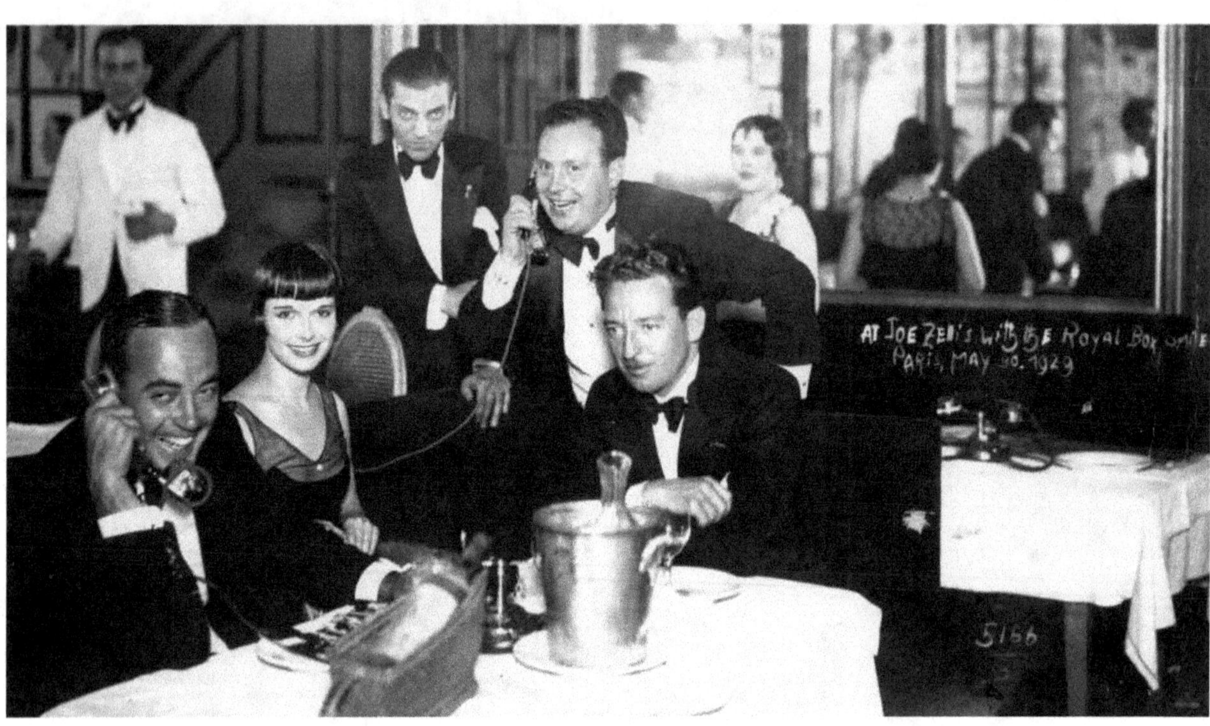

Image 92: With friends at Joe Zelli's Royal Box nightclub in Paris, May 1929.

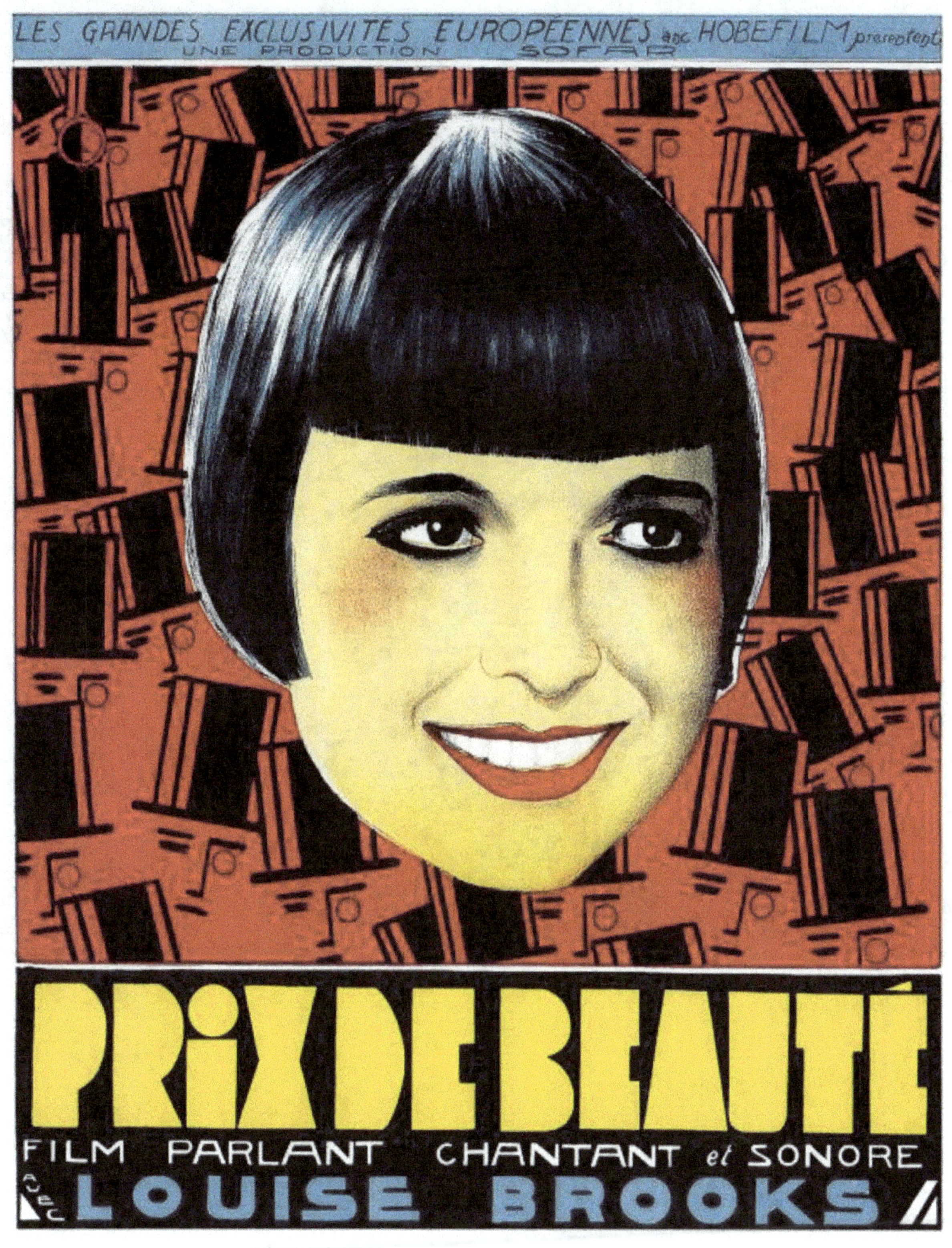

Image 93: French Poster for *Miss Europa,* 1930.

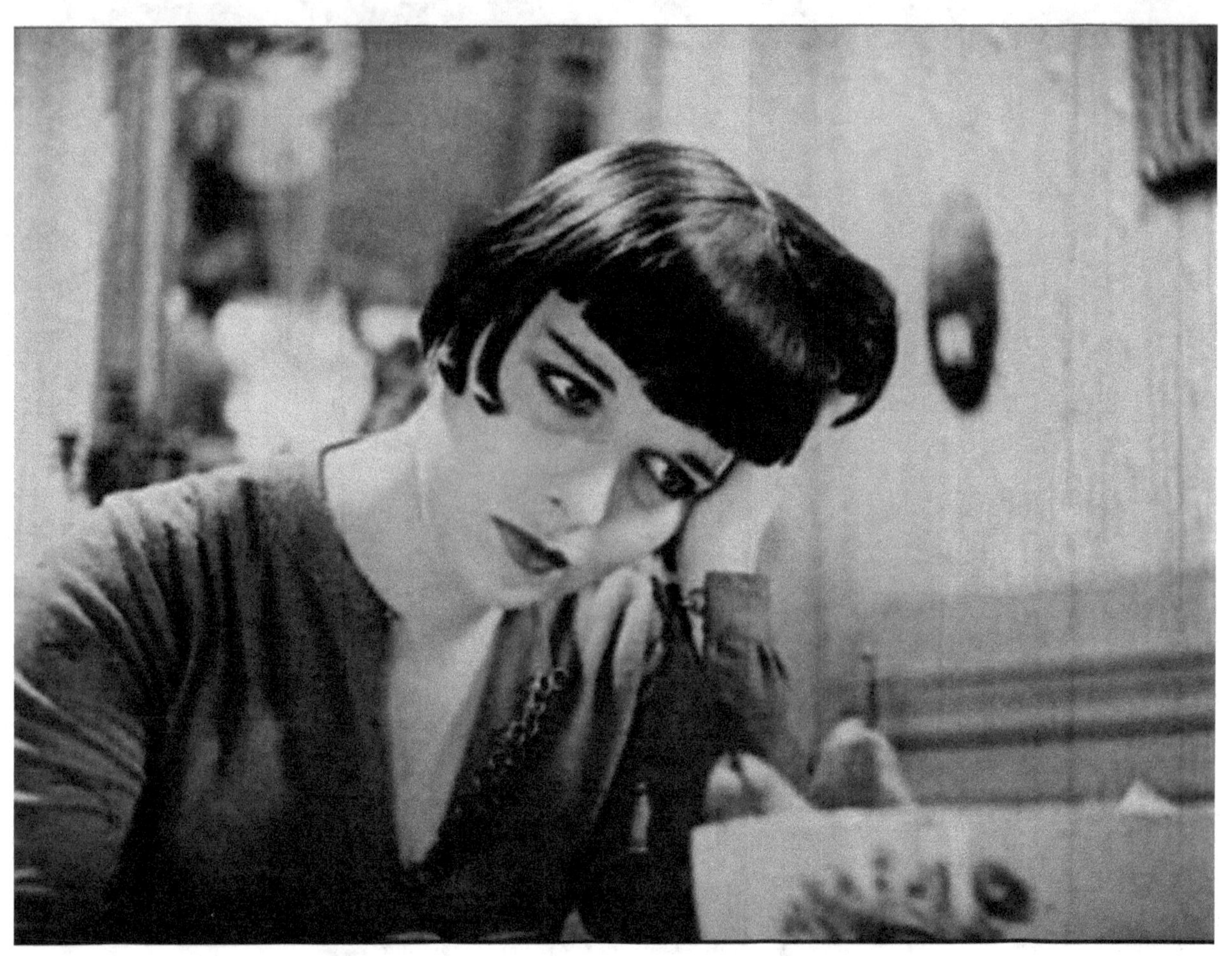

Image 94: *Miss Europa*, 1930.

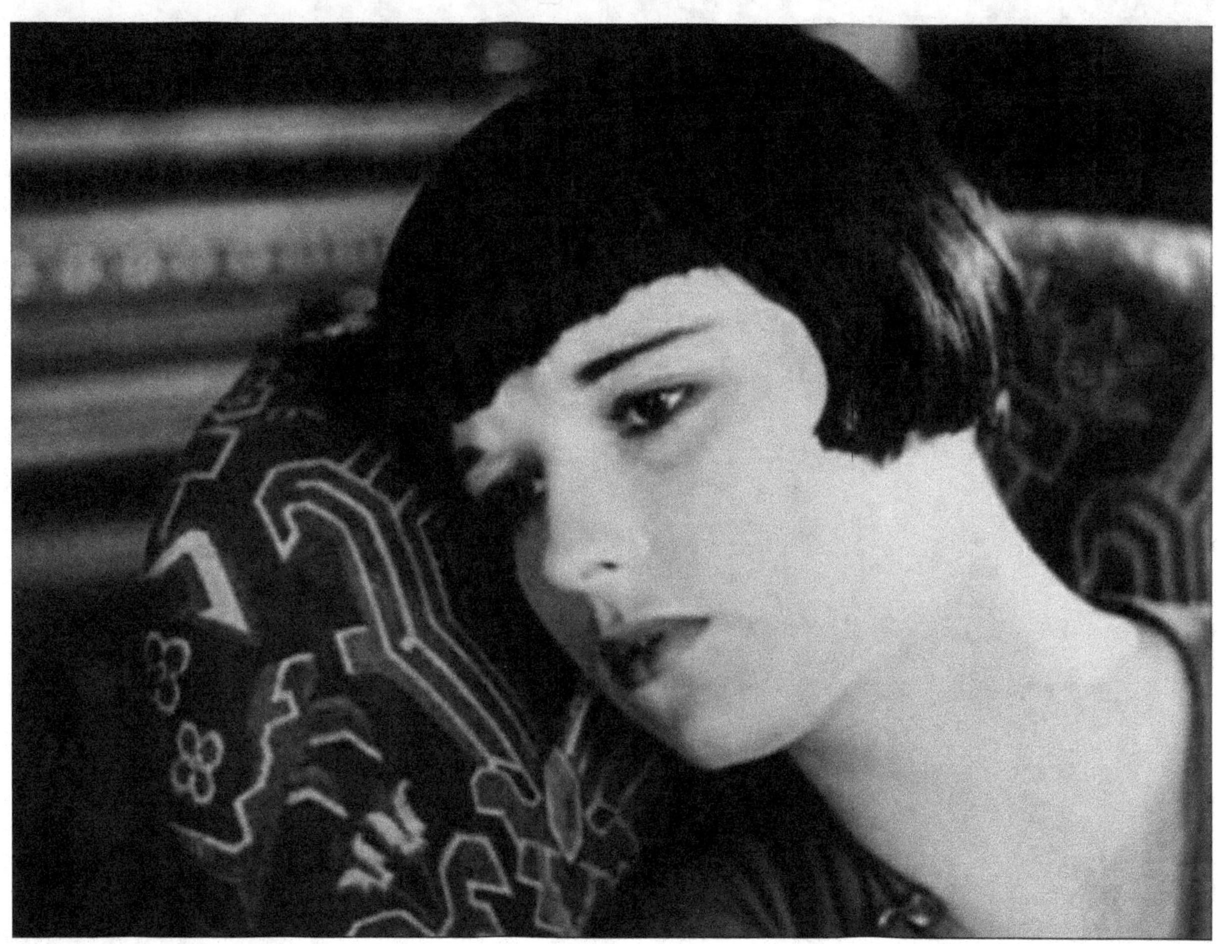

Image 95: *Miss Europa*, 1930.

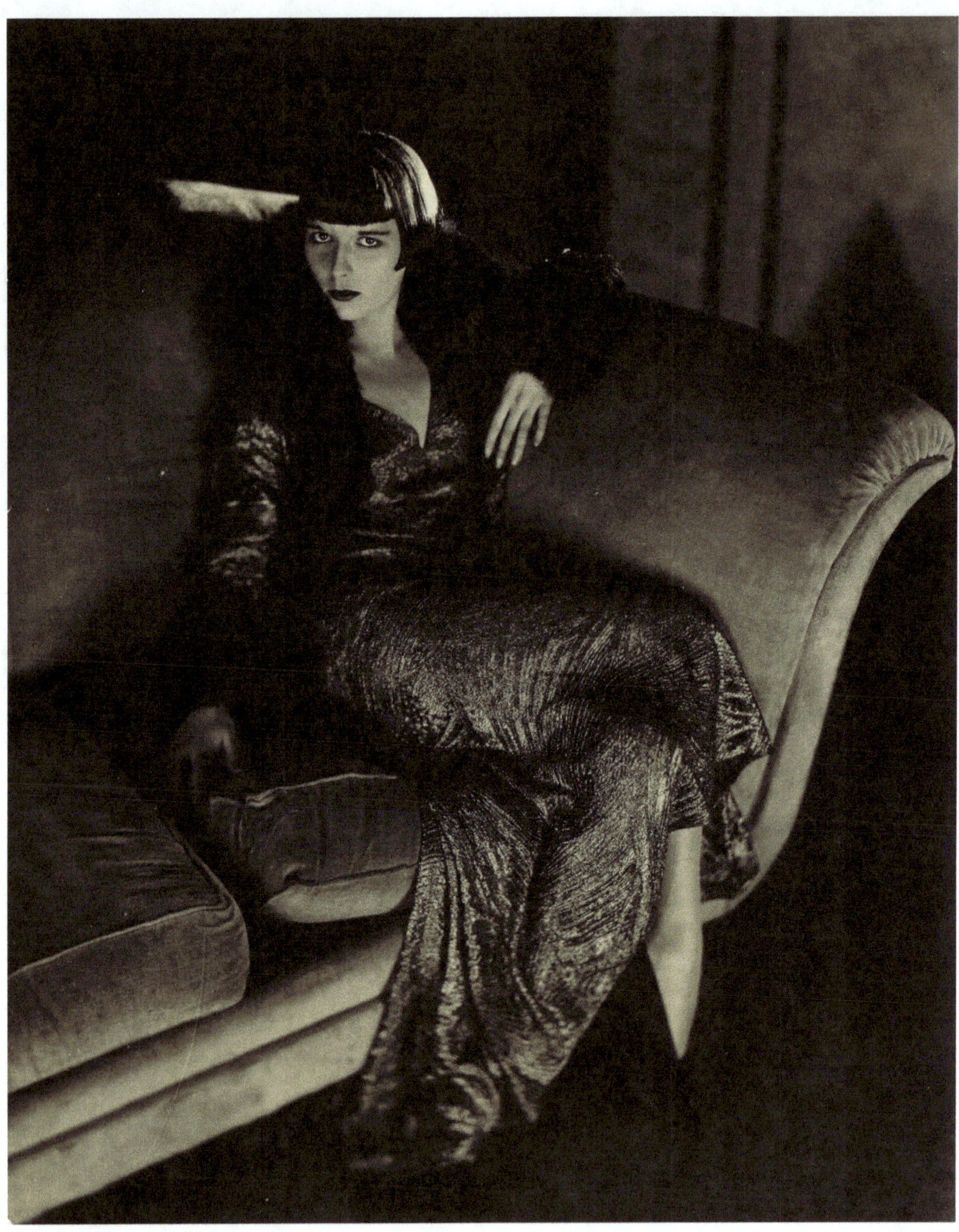

Image 96: *Miss Europa,* 1930.

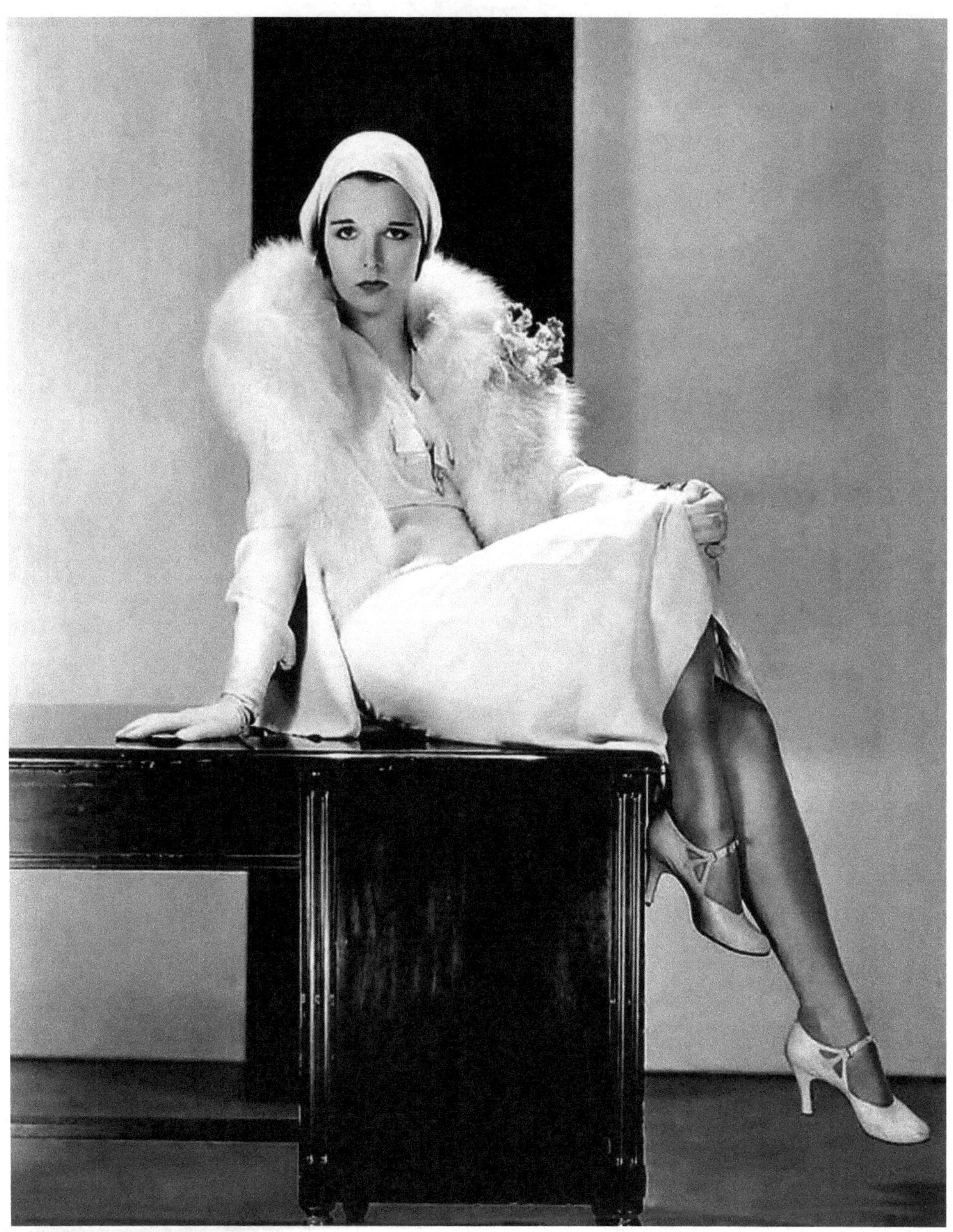

Image 97: *It Pays to Advertise,* 1931.

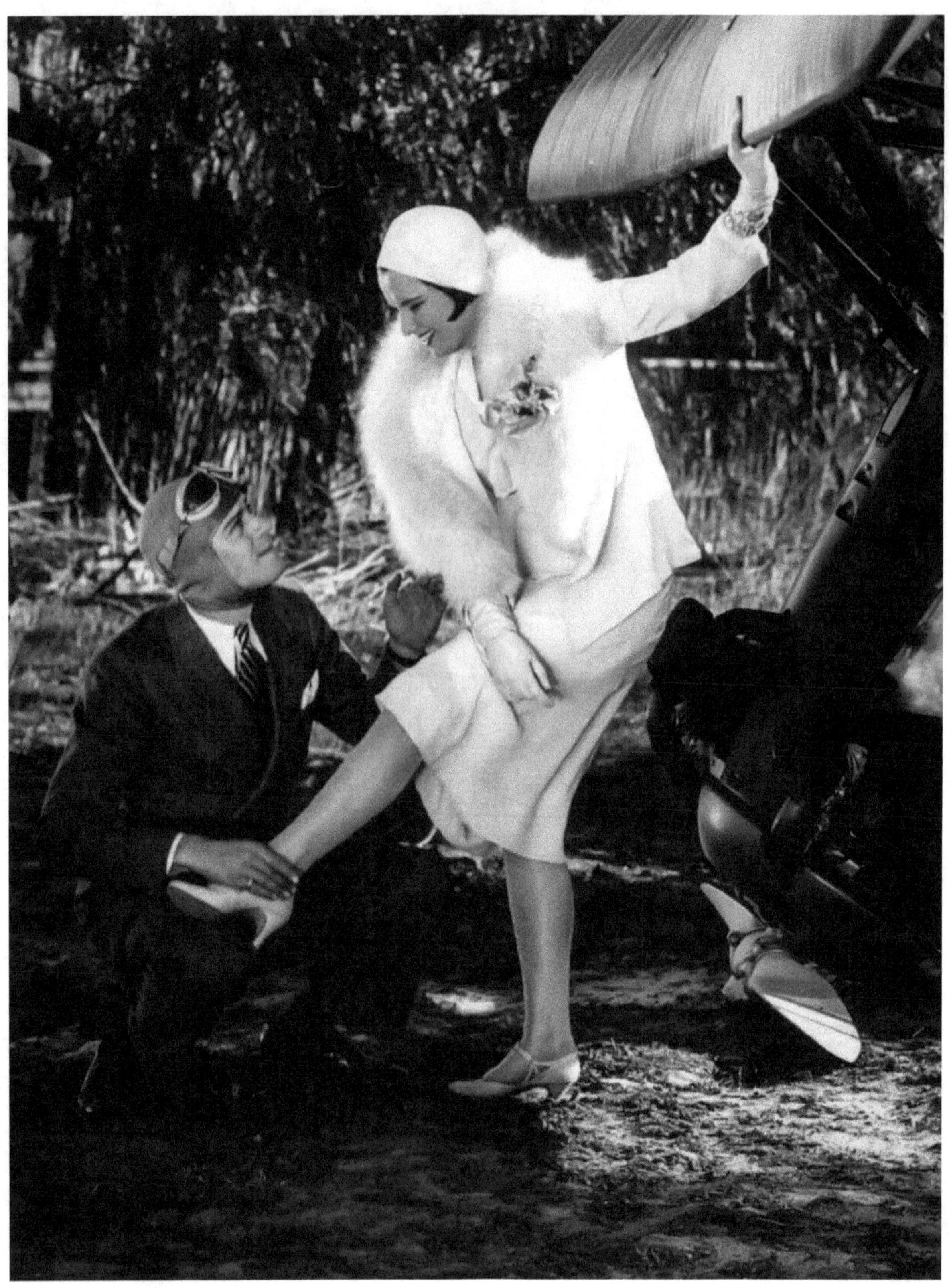
Image 98: *It Pays to Advertise*, 1931.

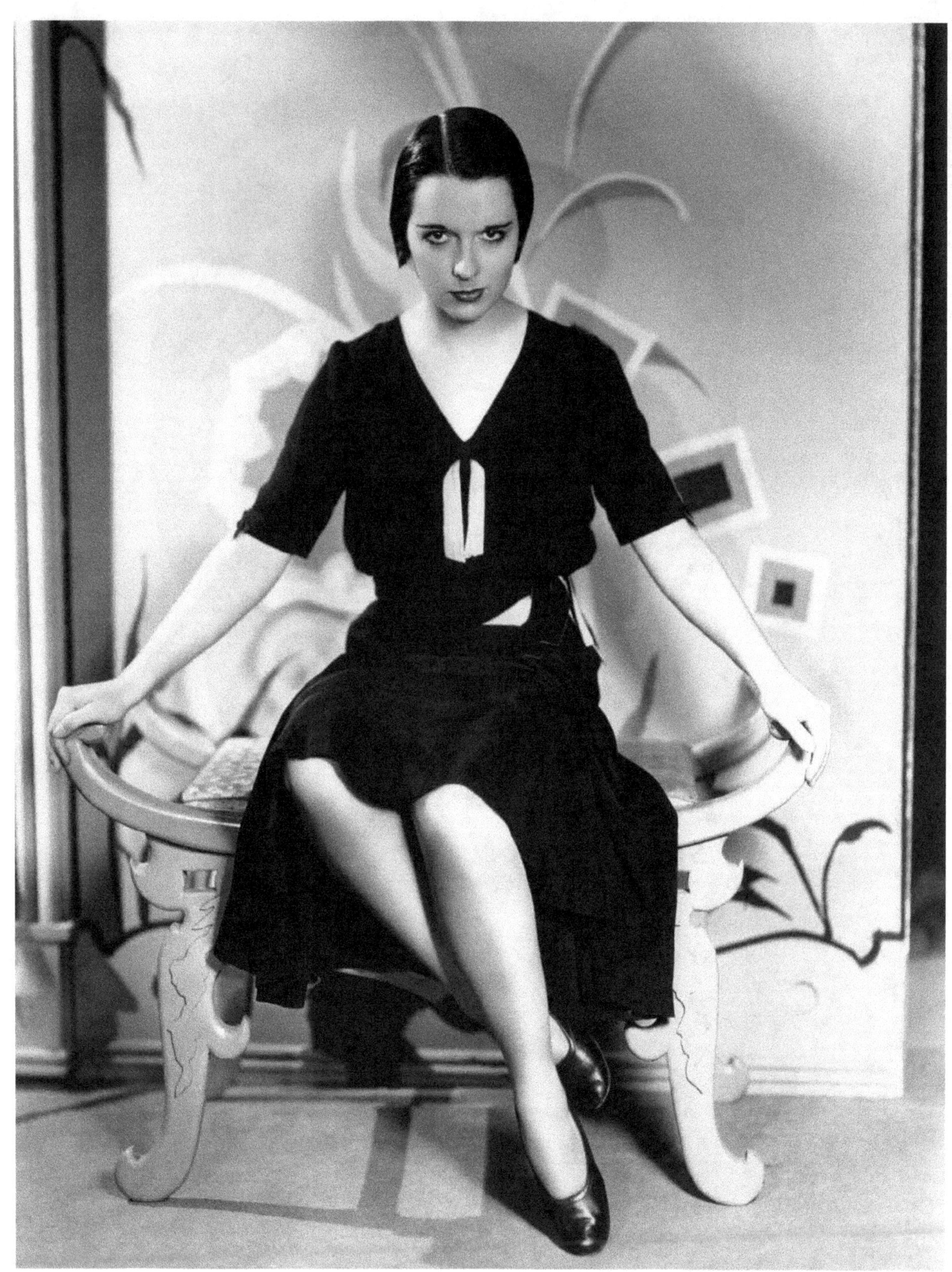

Image 99: *God's Gift to Women*, 1931.

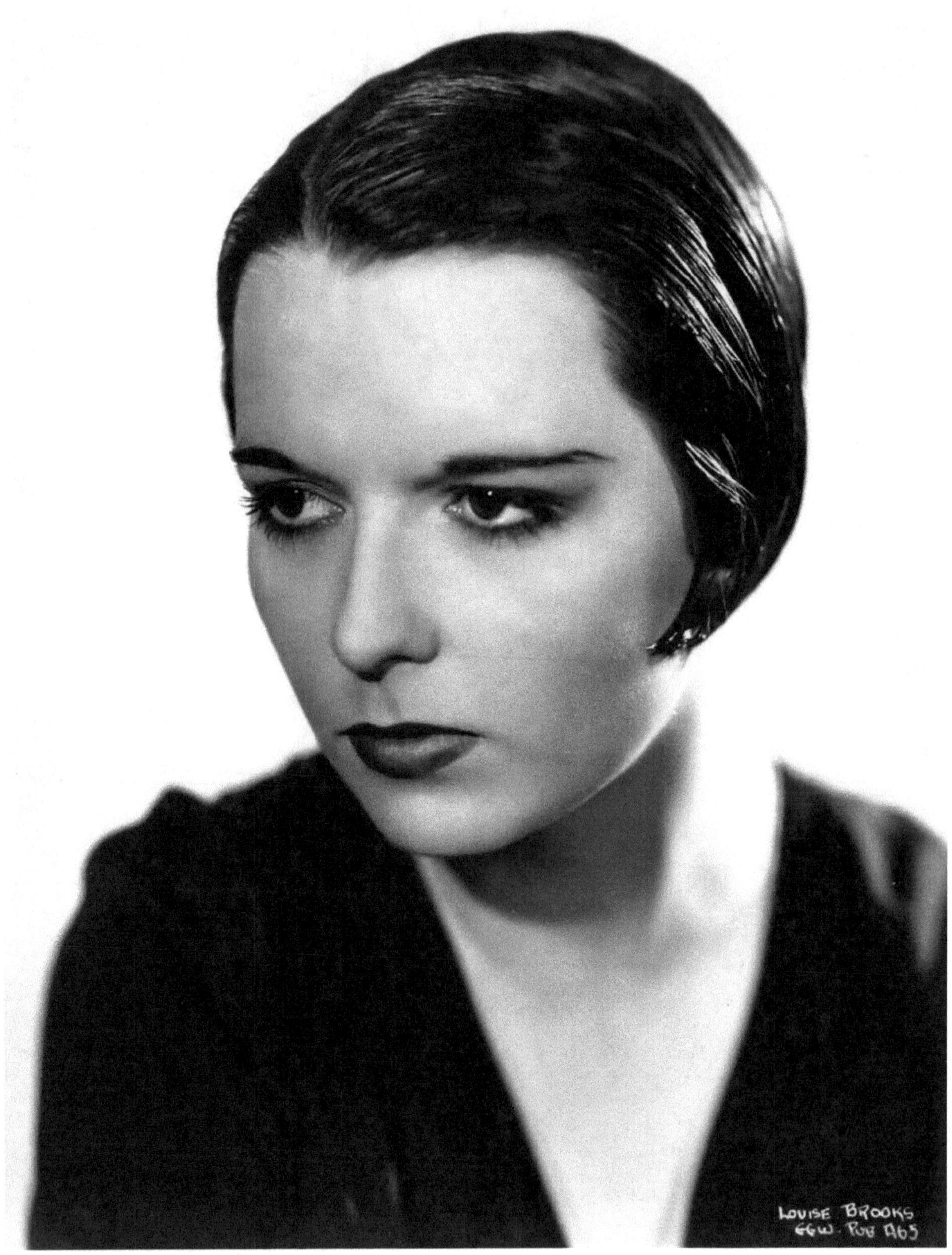

Image 100: *God's Gift to Women*, 1931.

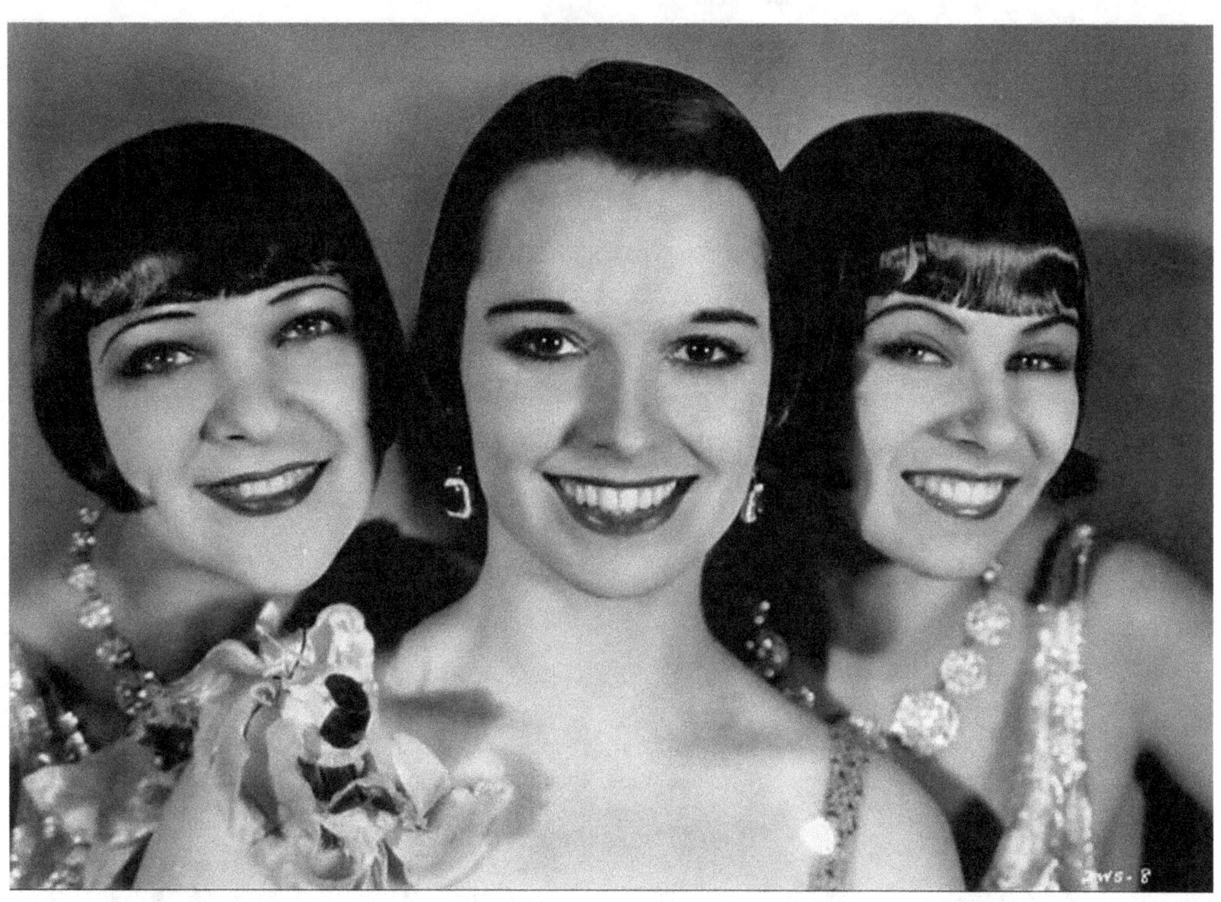

Image 101: With Eleanor and Karla Gutöhrlein, aka "The Sisters G," *God's Gift to Women*, 1931.

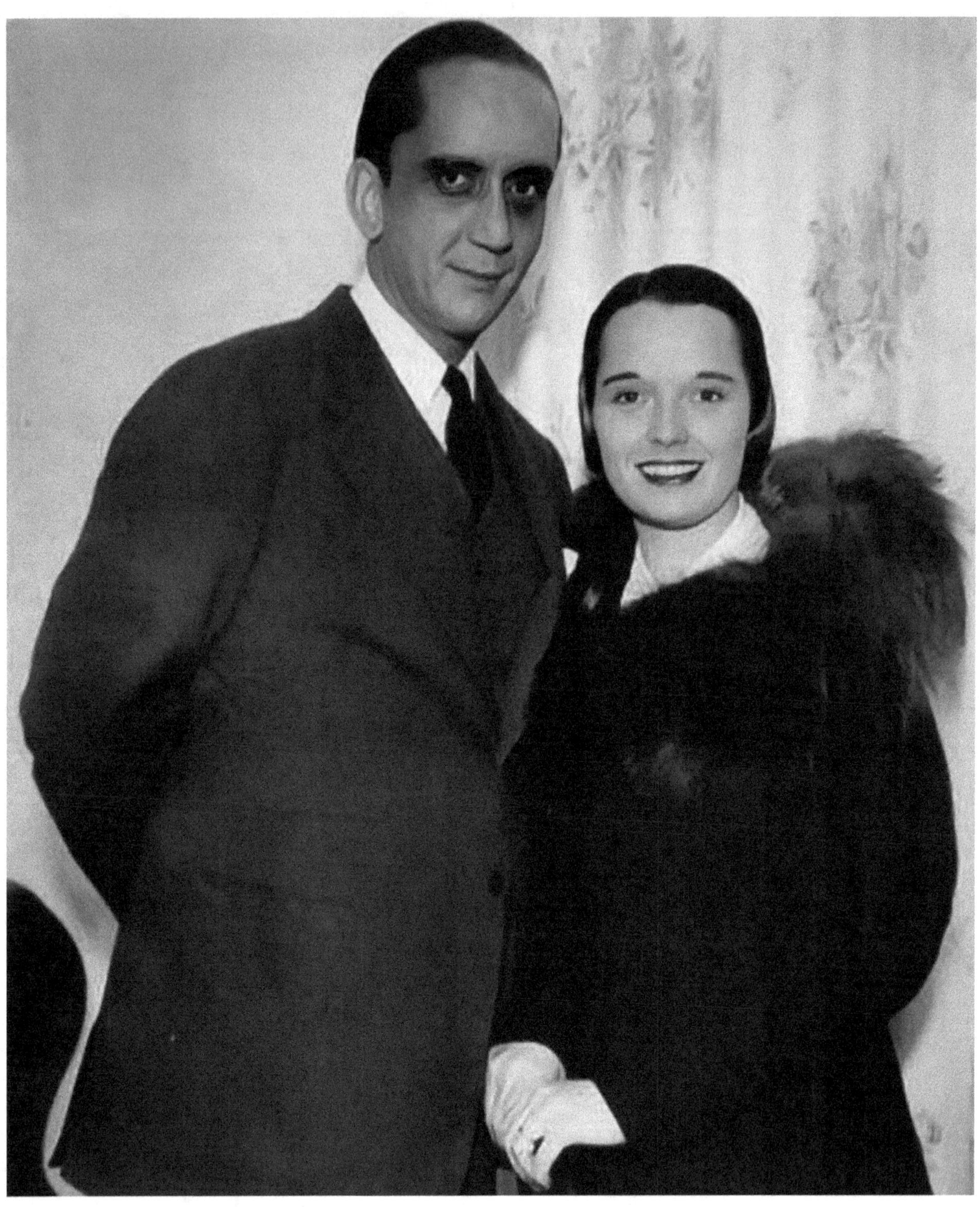

Image 102: With second husband Deering Davis, 1933.

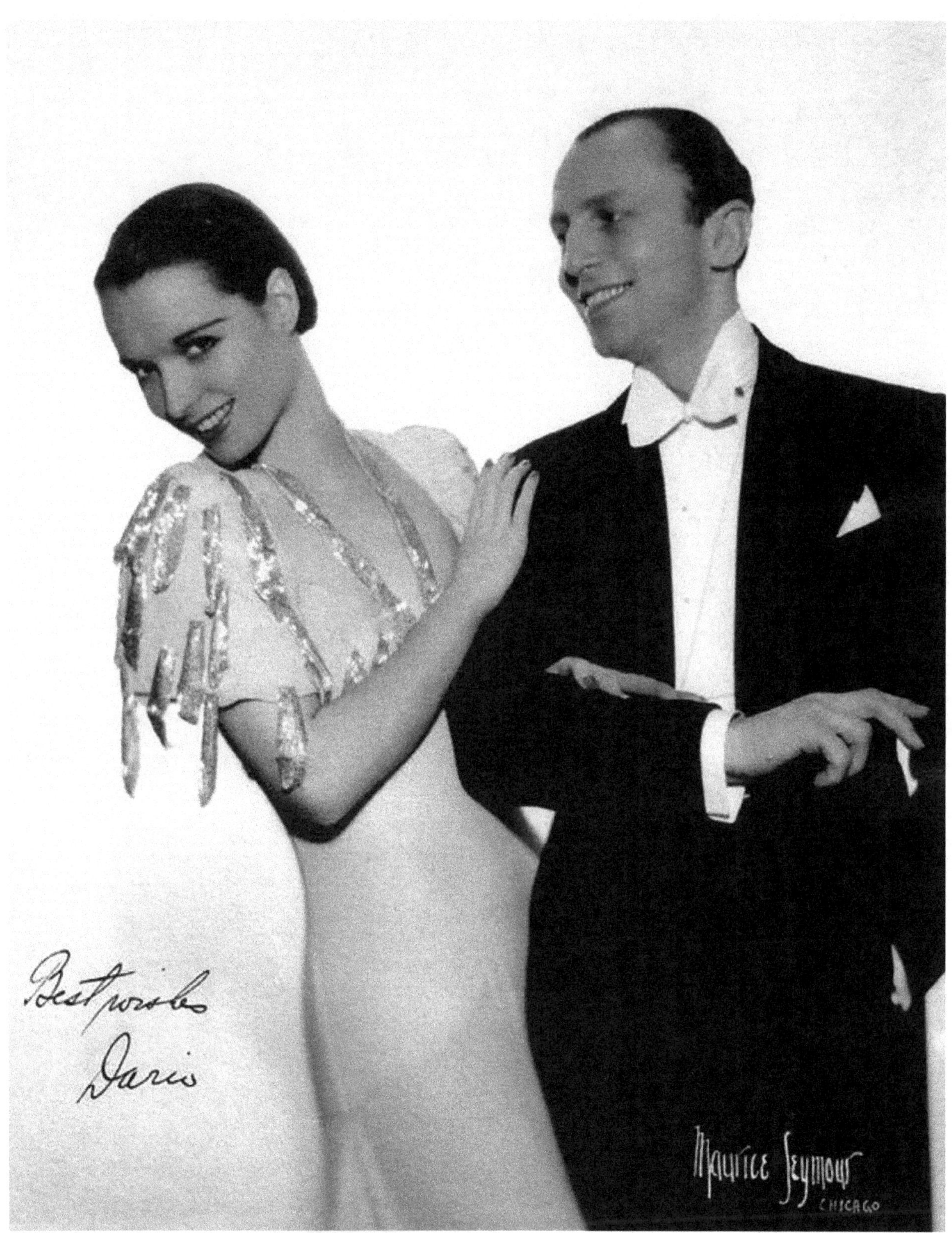

Image 103: With ballroom dance partner Dario Banzani, 1934.

LOUISE BROOKS FILMOGRAPHY

Year	Title	Role
1925	The Street of Forgotten Men	A Moll
1926	The American Venus	Miss Bayport
1926	A Social Celebrity	Kitty Laverne
1926	It's the Old Army Game	Mildred Marshall
1926	The Show Off	Clara
1926	Just Another Blonde	Diana O'Sullivan
1926	Love 'Em and Leave 'Em	Janie Walsh
1927	Evening Clothes	Fox Trot
1927	Rolled Stockings	Carol Fleming
1927	Now We're in the Air	Griselle/Grisette
1927	The City Gone Wild	Snuggles Joy
1928	A Girl in Every Port	Marie, Girl in France
1928	Beggars of Life	The Girl (Nancy)
1929	The Canary Murder Case	Margaret Odell
1929	Die Büchse der Pandora (Pandora's Box)	Lulu
1929	Tagebuch einer Verlorenen (Diary of a Lost Girl)	Thymian
1930	Prix de Prix de Beauté (Miss Europa)	Lucienne Garnier
1931	It Pays to Advertise	Thelma Temple
1931	God's Gift to Women	Florine
1931	Windy Riley Goes Hollywood	Betty Grey
1936	Empty Saddles	"Boots" Boone
1937	When You're in Love	Chorus Girl
1937	King of Gamblers	Joyce Beaton
1938	Overland Stage Raiders	Beth Hoyt

SUGGESTIONS FOR FURTHER READING

Böhme, Margarete, and Thomas Gladysz. *The Diary of a Lost Girl*. Louise Brooks editor, Pandora's Box Press, 2010.

Brooks, Louise. *Lulu in Hollywood*. Expanded edition, University of Minnesota Press, 2000.

Cowie, Peter. *Louise Brooks: Lulu Forever*. Rizzoli, 2006.

Gladysz, Thomas. "Louise Brooks Society." The Louise Brooks Society website, https://www.pandorasbox.com/.

---. *Louise Brooks, the Persistent Star: Articles, Essays, Blogs and Interviews*. Louise Brooks Society :, 2018.

Jaccard, Roland, editor. *Louise Brooks: Portrait of an Anti-Star*. Columbus, 1988.

Paris, Barry. *Louise Brooks*. Anchor Books, 1990.

Wahl, Jan, and Louise Brooks. *Dear Stinkpot: Letters From Louise Brooks*. BearManor Media, 2016.

PLEASE REVIEW THIS BOOK!

I hope you liked this book.

I'd very much appreciate your review on Amazon. Your review helps other people find books they might want to read. Thank you!

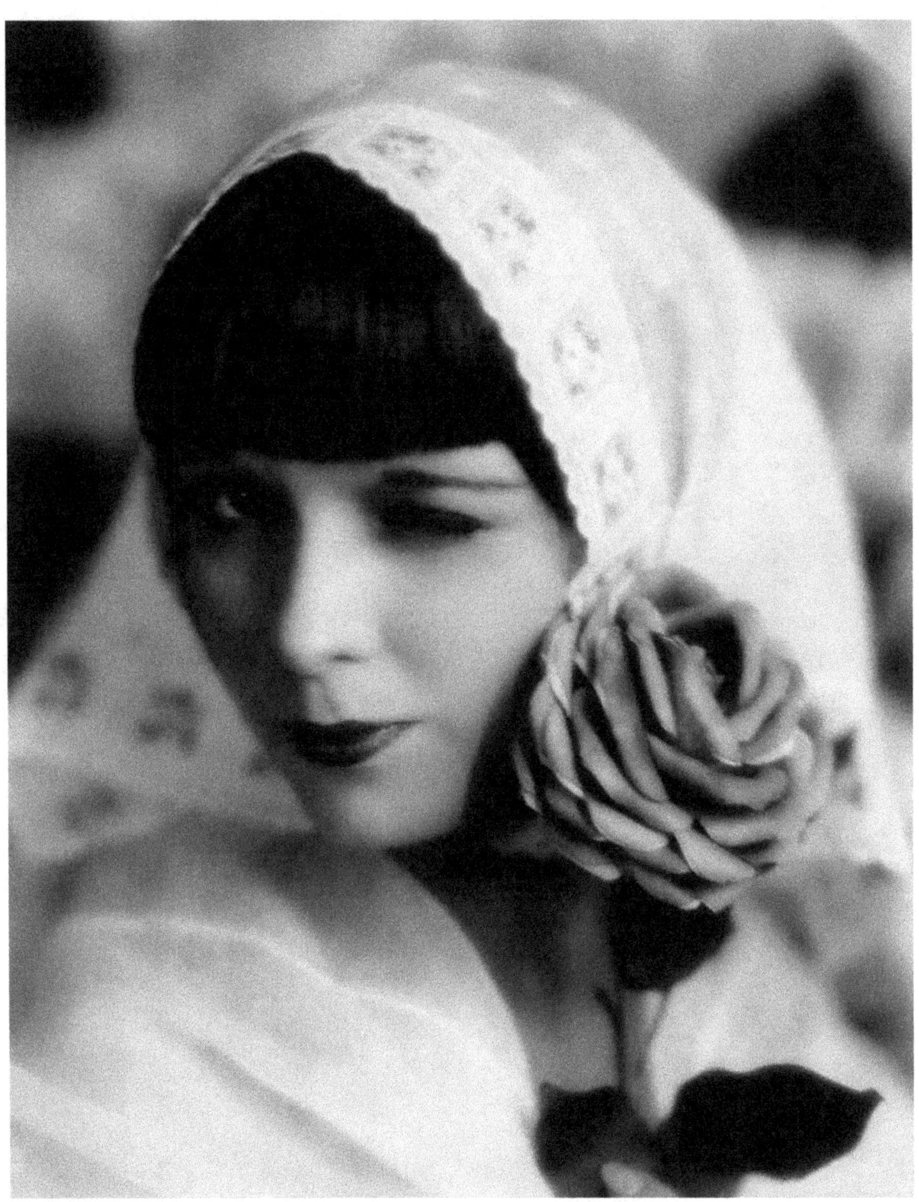

Image 104: Publicity photo from *Now We're in the Air*, 1927

www.ingramcontent.com/pod-product-compliance
Lightning Source LLC
LaVergne TN
LVHW061204120826
845149LV00011B/1902